JAPANESE INTERNATIONAL TRADE
AND INVESTMENT LAW

JAPANESE INTERNATIONAL TRADE AND INVESTMENT LAW

MITSUO MATSUSHITA
University of Tokyo

THOMAS J. SCHOENBAUM
University of Georgia

Foreword by
MIKE MANSFIELD

UNIVERSITY OF TOKYO PRESS

Publication of this volume was assisted by grants from the Suntory Foundation and the Egusa Foundation for International Cooperation in the Social Sciences.

© 1989 UNIVERSITY OF TOKYO PRESS
ISBN 0–86008–449–3
ISBN 4–13–037016–2

Printed in Japan

CONTENTS

3. REGULATION OF IMPORT AND SALES ACTIVITIES

4. EXPORT REGULATIONS

5. INVESTMENT AND ESTABLISHMENT

6. ANTITRUST LAW

7. FOREIGN SERVICES IN JAPAN

8. INTELLECTUAL PROPERTY

9. TAXATION

ABBREVIATIONS

Gyōsai Reishū	*Gyōsei Jiken Saiban Reishū* (Administrative Cases Reporter)
Haijo Meireishū	*Kōsei Torihiki Iinkai Haijo Meireishū* (Fair Trade Commission Excluding Orders Reporter)
Hanrei Jihō	(Current Cases Reporter)
Hanrei Taimuzu	(Current Cases Times)
Kakyū Keishū	*Kakyū Saibansho Keiji Saiban Reishū* (Lower Court Criminal Cases Reporter)
Kakyū Minshū	*Kakyū Saibansho Minji Saiban Reishū* (Lower Court Civil Cases Reporter)
Kampō	(Official Gazette)
Keishū	*Saikō Saibansho Keiji Hanreishū* (Supreme Court Criminal Cases Reporter)
Kōsai Minshū	*Kōtō Saibansho Minji Hanreishū* (High Court Civil Cases Reporter)
Minshū	*Saikō Saibansho Minji Hanreishū* (Supreme Court Civil Cases Reporter)
Mutai Reishū	*Mutaizaisanken Kankei Minji Gyōsei Saiban Reishū* (Civil and Administrative Cases on Intellectual Property Rights Reporter)
Shinketsushū	*Kōsei Torihiki Iinkai Shinketsushū* (Fair Trade Commission Decisions Reporter)
B.I.S.D.	Basic Instruments and Selected Documents

BNA	Bureau of National Affairs
Cir.	Circuit
Dist. Ct.	District Court
F. Supp.	Federal Supplement
H. Ct.	High Court
Sup. Ct.	Supreme Court
T.I.A.S.	Treaties and Other International Acts Series
T.S.	Treaty Series
U.N. Doc. A/CONF	United Nations Documents A/Conferences
U.N. GAOR	United Nations General Assembly Organization
U.N.T.S.	United Nations Treaty Series
U.S.C.	United States Code
U.S.T.	United States Treaties

FOREWORD

MIKE MANSFIELD

FORMER UNITED STATES SENATOR FROM MONTANA AND
UNITED STATES AMBASSADOR TO JAPAN

Forty years ago, it would have been impossible to predict the
speed with which our relationship with Japan would grow or
the fact that this relationship would eventually touch every aspect
of our national lives. But grow it did, and now that bilateral
relationship between Japan and the United States is the most
important in the world—bar none.

Very early in our relationship, we discovered the remarkable
fact that, despite our different histories and traditions, we both
had come to cherish political and personal freedoms, respect
for the rule of law, and the limits of government. Also, we learned
that, despite difficult language and cultural barriers, it was possible for us to communicate with each other.

Japan and the United States have developed a relationship
which has become more integrated and interlocked with the
passage of time. It will continue to do so in the future. In the
meantime, we will have problems to face up to mostly in the
economic and trade area, but as good friends and allies we have
to expect that.

It would be my hope that while we have to pursue our present
policy of considering our trade differences on a single or sectoral
basis, we seek other means, such as a free trade agreement or
something approximating it, that would allow us to face up to
the trade factor as a whole rather than in bits and pieces. This,
of course, would mean a redirection of our policy from the present

necessary one to one of wider proportions. The key word is "access" to the Japanese market by Americans and vice versa, and it should be based on reciprocity, mutual understanding, and equality.

In sum, two nations that historically have acted quite independently have become interdependent. Neither nation can survive at the current level of economic welfare and security without the active cooperation of the other.

In writing this book, Professor Matsushita and Professor Schoenbaum have made an excellent contribution to understanding the inner workings of the Japanese market and legal system.

PREFACE

This book is a product of a joint effort of two authors: a Japanese law professor and an American law professor who are both specialists in international trade law. Mitsuo Matsushita is Professor of Law at the University of Tokyo and teaches courses on both domestic and international economic laws. Thomas J. Schoenbaum is Dean Rusk Professor of Law at the University of Georgia Law School and teaches courses on international trade law, maritime law, and environmental law. He is also the Executive Director of the Dean Rusk Center for International and Comparative Law at the University of Georgia.

As Japan has emerged as a major economic power and the impact of its presence has been felt by other countries, it has become its responsibility to open its economy to the world. Accordingly, Japan has engaged in a massive effort to internationalize its economy. Many books and articles have been written in English on the Japanese economy, corporate structure, management, labor relations, and the distribution system, as well as cultural matters. Surprisingly, however, there are few publications in English on legal subjects. This is especially true with regard to Japanese international trade and investment law. This is the reason that the authors undertook to write this book.

In this volume, the authors have attempted to present a critical analysis of the major public laws and regulations in Japan which have some bearing on doing business with Japan in order to provide a guide to foreign businesspeople, lawyers, government officials, and scholars and students who deal with Japan. The public regulation of international trade and investment is a vast subject that is difficult to summarize in a book of this size. However, the authors believe that they have covered the essentials of Japanese foreign trade and investment law and that this book will be serve as a basic reader for students of this subject and a useful guide to practitioners.

The following sections were drafted by Matsushita and reviewed by Schoenbaum. They reflect primarily the research and views of Matsushita, who is responsible for these sections: Chapter 3: §3–6, §3–7, §3–9, §3–10, §3–11, §3–12; Chapter 4: §4–1, §4–2; Chapter 6: §6–1, §6–2, §6–3, §6–4, §6–5, §6–6; Chapter 8: §8–4, §8–7; Chapter 9: §9–3, §9–5.

The following sections were drafted by Schoenbaum and reviewed by Matsushita. They reflect primarily the research and views of Schoenbaum, who is responsible for these sections: Chapter 1: §1–1, §1–3, §1–4; Chapter 3: §3–1, §3–2, §3–3, §3–4; Chapter 5: §5–1, §5–2, §5–3, §5–4, §5–5, §5–6, §5–7, §5–8, §5–9; Chapter 7: §7–1, §7–2, §7–3, §7–4; Chapter 8: §8–1, §8–2, §8–3, §8–5, §8–6, §8–9; Chapter 9: §9–1, §9–2, §9–4.

The following sections were jointly drafted, and both authors are responsible for them: Chapter 1: §1–2, §1–5; Chapter 2: §2–1, §2–2, §2–3, §2–4, §2–5, §2–6, §2–7; Chapter 3: §3–5, §3–8; Chapter 8: §8–8.

The authors' are grateful to the staff of the University of Tokyo Press for its encouragement and excellent editorial work which made the publication of this book possible. The Suntory Foundation and the Egusa Foundation for International Cooperation in the Social Sciences provided generous publication subsidies without which this book could not have been published. The authors wish to express their thanks to Mr. Tadashi Shiraishi, research associate at the Faculty of Law, University of Tokyo, who assisted in the preparation of the manuscript.

It is the sincere hope of the authors that the book will be read by those concerned with international transactions with Japan and will contribute to a better understanding of Japan.

RESOLVING TRADE FRICTION WITH JAPAN THROUGH FREE TRADE

In the decade of the 1980s, Japan became an economic superpower, transforming itself from a relatively closed, controlled, and backward economy into a liberalized, more open society confident of its global political and economic power. Prodded by its trading partners, especially the United States, Japan has reformed its trade policy to stimulate domestic demand and to increase imports. International monetary reforms were adopted that resulted in both a higher value and a stronger international role for the yen. Financial markets were liberalized and restrictions on capital flows eliminated so that Tokyo is now a financial capital of global importance. Trade policies favoring farmers are being revised despite resultant domestic political difficulties. Import and export rules are being revamped. In order to recycle its still-impressive trade surplus, Japan has adopted an ambitious $50 billion plan for aid to developing countries.

Japan has carried out this historic transition with remarkable ease. To cope with a narrowing trade surplus and the high value of the yen, Japanese industry invested heavily overseas, cut costs, and stimulated domestic demand. As a result, Japan's rate of economic growth has remained high. It has become the second largest economy in the world. Imports of raw materials and even manufactured goods have increased dramatically; but exports have also soared so that Japan's trade surplus remains high.

Japan's rise to economic prominence in the 1980s has posed attendant difficulties for many other countries, especially the United States and Europe. Current account deficits with Japan have resulted in controls on trade in automobiles, semiconductors, steel, and other industries. Japan is accused by its trading partners of maintaining protectionist barriers while taking advantage of the openness of the world economy.

Much of this criticism is valid, and the trade friction has had a positive effect by compelling reform in Japan. Some of the outcry, however, is plainly scapegoating, blaming Japan for the loss of competitiveness in domestic American and European industries that have become too complacent about the quality of their products and the ability to dominate their traditional markets.

As the decade of the 1980s draws to a close, Japan has reached a historic transition point in its relations with its major trading partners. There is a new mood of confrontation as trade conflicts compounded by cross-cultural differences persist. But continued confrontation can only be harmful to both Japan and other nations.

The question for the 1990s is how to cooperate with Japan to enhance political and economic security and peace and prosperity in the world. This involves creating a new political and economic order to govern relations with Japan. The concept of Japan as a defeated power under the tutelage of the United States has clearly run its course, as has the era of trade friction, Japan bashing, and "us versus them." New ties and institutional arrangements must be forged between Japan and other nations in order to establish a better basis of understanding and cooperation.

There is a school of thought, particularly in the United States, that believes in a new relationship with Japan consisting of what is called "managed trade."[1] Under this scheme the United States would abandon its traditional stance of favoring open and fair competition and pursue a trade policy that would be result-oriented, concentrating on outcomes and mandating a more even balance of trade by government fiat. This view is the antithesis of free trade; it amounts to a new protectionism that would stifle competition and world economic growth.

According to this theory, Japan's rise is due to economic stagnation in the United States and Europe. Nothing could be further from the truth. By any measure, the United States and Europe

---

[1] See, e.g., C.V. Prestowitz, *Trading Places: How We Allowed Japan to Take the Lead* (1988).

remain vital and competitive. The European Community has recently expanded, and progress toward economic union as well as political cooperation has been substantial. The United States also remains strong. The "deindustrialization" notion that is central to the myth of the United States's demise is untrue. As a share of GNP, U.S. manufacturing output increased in the 1980s, surging ahead of most European countries. In technological innovation, too, the United States remains a leader.[2] The U.S. economy is the largest in the world, half again as large as its nearest rival.

What has happened is not that Japan surpassed the United States and Europe—Japan has merely matured, achieving a state of development comparable to that of the United States and Europe. This was accomplished so quickly and easily precisely because the United States and Europe led the way. In becoming a global economic power, Japan used economic interaction with other nations as the mainspring of its progress. As a result, Japan, the United States, and Europe have become increasingly interdependent. The economic and political destinies of these three advanced industrial economies are so intertwined that a rupture between them is unthinkable.[3] There is also a new equality between Japan and the other principal industrialized countries based on recognition of Japan's new wealth and influence in the world.

We must, therefore, resist the siren call of protectionism and reject politically determind, quantity-oriented bilateral trade arrangements. Instead, Japan and the United States should coordinate their policies to preserve free trade and the market focused multilateral world trade arrangement of the GATT (General Agreement on Tariffs and Trade).

[2] "High Technology: Clash of the Titans," *The Economist*, 23 Aug. 1986, pp. 4, 18. In the 1980s, Japan, in contrast to the United States, was still a technology-importing nation. Ibid.

[3] See E.L. Frost, *For Richer, For Poorer: The New U.S.-Japan Relationship* (1987).

JAPANESE INTERNATIONAL TRADE
AND INVESTMENT LAW

CHAPTER ONE

JAPAN AND THE INTERNATIONAL TRADING SYSTEM

§ 1–1. JAPANESE PARTICIPATION IN THE WORLD ECONOMIC ORDER

Japan today has the world's second largest economy and is the second leading industrial power. Out of the ashes of World War II, Japan rose to achieve the highest rate of economic growth of any nation. Although much of this spectacular progress is based on exports, Japan (with a population of about 120 million) is a large and important internal market as well.

Beginning in the 1970s, Japan became an important exporter of technologically advanced manufactured products, overtaking the United States and Europe in certain areas, such as electronics, autos, and machine tools. In the 1980s, its trade surplus soared, reaching $85.8 billion in 1986.

By 1987, however, the Japanese trade surplus began to stabilize, reflecting a leveling-off of exports and an increase in imported products. This was the result of a number of factors. First, under pressure from its trading partners, particularly the United States and the European Community, Japan has dismantled most of the formal barriers to trade, capital movements, and investments, a process that began about 1980. Second, following the so-called Plaza Agreement between the Group of Seven major industrialized nations in September 1985, the Japanese yen increased dramatically in value against the dollar, making Japanese exports more expensive and correspondingly decreasing the prices of imported products in Japan. Third, the Japanese government undertook a succession of "Action Programs," pump-priming economic measures designed to encourage imports. Accordingly, the Japanese economy has become more international

3

in character, and Tokyo has become one of the world's leading capital markets.

Japan is not a member of any economic bloc; its most important trading partners are the United States and the European Community. Japan also has an important informal "partnership" with ASEAN, the nations of the Association of Southeast Asian Nations (Brunei, Singapore, Thailand, Malaysia, Indonesia, and the Philippines),[1] and has been a leader in developing trade with nations of the Pacific Rim, especially China, Canada, Mexico, Australia, and Chile. Important economic links are maintained with other nations as well, so that Japan is in every sense a global economic power.

The international law norms governing Japanese trade relations flow from Japan's acceptance of the multilateral treaties and other arrangements. Japan became a member of the General Agreement on Tariffs and Trade (GATT) in 1955 and joined the Organization for Economic Cooperation and Development (OECD) in 1964. Japanese membership in the GATT caused many nations to invoke article XXXV of this agreement, which allows any contracting party to "opt out" of extending GATT benefits to any other contracting party if the two countries concerned have not "entered into tariff negotiations," meaning that they have not previously held a first meeting scheduled by a tariff negotiations committee at which lists of offers were exchanged.[2] However, most of the invocations of article XXXV against Japan have now been withdrawn.[3]

Japan is also an important member of both the International Monetary Fund (IMF) and the International Bank for Reconstruction and Development (the World Bank). Since 1963, Japan has observed article VIII of the IMF Agreement,[4] which prohibits foreign exchange restrictions on current payments for balance of payment reasons.

In addition to its status as a prominent member of multilateral organizations and agreements concerned with trade and economic

---

[1] Japan has created a $2 billion ASEAN-Japan Development Fund to boost industrial projects in the ASEAN region.

[2] See GATT B.I.S.D., Vol. II, 35 (1952).

[3] Only Cyprus and Haiti still apply art. XXXV against Japan.

[4] International Monetary Fund Articles of Agreement, art. VIII (1978).

matters, Japan has bilateral trade relations with most of the nations of the world. Such bilateral agreements range from broadly general treaties of friendship, commerce, and navigation[5] and tax treaties[6] to narrow and specific pacts resolving trade friction in certain product areas or restricting trade in particular commodities.[7] Because of Japan's formidable status as exporter, many nations have sought special bilateral arrangements that function as exceptions to the multilateral trading system.

§ 1–2. THE STATUS OF TRADE AGREEMENTS IN JAPANESE CONSTITUTIONAL LAW

There are various terms for international agreements between Japan and foreign governments. The most common are *jōyaku* (treaty), *kyōyaku* (convention), *kyōtei* (agreement), *torikime* (arrangement), *sengen* (declaration), *giteisho* (protocol), *ketteisho* (act), *kōkanbunsho* (exchange of notes), *kōkanshokan* (exchange of letters), and *oboegaki* (memorandum). The distinctions between these terms are important, because, under article 73(3) of the Constitution of Japan,[8] only a treaty requires the approval of the Diet, the Japanese parliament. Other agreements may be concluded by the executive—the Cabinet[9]—acting alone.

Whether an agreement between Japan and a foreign government falls in the category of "treaty" under article 73(3) depends on its substance rather than its name. In general, any agreement

[5] Compare the Treaty of Friendship, Commerce, and Navigation between the United States and Japan signed at Tokyo, 2 April 1953, entered into force 30 Oct. 1953, 4 U.S.T. 2063, T.I.A.S. 2863, 206 U.N.T.S. 143 with the Treaty of Commerce Establishment and Navigation between the United Kingdom and Japan signed in London, 14 Nov. 1962, *International Legal Materials*, Vol. 2, p. 151 (1963).

[6] E.g., Income Tax Treaty between Japan and the United States, entered into force 9 July 1972, *CCH Tax Treaties*, Vol. 2, pp. 4393.

[7] An example of this is the Market Oriented Sector Specific (MOSS) talks extending over several years and concluded in 1987 between the United States and Japan.

[8] The Constitution of Japan (Nihon Koku Kempō) entered into force 3 May 1947. The official English translation is reprinted in *Constitutions of the World*, Vol. 9, A. Blaustein and G. Flanz, eds. (1973). Some references to the Constitution available in English are .S. Fuji, *The Constitution of Japan: A Historical Survey* (1965); D. Henderson, *The Constitution of Japan: Its First Twenty Years*, 1947–1967 (1969); H. Itoh and L.W. Beer, *The Constitutional Law of Japan: Selected Supreme Court Decisions, 1961–70* (1978).

[9] Arts. 65 and 73 of the Constitution provide that the executive power is vested in the Cabinet.

that affects the rights of individuals—binding or prohibiting their conduct—is regarded as a treaty under Japanese law. Some examples of international agreements that are not considered treaties and for which the approval of the Diet is not necessary are: (1) an agreement pertaining to technical details of diplomacy; (2) an agreement providing for detailed rules implementing a treaty already approved by the Diet; and (3) an executive agreement within the framework of the powers delegated to the Cabinet by legislation.

Although the requirement of Diet approval of treaties is interpreted very flexibly by the Japanese government, the GATT as well as most of the Multinational Trade Negotiation (MTN) Codes adopted under the auspices of the GATT are considered treaties and were approved by the Diet.[10] However, many trade agreements of lesser scope than the GATT are routinely entered into and approved by the government without the formality of consent of the Diet. Japanese government officials take the view that if an international agreement is not self-executing but requires domestic legislation to implement it, the Cabinet need not submit the agreement to the Diet for approval; rather, implementation will take place either through domestic legislation already enacted by the Diet or, if such legislation is lacking, the government will introduce the necessary legislation for Diet approval. This view was summarized by the Director General of the Cabinet Legislation Bureau as follows:

> If . . . an international agreement is enforced not as such but through a domestic law, then restrictions of the rights of individuals are governed by that domestic law. In this situation, we believe that such an agreement need not be submitted to the National Diet. When our government and a foreign government have agreed on a matter under the Constitution, it is not necessary to put such an agreement under the democratic control of the Diet as long as such agreement is not enforced directly (that is, such agreement does not impose obligations and restrictions upon the conduct of citizens in Japan) and is

[10] J. Jackson, J.-V. Louis, M. Matsushita, *Implementing the Tokyo Round* (1984), pp. 84–85.

not in conflict with a treaty which has been approved by the Diet. It is to be understood as an executive agreement of which no such approval is necessary.[11]

Nevertheless, there is an important difference in legal effect between a treaty approved by the Diet and other types of international agreements. Only a treaty approved by the Diet will override a conflicting domestic statute or legislation, regardless of whether the Diet approves the treaty before or after the conflicting statute or regulation.[12] An international agreement which has not been approved by the Diet has no such legal effect. This conclusion is derived from the doctrine that the Diet's approval of a treaty is required to guarantee that the legislative power of the Diet is not infringed by the Cabinet's treaty-making power. Thus domestic legislation in Japan takes precedence over non-treaty executive agreements, but treaties enjoy complete supremacy.

It is unsettled whether treaties prevail over the Constitution in Japan. There are two conflicting schools of thought, one maintaining that the Constitution prevails and the other asserting that a treaty prevails. The first bases its rationale on, among other things, the amendment procedure of the Constitution. In order to amend the Constitution a referendum is required, but the conclusion of a treaty needs only the approval of the Diet. Thus, should a treaty be given priority over the Constitution, it would mean that the Constitution, which must otherwise be amended by means of a national referendum, can be amended in substance by the conclusion of a treaty. This would be contrary

[11] Testimony of the Director of the Cabinet Legislation Bureau in Hearing of the Committee of Budget of the House of Councillors, Hearing No. 7, 67th Diet, 15 (9 Jan. 1971). As long as the government holds the majority in both houses of the Diet, a legislative proposal made by the Cabinet is likely to pass unless there is an unusual situation. Normally, a Cabinet bill passes without amendment.

[12] Art. 98(2) of the Constitution declares that a treaty in the established international law shall be faithfully observed. To admit that there can exist a law that conflicts with a treaty would be contrary to this constitutional command.

This rule holding treaties supreme over conflicting domestic law is in contrast with U.S. law which holds that an act of Congress may supersede an earlier rule of international law or a provision of an international agreement if the purpose of the act is to supersede the earlier rule or if the act and the earlier rule or provision cannot be fairly reconciled. Whitney v. Robertson, 124 U.S. 190 (1888). See *Restatement (Third) of the Foreign Relations Law of the United States*, § 115(1)(a) (1987).

to the basic principle of the sovereignty of the people, which is regarded as one of the fundamental principles of the Constitution.

On the other hand, the theory that a treaty prevails over the Constitution holds that since the Constitution is the expression of the national will of only one nation, it must yield to a treaty, which is the expression of the will of the international community.

Without going into detail, it must be stated that the former theory is more persuasive than the latter, since to hold that a treaty prevails over the Constitution would mean that the most fundamental rights provided by the Constitution (such as the Bill of Rights) could be overridden if the Cabinet and the Diet decided to enter into a treaty repudiating them. This seems an absurd proposition.[13]

In the Sunakawa case, the Supreme Court in an indirect way took the position that the Constitution prevails over a treaty.[14] This case concerned the effect of the Status of Forces Agreement between the United States and Japan, which in turn was based on the Security Treaty between those two countries. The Supreme Court stated that the Security Treaty had great political importance and was not subject to judicial review of the courts "unless some of its provisions were clearly and obviously unconstitutional." In this particular case, the Court used the doctrine of political question to avoid ruling upon constitutionality of the treaty. In dicta, however, the Court recognized the possibility of judicial review of a treaty when some of its provisions seem clearly and obviously unconstitutional.

[13] The view that the Constitution is supreme is in accordance with U.S. law. In Reid v. Covert, 354 U.S. 1, 16–17 (1957), Mr. Justice Black, speaking for the court, stated that "no agreement with a foreign nation can confer power on the Congress, or on any other branch of government, which is free from the restraints of the Constitution. . . . The prohibitions of the constitution were designed to apply to all branches of the National Government and they cannot be nullified by the Executive or by the Executive and the Senate combined."

[14] Japan v. Sakata, *Keishū*, Vol. 13, p. 3225 (Sup. Ct., 16 Dec. 1959). In this case, a person was indicted for trespassing on a U.S. Air Force installation in Japan. The indictment was brought under the Criminal Special Measures Law (Law 138, 1952), which provides for the punishment of anyone who trespasses on the property of U.S. bases in Japan, to implement the Status of Forces Agreement and the Security Treaty between the United States and Japan. The defendant's counsel argued that this law, the agreement, and the treaty conflicted with art. 9 of the Constitution, which prohibits Japan from exercising military power for the purpose of solving international conflicts. The court allowed the indictment to stand.

A constitutional provision relevant to this issue is article 22, which guarantees the freedom of occupation, including the right to carry on a trade or business. There is a line of cases interpreting article 22 in which the Supreme Court had to decide the constitutionality of domestic legislation restricting the rights of individuals to engage in exporting or some other economic activity.[15] The court consistently holds that a judgment on whether a restriction is in fact necessary is best made by the legislative branch of the government and should in principle be left to the discretion of the Diet.[16] Under this reasoning, if a law that restricts the rights of individuals is designed to achieve some social or economic policy (for example, the protection of small enterprises), the court will refrain from making a judgment on the wisdom of the restriction. It is easy to see that under this rule any legislation that is designed to achieve an economic policy (including an international economic policy) will be considered justified unless it is flagrantly unreasonable.

§ 1-3. GATT: The Principal Obligations and Undertakings

In principle, Japan adheres to the GATT as the principal source

---

[15] See Shimizu v. Japan, *Keishū*, Vol. 9, p. 89 (Sup. Ct., 26 Jan. 1955), tr. in J. Maki, *Court and Constitution in Japan* (1964); Sumiyoshi v. Governor of Hiroshima Prefecture (1975), tr. in *Law in Japan*, Vol. 8, pp. 194–204 (1975). For a comment on this case, see Haley, "The Freedom to Choose an Occupation and the Constitutional Limits of Legislative Discretion: K.K. Sumiyoshi v. Governor of Hiroshima Prefecture," *Law in Japan*, Vol. 8, pp. 188–94 (1975).

[16] In Marushin Sangyō K.K. v. Japan, a company was indicted for having erected a building with compartments and leasing the compartments to retailers without a license. Under the Retail Business Adjustment Special Measures Law (Kouri Shōgyō Chōsei Tokubetsu Sochi Hō, Law 155, 1959), a developer of a building to be leased or assigned to small retail shopkeepers must file a report with the local government and obtain a license. The law also gives local governments the power to set conditions for leasing or assigning any such building. Osaka Prefecture requires new buildings to be at least 700 meters away from any existing building in order to protect small mom-and-pop stores. The defendant built the building and leased it to storekeepers without obtaining a license from the prefectural government, and the building was within 700 meters of existing shop buildings. The company argued that the law and the zoning regulation enacted under it were contrary to art. 22 of the Constitution. The Supreme Court stated that a decision on whether small shopkeepers need to be protected by such legislation is. best made by the Diet (*Keishū*, Vol. 26, p. 586; Sup. Ct., 22 Nov. 1972). This suggests that in matters relating to socioeconomic or industrial policy, the courts should refrain from ruling on the wisdom of such legislation.

of its international obligations concerning trade.[17] The GATT not only provides a permanent framework for international consultations relating to trade and economics but also embodies a common set of principles, rules, and undertakings—albeit quite vague and general—to guide the practices and policies of individual member nations. A full discussion of the GATT is beyond the scope of this book and is available elsewhere;[18] here, only the principal obligations and undertakings will be briefly summarized.

A central tenet of the GATT system is the principle of non-discrimination in levying customs duties. Article I obligates member states not to play favorites with respect to imports and exports. Any favors that are extended to one country must be extended equally to all GATT member states. This is known as "unconditional most favored nation" treatment, one of the GATT's proudest achievements.

It must be conceded, however, that a number of exceptions from this principle of non-discrimination have been permitted. First, article XIV of the GATT permits countries which form customs unions or free trade areas to extend special treatment to one another. Second, article XIV permits countries which apply import restrictions for balance of payments reasons to discriminate among sources of their imports. Third, the contracting parties of the GATT have granted special waivers to permit developed countries to extend tariff preferences to imports from developing countries as well as to allow developing countries to exchange preferential tariff treatment among themselves. Fourth, the GATT has granted waivers to individual countries to allow them to give preferential tariff treatment to particular imports from particular countries. Fifth, a special arrangement in textile prod-

---

[17] The General Agreement on Tariffs and Trade was agreed upon in 1947, when it became apparent that the creation of an international trade organization under the auspices of the United Nations was a controversial matter. The GATT was initially signed as a temporary agreement. See the protocol of provisional application of 30 Oct. 1947, 61 Stat. A2051, T.I.A.S. 1700, 55 U.N.T.S. 308. The temporary agreement has become permanent, and the GATT now has 96 members, including all the industrial states of the world except the Soviet Union.

[18] See K. Dam, *The GATT* (1970); J. Jackson, *World Trade and the Law of GATT* (1969); R. E. Hudec, *The GATT Legal System and World Trade Diplomacy* (1975); E. McGovern, *International Trade Regulation*, 2nd ed. (1986).

ucts, the Multifiber Arrangement, permits the imposition of quantitative controls on trade and textile products on a discriminatory basis under special conditions.

Article II of the GATT reinforces the most-favored-nation obligation by requiring each member state not to increase a tariff to a level above the rate to which it is bound by previous tariff negotiations. The GATT has sponsored several rounds of tariff negotiations: Geneva, 1947; Annecy, 1948; Torquay, 1950; Geneva, 1956; Geneva, 1960–61 ("Dillon"); Geneva, 1964–67 ("Kennedy"); and Geneva, 1973–79 ("Tokyo"). Another session known as the "Uruguay Round" is currently under way.

Japan has implemented these obligations in its customs and tariffs laws, which deal with such matters as tariff classification, customs valuation, retaliatory tariffs, emergency tariffs, quotas, and antidumping and countervailing duties.[19] Japan applied to the Tokyo Round tariff bindings ahead of schedule and presently has the lowest average tariffs of any country in the world. For customs purposes, Japan is divided into eight districts with 109 ports and eight airports open to foreign trade.

Article III of the GATT provides that internal taxes and other regulations and requirements shall not be applied to imported products in a way "to afford protection to domestic production." Article XVII obligates state trading enterprises to act solely in accordance with non-discriminatory commercial considerations with respect to imports, but there is an exemption for procurement by government agencies for their own use. Article VI permits an importing country to impose an antidumping duty in addition to the regular duty if an imported product is sold at less than its "normal" value. Article XVI imposes restrictions on subsidies of exports and permits countervailing duties to be levied under certain circumstances. Articles VII and VIII set out general rules for the valuation of imported products, the limitation of service fees other than duties, and the simplification of customs formalities. Article IX provides standards for national requirements of marks of origin of imported goods to prevent both fraudulent markings and unduly burdensome rules.

In principle, the GATT (article XI) prohibits the use of quan-

[19] See infra § 3–5.

titative restrictions to limit imports and exports,[20] but exceptions are permitted (1) for agricultural or fisheries products where these are used in support of governmental programs that restrict the production or sale of the product concerned; (2) for restrictions used by countries experiencing balance of payments difficulties (articles XII and XVIII); (3) for "safeguard" measures taken under the authority of article XIX; (4) for textiles and clothing under the Multifiber Arrangement; and (5) for various general law enforcement measures such as the protection of public health, national security, public morals, national treasures, and restrictive practices (articles XX and XXI). Quotas may not be applied to imports from one nation unless they are applied to all; and they must be allocated among supplying states so as to preserve the shares of imports they would normally have in the absence of restrictions (article XIII).

The GATT contains several "safeguard" clauses that allow a member state to avoid certain duties and obligations, usually on a temporary basis and only after consultations with other trading partners. Article XXVIII permits a revision of bound tariff duties if agreement can be reached with the exporting countries "primarily concerned." Resort to temporary quotas (but not increased tariffs) is permissible if a state encounters balance of payments difficulties (articles XII and XVIII). A state may also take emergency action, which may include both quotas and increased tariffs, if it finds that because of unforseen developments and concessions granted, a product is being imported in increased quantities so as to cause or threaten serious injury to domestic producers (article XIX). Japan has not had occasion to invoke any of these safeguard provisions.

While in its early years the GATT was concerned principally with reducing tariffs, in the 1970s, non-tariff barriers to international trade became the focus of attention. In 1979, the Tokyo Round was concluded, and a series of agreements emerged to deal with these issues: (1) The Subsidies Code; (2) The Antidumping Code; (3) The Customs Valuation Code; (4) The Agreement on Government Procurement; (5) The Agreement

---

[20] Japan was recently found to be in violation of this provision in connection with import quotas on various types of agricultural products. See infra § 3–8.

on Technical Barriers to Trade; (6) The Agreement on Import Licensing Procedures; (7) The Agreement on Trade in Civil Aircraft; (8) The International Dairy Agreement; (9) The Agreement on Bovine Meat.

Current GATT negotiations, the Uruguay Round, focus on a wide variety of issues, such as agricultural trade, services, intellectual property, investment, and improving GATT operation and enforcement.

§ 1–4. GATT: Dispute Resolution

The GATT provides an important framework and a series of procedures to resolve trade disputes between member states. Throughout, the principal emphasis is on encouraging bilateral negotiations and conciliation to settle disputes in order to preclude resort to retaliation and counter-retaliation.

The most important dispute resolution procedures of the GATT are set out in articles XXII (Consultation) and XXIII (Nullification and Impairment).[21] Article XXII commits each member state to consult with other member states concerning "any matter affecting the operation of this agreement." The other "contracting parties" to the GATT may also, if requested, be consulted if the dispute cannot be resolved by the parties themselves.

Article XXIII sets out a procedure for formal, written proposals and consultations between member states concerning a broad variety of problems if a member country considers that "any benefit accruing to it directly or indirectly under this agreement is being nullified or impaired or that the attainment of any objective is being impeded" because of (1) a violation of the agreement: (2) the application of any measure even though not in violation of the agreement; or (3) any other situation. Where bilateral consultations cannot resolve the issue, the contracting parties may be requested to "make appropriate recom-

---

[21] In addition to the dispute resolution procedures in arts. XXII and XXIII, procedures concerning disputes are found in the substantive articles of the GATT itself. For example, article XIX contains a specific set of consultation procedures to be followed. In addition, the Tokyo Round codes themselves contain procedures for resolving disputes that arise under them. The common pattern here is consultation, conciliation, panel investigation, and report, followed by action by the appropriate committees after further consultation with the parties.

mendations . . . or give a ruling on the matter." This can involve
referring the matter to a special working party or a dispute settlement panel which hears presentations from both sides as well
as from other interested parties and renders its findings and con-
clusions.[22]

The GATT is not an enforcement body, and there is little
power to compel a member state to correct a violation. In fact,
however, most problems are addressed within the limits of political feasibility. Moreover, as a last resort, the contracting parties
may authorize an injured party to retaliate, withdrawing or
suspending equivalent concessions if "circumstances are serious
enough to justify such action."

Reform and strengthening of the dispute resolution process
of the GATT was addressed in the Tokyo Round of 1979, and
a special agreement was concluded which provides an "agreed
description" of the procedures under article XXIII.[23] The 1982
GATT Ministerial Meeting adopted a Declaration on Dispute
Resolution which calls for prompt consideration of panel reports
and requires a party to whom a recommendation has been addressed to report an action taken or its reasons for not implementing the recommendation or ruling.

Japan fully supports and has implemented the GATT policy
of resolving disputes with its trading partners through bilateral
consultations and negotiations. Japan's trading practices have
also been the subject of investigation and reports by GATT
panels.[24]

§ 1–5. THE RELATIONSHIP BETWEEN THE GATT
AND DOMESTIC LAW IN JAPAN

An important but difficult issue is the relationship between GATT

---

[22] See Plank, "An Unofficial Description of How a GATT Panel Works and Does
Not," *Swiss Review of International Competition Law*, p. 81 (1985).

[23] See "The Understanding Regarding Notification, Consultation, Dispute Settlement, and Surveillance," 28 Nov. 1979, 26 B.I.S.D. 210 (1980). See also Hudec,
"GATT Dispute Settlement After the Tokyo Round: An Unfinished Business," *Cornell International Law Journal*, Vol. 13, p. 145 (1980).

[24] E.g., in October 1987 a GATT investigative panel ruled that punitive Japanese
taxes on liquor imports from the European Community are contrary to the GATT
rules and should be removed. *International Trade Reporter* (BNA), Vol. 4, p. 1385 (11
Nov. 1987). In December 1987, a GATT panel ruled that Japanese quantitative

and domestic law. Article 98(2) of the Constitution provides that treaties and established international law should be given due respect. This constitutional provision has been interpreted to signify the supremacy of a treaty or customary international law. Therefore, when a domestic law or an administrative regulation is contrary to a treaty provision or a rule of customary international law, the treaty or rule should prevail.[25] The GATT enjoys treaty status in the Japanese legal system since it was signed by the Cabinet as a treaty and approved by the Diet. Therefore, when a conflict arises between a provision in the GATT and a domestic law or regulation, the GATT should be interpreted as supreme.

A case dealing with these issues was decided by the Kyoto District Court in 1984, involving a law establishing a price stabilization scheme for domestically produced raw silk.[26] Under this law, the Ministry of Agriculture, Forestry, and Fisheries is empowered to establish upper and lower prices for raw silk, and when the market price dips below the minimum, the agency may purchase raw silk to support the price. When it goes above the upper limit, then the agency may sell raw silk to bring the price down. Even though this legislation deals with both lower and higher prices, its main concern is to establish a minimum support price for silk.

To effectively operate this price stabilization program, it was necessary also to restrict the import of raw silk. This is because the stabilization program would be disrupted if raw silk from abroad were allowed to come in freely when the domestic price was too low. In light of this, the law was amended to provide for import restrictions. Under this amendment, a government agency (Sanshi Jigyōdan, the Silk Business Agency) has exclusive power to import raw silk. Moreover, when the agency sells the imported raw silk, the sale price must not be below the standard price as determined by the government. As can readily be seen, this system is designed to protect the domestic raw silk

---

restrictions on the import of certain cultural products were in violation of the GATT. *International Trade Reporter* (BNA), Vol. 4, p. 1490 (2 Dec. 1987).

[25] See supra § 1–2.

[26] Decision in Endō v. Japan, *Hanrei Taimuzu*, No. 530, p. 265 (Kyoto Dist. Ct., 29 June 1984).

producers, and the price of raw silk in Japan is much higher than the international market price.

Although raw silk imports are restricted, there are no restrictions on the importation of silk fabrics. As a result, even with existing tariffs on imported silk fabrics and ties, European tie manufacturers can purchase raw silk from the People's Republic of China and South Korea, the two major producing countries, and produce ties at much lower cost than the Japanese manufacturers.

The Japanese fabric producers accordingly complained that they could not compete with European ties imported into Japan and filed suit against the government, alleging that the raw silk law was contrary to article 22(1) and article 29(2) of the Constitution (which guarantee freedom of trade and private property, respectively) and article XVII of the GATT which provides that a state trading agency must act on the basis of commercial considerations in foreign trade operations.

The Kyoto District Court, however, ruled in favor of the government and upheld the law. The court first held that freedom of trade and the guarantee of private property are not absolute but are subject to restrictions for the public welfare. The question of what kind of policy should be adopted and enforced in socioeconomic matters is best left to the judgment and discretion of the Diet as the organ most suitable for examining such questions on the basis of empirical data and adjusting the various adverse interests involved.

The court also stated that the government provided aid to the Japanese producers of tie fabrics by imposing high tariffs. And if the condition of the Japanese fabric industry seriously deteriorated, the government would be able to invoke an import restriction of necktie fabrics under article XIX, the Escape Clause of the GATT. In view of these compensatory measures, the court concluded that the raw silk law did not unreasonably restrict the freedom of trade of Japanese fabric producers.

Another issue raised by the fabric producers was the legality of this legislation under article XVII(1)(a) of the GATT, which stipulates that each contracting party agrees that a state trading agency under its control should operate its transactions on the basis of commercial considerations only in terms of price, quality, and availability. Article II(4) of the GATT also stipulates that, whenever a tariff concession under the GATT has been made for a commodity which is an object of state trading, a contracting party shall not sell the commodity in the domestic market at a price above the actual import price plus the applicable tariff.

The Japanese fabric producers argued that the government agency in charge of importing raw silk amounted to a state trading agency, and since the agency was not allowed to sell imported raw silk in the domestic market below the stabilization price, the sales policy envisaged in the legislation violated articles II and XVII of the GATT.

In rejecting this argument, the court gave the following reasons for upholding the validity of the legislation:

> The exclusive importership and the price stabilization system under consideration . . . are designed to protect the business of raw silk producers from the pressure of imports for a while, and this has the same substance as the emergency measure permitted under article XIX of the GATT. Even though it is reasonable to state that, judging from the nature of such an emergency measure, there should be a limit to the duration of it, such a limit should not be regarded as absolute. Since this duration should be decided in relation to the duration of the pressure of imports, article 12–13–2 of the law providing for enforcing the exclusive importership for a while cannot be regarded as unreasonable.

Regarding the effectiveness of GATT articles in relation to domestic laws, the court stated:

> A violation of a provision of GATT pressures the country in default to rectify the violation by being confronted with a request from another member country for consultation and possible retaliatory measures. However, it cannot be interpreted to have more effect than this. Therefore, it cannot be held that the legislation in question is contrary to the GATT and null and void. . . .

The validity of the court's holding on the relationship between the GATT and a domestic regulation is rather dubious. The court held that the import restriction in question would be held lawful since the same kind of measure would be allowed under article XIX of the GATT. However, article XIX requires that a country invoking a safeguard measure find "serious injury" caused by an increase in imports. In this case, however, not only was "serious injury" not found, but there was no procedure in the law to find such an injury. Moreover, this exclusive importership was established in 1976, and there is no sign yet that it will be relaxed or abolished. Even admitting that the duration of the restriction may be determined relative to import pressure against which the restriction provides protection, the raw silk law's unlimited duration seems excessive.

Finally, the court seems to imply that the fact that a domestic law is contrary to a provision of the GATT will not affect the validity of the law in Japan, although it may trigger a request for consultation or even retaliation by another GATT member country. This view seems to ignore article 98(2) of the Constitution, which provides that a treaty and established rules in international law should be accorded due respect, as well as the established legal interpretation in Japan that a treaty overrides a contrary domestic law regardless of the order in which the treaty and the domestic law were enacted.[27]

Nevertheless, the decision of the Kyoto District Court in the Chinese Silk case is remarkably consistent with similar cases interpreting the GATT in the European Community and the United States. In International Fruit v. Produktshap,[28] the Court of Justice of the European Community held that although the Community was bound by its provisions, the GATT, because of the flexibility of its terms, is not capable of conferring on individual companies' and citizens' rights which they can invoke before the courts. In the United States as well, with rare exceptions, the GATT is held not to provide rights to private parties.[29]

---

[27] See supra § 1–2.

[28] Court of Justice of the European Communities, Case Nos. 21–24/72, (1972) *European Community Review*, 1219.

[29] See *Restatement (Third) of the Foreign Relations Law of the United States*, Part VIII, Chapter One, Introductory Note, p. 264 (1987).

CHAPTER TWO

GOVERNMENTAL AUTHORITY OVER TRADE IN JAPAN

§ 2–1. CONSTITUTIONAL POWERS OVER TRADE

Under the Japanese Constitution, there are three basic branches of government: the National Diet (Kokkai), the Cabinet (Naikaku), and the Judiciary (Saibansho). The National Diet is made up of the House of Representatives (Shūgi-in, the lower house) and the House of Councillors (Sangi-in, the upper house) (See Appendix).

The Constitution declares that the National Diet is the highest organ and the sole lawmaking organ of the state, and that members of both houses are elected by the people (article 43(1)). It also states that a legislative proposal becomes a law when it has been approved by both houses (article 59(1)). The House of Representatives has the right to pass a no-confidence resolution in the Cabinet. In the event that such a resolution is passed, the Cabinet must either resign or dissolve the lower house (article 69), in which case an election must be held (article 54(1)). The lower house, which is composed of 511 members at present, may also be dissolved by the prime minister before the full term is up, at a time politially favorable to him or his party (article 7(3)).

The House of Councillors is also a popularly elected body, but it is elected in a different way from its counterpart. At present one hundred of the councillors are chosen through a proportional representation system, while the other 152 are chosen from local constituencies. Half of each group is chosen every three years for the six-year term of office (article 46). The House of Councillors' power is clearly subordinate to that of the House of Representatives (see articles 59–61, 67). Each house has the same sixteen standing committees and creates special committees as needed

19

for special issues. Most of the committees correspond to major ministerial divisions of the Cabinet and bureaucracy.

Administrative power is vested in the Cabinet (article 65) which consists of the prime minister and other ministers of state (article 66(1)). While the prime minister may be elected from among the members of either house by a resolution of the Diet (article 67), he is invariably elected from the lower house. The Cabinet is responsible to the Diet in the exercise of administrative power (article 66(3)). The prime minister appoints the Cabinet ministers (20 at present), a majority of whom must be chosen from among the members of the Diet (article 68(1)). The Cabinet is charged with general administrative duties, including executing the law, managing foreign affairs, concluding treaties, preparing and presenting the budget, issuing Cabinet orders, and granting clemency (article 73). The work of carrying out these functions is divided among 12 ministries, each of which is headed by one of the ministers of state. The Cabinet must resign when the House of Representatives passes a non-confidence resolution or rejects a confidence resolution, unless the House is dissolved within ten days of the resolution (article 69).

The third branch of the government is the Judiciary, which is made up of the Supreme Court (Saikō Saibansho) and lower courts (article 76(1)), and the Constitution declares that all judicial power is vested in the judiciary (article 76(1)). The Supreme Court is at the heart of the judicial power. It nominates the judges of the lower courts (article 80(1)) and has the ultimate power to determine the constitutionality of all laws (article 81), like its counterpart in the United States. Article 98(1) states that the Constitution is the supreme law of the nation, and laws, orders, imperial decrees, and other regulations contrary to its provisions are null and void. The chief justice as well as the other justices of the Supreme Court are appointed by the Cabinet (articles 8(2) and 79(1)). After their appointment, the justices of the Supreme Court cannot be removed except by public impeachment (article 78).

§ 2–2. THE JAPANESE LEGAL SYSTEM

Japan is a unitary state with a civil law system largely derived from Continental Europe.[1] In addition to the Constitution, there are five major codes: (1) the Civil Code,[2] (2) the Code of Civil Procedure,[3] (3) the Criminal Code,[4] (4) the Code of Criminal Procedure,[5] and (5) the Commercial Code.[6]

The Civil Code and the Commercial Code provide the basic framework governing the legal relationships between individuals and legal transactions. The Civil Code, which was enacted in 1898, is modeled after its German counterpart, although with influences from French, English, and Japanese customary law as well.[7] The Civil Code has five divisions: (1) The General Part (Sōsoku), (2) Real Rights (Bukken), (3) Obligations (Saiken), (4) Domestic Relations (Shinzoku), and (5) Inheritance (Sōzoku). The Commercial Code, enacted in 1899, was modeled after its German counterpart. However, after World War II, some new provisions (such as those relating to authorized capital and a representative suit) based on American corporation laws were incorporated. The Commercial Code is divided into: (1) the General Part (Sōsoku), (2) Corporations (Kaisha), (3) Commercial Acts (Shōkōi), and (4) Maritime Law (Kaishō). There are several related laws, such as the Limited Company Law and the laws relating to bills and notes. The codes are formulated in abstract terms and are subject to judicial interpretation by the courts, which must decide cases involving particular fact situations. Although judges in Japan are not bound by judicial precedents, as a practical matter, well-established decisional rules will be followed.

The public law of Japan—dealing with the rights of individuals and companies in relation to the state—is governed by subject-specific statutes passed by the Diet. Also important are official and unofficial governmental regulations and pronouncements that interpret and implement these statutes. Governmental agen-

---

[1] See, generally, Y. Noda, *Introduction to Japanese Law* (1976); H. Tanaka, *The Japanese Legal System* (1976).
[2] Minpō, Law 89, 1896, and Law 222, 1947.
[3] Minji Soshō Hō, Law 29, 1890.
[4] Kei Hō, Law 45, 1907.
[5] Keiji Soshō Hō, Law 131, 1948.
[6] Shō Hō, Law 48, 1899.
[7] See, generally, Young, "The Japanese Legal System: History and Structure," in *Doing Business in Japan*, Vol. 2, Z. Kitagawa, ed. (1984).

cies have the authority to issue general regulations (*meirei*), but the most important category of regulations is *seirei*—cabinet orders. Government ministers may issue ministerial orders (*shōrei*) in order to implement a statute or *seirei*. Heads of administrative committees may issue subsidiary rules called *kisoku*. If further interpretation is necessary, circulars (*tsūtatsu*) or directives (*kunrei*) may be issued.

In addition, various informal methods of administration are used by government agencies; this is known as administrative guidance (*gyōsei shidō*). Administrative guidance may take the form of requests (*yōbō*), direction (*shiji*), warnings (*keikoku*), suggestions (*kankoku*), and encouragements (*kanshō*).

§ 2–3. The Policymaking Process

Extraparliamentary processes are vitally important in the policymaking process in Japan. Policies, including economic policies, often take the form of legislation. Even though, as explained above, a law is passed by the Diet, in reality the process preceding the parliamentary process is vitally important. Often, ideas for policies are conceived in various ministries and in the Liberal Democratic Party (LDP), which is the party currently in control. And sometimes the LDP itself formulates policies. The process involved is very complex, and a brief sketch must suffice.[8]

When an idea for a policy is formulated in a ministry, officials in charge discuss the matter with key LDP members, and after obtaining their informal approval, draft a legislative proposal that is sent to the Legislation Bureau of the Cabinet (Naikaku Hōsei Kyoku). After the Legislation Bureau looks it over, the proposal is sent again to the LDP for a more formal examination. Then it is discussed in a Cabinet meeting. When the Cabinet has given its approval, it is introduced in the Diet.[9] As long as the LDP holds the majority in both houses, a legislative proposal made by the Cabinet after extraparliamentary consent by the

---

[8] In spite of the importance of this issue, there has been little writing on the extraparliamentary process in decision making in Japan. The following book describes the details of this process: I. Murakawa, *Seisaku Kettei Katei* (The Policy-Making Process) (1981).

[9] Id., pp. 125–63.

LDP is likely to pass, unless there is an unusual situation—if, for example, the opposition party obstructs the debate or the Diet runs out of time to examine the proposal. Normally, however, the Cabinet bill passes without amendment.

The extraparliamentary process, therefore, is as important, or perhaps more important, than the parliamentary process in formulating economic policies. Most of the bills are formulated through this process by the government and introduced in the Diet.

The Policy Research Council of the LDP is also an essential element of the policymaking process. This body conducts research in all fields of national policy and initiates new policy measures. All matters that are to be adopted as policy by the LDP must be approved by this council.

The council consists of 17 committees (*bukai*) corresponding to the chief ministries of the government and their Diet committees. There are also 84 special committees or task forces (*chōsakai* or *tokubetsu iinkai*).[10] For example, they include the Research Commission on Foreign Affairs, Research Commission on the Tax System, Research Commission on Comprehensive Agriculture, Research Commission on Fundamental Policies for Telecommunications, Investigations Committee for the Revision of Antimonopoly Laws, and Special Research Commission on International Economic Measures. Under the 17 committees and the special committees or task forces, there are 143 subcommittees (*shō iinkai*). The committees have a small number of regular staff members in addition to the LDP Diet members.[11] All of the LDP Diet members are usually members of one or more of the main committees or the special committees. The committees present the LDP Diet members with a forum in which the various opinions of the Diet members can be blended with one another and coordinated with the expert views of the ministerial bureaucracies. In carrying out this process, LDP Diet members and Diet members and the relevant ministerial bureaucrats hold intensive consultations behind the scenes.

[10] See *Gendaijin No Tame No Seiji No Jōshiki Dai Hyakka* (Encyclopedia of Common Sense in Politics for Contemporaries) No. 169, K. Iijima, Y. Miyazaki, and T. Watanabe, eds. (1983).

[11] See Murakawa, supra note 8, pp. 37–42.

§ 2–4. The Role of the Ministries

Although there is relatively little legislative opposition in the area of foreign or international economic policies, there is often tension and conflict among the various agencies and ministries in charge of formulating and executing them. The major government agencies in charge of economic policy include the Ministry of International Trade and Industry (MITI), the Ministry of Agriculture, Forestry, and Fisheries (MAFF), the Ministry of Finance (MOF), the Economic Planning Agency (EPA), the Ministry of Health and Welfare (MHW), and the Ministry of Foreign Affairs (MFA). Except for the MFA, which is in charge of foreign diplomacy, and the EPA, which oversees global economic policies, each ministry supervises and promotes certain industrial sectors, and it is the ministry in charge of an industry that is usually responsible for formulating the industrial agricultural policy concerning it.

Inevitably, the policies of various ministries sometime collide. For example, the MFA has a policy of maintaining friendly relations with foreign nations and has advocated the ending of import quotas for agricultural products. However, MAFF, as the advocate and promoter of the Japanese agriculture, has been in favor of restricting agricultural imports. MITI is in charge of supervising and promoting mostly industrial goods and may have a restrictive policy for industrial products that are not internationally competitive and a liberal trade policy for products that are. Even though the Cabinet is the forum in which such disagreements are to be reconciled, sometimes such conflicts persist and are difficult to resolve. In these cases, the LDP may act as a mediator and may try to reconcile the different points of view by suggesting a compromise.[12]

In any event, the bureaucracy plays a vital role in politics and also in economic policy because it is the key ministries where the best human resources and information about industries are pooled together. It is natural, then, that the real struggles take place there, in the very heart of the power structure. In this sense, something comparable to the conflict and tension between the

[12] Id., pp. 128–29.

Congress and the executive branch in the United States is present in the relationship among the key ministries.[13] This pluralism belies the concept of "Japan, Inc.," the view prevalent in Western circles that the Japanese always speak with one voice.

§ 2–5. INDUSTRIAL POLICY

Industrial policy may be defined as government intervention in "certain sectors of the economy to enhance the nation's economic welfare, especially where the competitive market mechanism is found to fail in achieving that end."[14]

The legal basis for industrial policy in Japan is the array of economic laws administered by MITI, the MOF, and other government ministries. The MOF has specific authority on such matters as fiscal and monetary policy, banking, securities, insurance, and some tariff measures through emergency tariff, antidumping, and countervailing duties. The MITI Establishment Law[15] grants MITI comprehensive powers over many sectors of industrial production. MITI also has specific authority over international trade through the Foreign Exchange and Foreign Trade Control Law and the Export and Import Transactions Law.[16]

MITI also has extensive legal powers to promote desirable industrial activities. Examples of this are the Petroleum Business Law, the Small Enterprises Modernization Promotion Law, Small Business Organization Law, and the Research Association Law. Tax incentives may also be used to achieve regional economic development, environmental protection, and efficient use of energy and mineral resources and to stimulate research and development.[17]

Many other laws give MITI and other agencies active power

---

[13] Peter Drucker characterizes this process as "unremitting guerilla warfare." Drucker, "Behind Japan's Success," *Harvard Business Review* (Jan.-Feb. 1981), p. 83.

[14] Okuno-Fujiwara and Suzumura, "Economic Analysis of Industrial Policy: A Conceptual Framework Through the Japanese Experience," *PAFTAD Conference Proceedings on the Industrial Policies for Pacific Growth*, 1 (1985).

[15] Tsūshō Sangyō Shō Setchi Hō, Law 275, 1952, as amended.

[16] On these laws, see Matsushita, "Economic Regulation," in *CCH Japan Business Law Guide* (1988), paras. 30-110–37-880.

[17] On these laws and measures, see Matsushita, "The Legal Framework of Japanese Industrial Policy," *Brigham Young University Law Review*, Vol. 1987, No. 2 (1987), pp. 541–70.

to manage sectors of the economy. The Law Concerning the Adjustment of Business of Large Retail Stores[18] requires any person who wishes to open a supermarket to notify MITI, which can compel measures to protect small retailers. MITI also manages the insurance program for exports and overseas direct investment, the system of regional industrial parks, and industrial research and development laboratories.

These and other laws under which MITI and government ministries exercise power over the economy provide only very broad and vague limits on administrative discretion. The bureaucracy thus is able to manage the economy with virtually no statutory restrictions. Moreover, the ministries commonly rely on administrative guidance[19]—the general term for a variety of practices through which the government makes informal suggestions and recommendations—as their chief tool for implementing industrial policies.

1. A BRIEF HISTORY OF JAPANESE INDUSTRIAL POLICY

Since the end of World War II, Japanese industrial policy has concentrated on a series of changing goals. The effort immediately after the war was to reconstruct the economy and to expand coal mining and basic industry, such as steel. Because this demanded concentrated capital and financial resources, there were detailed government regulations, price fixing, and allocation of markets.

In the 1960s, however, Japan began to concentrate on achieving economies of scale to build its industrial enterprise and to make them more efficient. Leading industries were encouraged to import technology from abroad and to implement the most modern production techniques at home. Basic industries such as steel, metal, oil refining, chemicals, and machinery were given first priority. In order to achieve further economies of scale, exporting was greatly emphasized. At the same time, the government maintained tight restrictions on imports and foreign investment.

---

[18] Daikibo Kouri Tempo ni okeru Kourigyō no Jigyō Katsudō no Chōsei ni kansuru Hōritsu, Law 109, 1973.

[19] See infra § 2–6.

During the 1970s, Japanese industrial policy began to shift toward more diversified goals.[20] The government began to emphasize knowledge-intensive industries—high technology, computers, software, and other industries with high value-added potential. A variety of new goals came to the fore, such as environmental quality, timber production, assuring adequate energy supplies, and allaying overseas trade frictions. During this period, Japan began to dismantle its formidable trade barriers to imports and foreign investment.

In the 1980s, Japan came to the realization that it was an important part of the world economy and had to adopt the policies of a global economic power.[21] Major elements of Japanese industrial policy today are: (1) to achieve an appropriate industrial structure by continuing to concentrate on high-value-added industries; (2) to encourage imports and to stimulate domestic demand; (3) to liberalize services and capital markets; (4) to assure a diverse and stable supply of natural resources and energy; (5) to promote research and development; and (6) to reduce international trade friction.

2. RESEARCH AND DEVELOPMENT

For purposes of analysis, research and development may be classified as: (1) basic research, (2) applied research, and (3) development research.[22] In basic research, there is no immediate link between the research and the development of a particular product; research is conducted only for the purpose of proving a hypothesis. In development research, the direct objective is to employ technology to produce a new product. Applied research is the intermediate stage between these two. Since basic research involves a great deal of money and risk, private enterprises are unlikely to engage in such research unless some incentives are provided.

As a result, several laws encourage basic research and development. The Research Association Law permits private enterprises

---

[20] See, generally, C. Johnson, *MITI and the Japanese Miracle: The Growth of Industrial Policy, 1925–1975* (1982).

[21] See, generally, I. C. Magaziner and T. M. Hunt, *Japanese Industrial Policy* (1980); T. Nakamura, *The Postwar Japanese Economy: Its Development and Structure* (1981); R. Komiya, M. Okuno, and K. Suzumura, eds., *Industrial Policy in Japan* (1988).

[22] On this topic, see, generally, Matsushita, supra note 17.

to form an association for the purpose of carrying out specific technological tasks. An association created under this law can apply for a joint patent for the technology developed. In addition, there are various tax incentives and subsidies; and the government sometimes establishes a research association to carry on the research.

Another important law is the Basic Technology Research Facilitation Law, which was enacted in 1984. This law established the Basic Technology Research Facilitation Center, which provides funds and facilities to private enterprises doing research, organizes the research, arranges joint research projects between private enterprises and governmental research agencies, and collects technical information.

3. DECLINING INDUSTRIES

A feature of Japanese industrial policy is to provide for a system of measures to cope with depression. To deal with "cyclical depression," which occurs together with the general slowdown of the economy, depression cartels are allowed under article 24-4 of the Antimonopoly Law (AML). When the economy has plunged into a state of depression in which the price level falls below the cost of production and, due to it, the continuation of business activities in a certain industrial sector is difficult, enterprises in the industry may agree on a cutback of production and, when it is not effective, fixing of price. Such an agreement must be approved by the Fair Trade Commission (FTC), and, when it is, it is exempted from the application of the AML.

In structural depression, in contrast with cyclical depression, an industrial sector is in a state of depression, regardless of the state of the economy as a whole. Structural depression occurs due to, *inter alia*, the loss of comparative advantage vis-à-vis similar products imported from other countries, competing products produced domestically or abroad, and a shift in demand to other products. To deal with structural depression, a law passed in 1978, the Depressed Industry Law, permitted enterprises to utilize cartels to cut back excess production facilities. This legislation, however, expired in 1988 and was supplanted by a new law, the Law to Provide for Temporary Measures to Facilitate the

Industrial Structure Adjustment.[23] This law provides that enterprises may jointly formulate a "business adaptation program" or "business cooperation program." The programs must be approved by MITI and, when they are, the enterprises involved enjoy tax reduction and financial aids. Before approving the programs, MITI consults the FTC to make sure that the programs do not go counter to the AML.

4. SMALL BUSINESSES

A "small business enterprise" is generally defined as a business whose employees number 300 or less and whose capital is less than ¥100 million. The Small Business Organization Law[24] permits small enterprises to organize a commerce and industry association which is in essence a depressed-industry cartel. However, this differs from a depressed-industry cartel under article 24–4 of the AML in that a commerce and industry association under the Small Business Organization Law is allowed under more lenient standards. Small enterprises may form a commerce and industry association to cut back production and engage in other restrictions of competition whenever there exists "excessive competition" and "instability of management" among the member enterprises, while under article 24–4 of the AML, a depressed-industry cartel is allowed only when the price goes below the average cost of production and the majority of enterprises in the industry are faced with difficulty in continuing their operations. The purpose of allowing small businesses to cooperate is so that they can play a role as a countervailing force to large enterprises and to improve the business of the member enterprises through technological development and rationalization of management.

The activities of small business associations are exempt from the AML under article 24, since their activities are designed to strengthen small enterprises vis-à-vis large companies and to make them more competitive. Obviously, however, such combined power may be used to raise the prices and to eliminate competition. Nevertheless, there are thousands of such associations operating in Japan.

---

[23] Sangyō Kōzō Tenkan Enkatsuka Rinji Sochi Hō, Law 24, 1987.
[24] Chūshō Kigyō Dantai no Soshiki ni kansuru Hōritsu, Law 185, 1957, as amended.

The Small Business Opportunities Adjustment Law[25] authorizes a small business organization to petition MITI to regulate the entry of a large-scale enterprise into a field of business in which small business enterprises have been traditionally engaged, and the Large Retail Stores Law[26] likewise authorizes small shopkeepers in a specific locality to petition MITI or a local government to forbid a large-scale retail store like a supermarket or a department store from doing business in the area. If the enforcement agency has decided that the business of small enterprises in the area will be unduly disturbed by the entry of a large-scale enterprise, it can order the large enterprise to refrain from entering the market or to reduce its intended business. Ordinarily, these laws are enforced through administrative guidance instead of through a formal recommendation or order.

5. PRICE CONTROLS

Laws authorizing price controls may be divided into: (1) those that are applied only in emergencies and (2) those that are designed to stabilize prices in specific sectors, such as agriculture.

During the Oil Crisis of the 1970s, prices soared when it was learned that the oil supply would be reduced. To cope with such emergencies, the government passed laws that authorize the control of prices at such times. Examples are the Price Control Order,[27] the National Life Stabilization Law,[28] and the Law Against Speculation and Hoarding.[29] Each of these contains provisions stating that the government may intervene to control prices in emergency situations. The Price Control Order authorizes a price-freeze, the most direct form of government intervention. By contrast, the National Life Stabilization and the Petroleum Products Laws authorize the government to set standard prices for designated products in an emergency. A standard price is only a guideline issued by the government, and disobedience

[25] Chūshō Kigyō no Jigyō Katsudō no Kikai no Kakuho no tame no Dai Kigyō-sha no Jigyō Katsudō no Chōsei ni kansuru Hōritsu, Law 74, 1977.
[26] See supra note 18.
[27] Bukka Tōsei Rei, Decree 118, 1946.
[28] Kokumin Seikatsu Antei Kinkyū Sochi Hō, Law 121, 1973.
[29] Seikatsu Kanren Busshi Tō no Kaishime oyobi Urioshime ni taisuru Kinkyū Sochi ni kansuru Hōritsu, Law 48, 1973.

does not incur criminal liability. If the standard price is ignored, however, the name of the violating enterprise is published, and the government may order it to pay as a penalty the difference between the standard price and the actual price charged. Under the Law Against Speculation and Hoarding, the government can order a hoarding enterprise to reduce its stockpile in an emergency.

Some laws permit permanent price controls in certain fields. Under the Foodstuff Control Law,[30] the government is the exclusive buyer of rice, and the purchase price is set in order to guarantee farmers a reasonable income. But consumer prices for rice are fixed at a lower price, and the resultant deficit is paid for through taxes.

The prices of certain other agricultural products, such as meat, dairy, sugar, and raw silk production, are controlled by the government through price stabilization programs. Price controls are probably jusified in emergencies as long as their duration is limited. However, comprehensive measures to stabilize the price of agricultural products and to control imports are difficult to justify. The economic cost of maintaining the present protection of agricultural products is disproportionately high in relation to the benefits.

§ 2–6. ADMINISTRATIVE GUIDANCE

Administrative guidance (*gyōsei shidō*) appears nowhere in any Japanese statutes, and it is not a legal term. Rather, it is a phrase used by journalists, businesspeople, and government officials to describe a category of informal regulation of private industry that is widespread in Japan. Perhaps the best meaning of the term is: a request made by an administrative body for voluntary cooperation.

Administrative guidance is often preferred over more formal administrative decisions, such as directives or orders, because it preserves the important values (which are often illusory) of harmony and consensus between government and industry. Admin-

---

[30] Shokuryō Kanri Hō, Law 40, 1942.

istrative guidance usually consists of suggestions to take or avoid a particular course of action, advice on interpretation of laws or regulations, and veiled warnings about the unpleasant consequences of certain types of actions.

Administrative guidance is not a technical term, and its wide usage in the media and among government officials makes it difficult to devise a precise legal definition.[31] A government official, when asked in the Diet to define administrative guidance, gave the following answer:

> [Administrative guidance] is not legal compulsion restricting the rights of individuals and imposing obligations on citizens. It is a request or guidance on the part of the government within the limit of the task and administrative responsibility of each agency as provided for in the establishment laws, asking for a specific action or inaction for the purpose of achieving some administrative objective through cooperation on the part of the parties who are the object of the administration.[32]

There are at least three different categories of administrative guidance: (1) promotional or "protective" administrative guidance, (2) conciliatory administrative guidance, and (3) regulatory administrative guidance.

Promotional administrative guidance is advice and information given to enterprises to advance and promote their own interests. In agriculture, for example, government officials disseminate information about new technology and assist as to improvements regarding the production, processing, and storage of agricultural products. Likewise, government agencies in charge of small business provide financial assistance and management advice.

---

[31] Articles in English on administrative guidance written from a legal standpoint include: Young, "Administrative Guidance in the Courts: A Case Study in Doctrinal Adaptation," *Law in Japan*, Vol. 17, p. 120, 130 (1984); Smith, "Prices and Petroleum in Japan: 1973–1974—A Study of Administrative Guidance," *Law in Japan*, Vol. 10, p. 81 (1977); Yamanouchi, "Administrative Guidance and the Rule of Law," *Law in Japan*, Vol. 7, p. 22 (1974); Narita, "Administrative Guidance," *Law in Japan*, Vol. 2, p. 45 (1969); Yeomans, "Administrative Guidance," *Law in Japan*, Vol. 19, p. 125 (1986).

[32] Testimony by the Bureau Chief of the Legal Department of the Cabinet in a hearing held by the Committee on Commerce and Industry of the House of Councilors (26 March 1974), quoted in Office of Industrial Organization, *Gyōsei Shidō to Dokusen Kinshi Hō* (Administrative Guidance and the Antimonopoly Law) p. 62, (Oct. 1981).

Conciliatory administrative guidance is used to aid private enterprises to solve disputes among themselves. For example, MITI and local governments commonly mediate disputes between large and small enterprises.[33]

Regulatory administrative guidance is used by government agencies to regulate the conduct of business enterprises and persons, often as a substitute for a more formal order. Administrative guidance used in this way is a substitute for legal compulsion.[34]

Despite its informality and a recent decline in its effectiveness, administrative guidance is still a powerful governmental tool. Japanese businessmen generally feel that government directives must be respected, whether they are based on legal authority or not. Business in Japan prefers to submit to government direction and avoid confrontations, even if the government direction is wrongful.

Another reason for the effectiveness of administrative guidance is the wide range of powers of some government agencies. For example, MITI derives its authority from about 130 statutes covering a wide variety of areas, such as international trade, safety standards, and pollution control, which makes it a formidable adversary for any company likely to be affected by one or more of those statutes. Faced with MITI administrative guidance, most companies will think twice before resisting it.

Nevertheless, administrative guidance is not sacrosanct. It is most effective when: (1) based on a consensus within the industry which is the object of administrative guidance; (2) supported by legislation which could achieve a similar purpose by compulsory process; and (3) the government can offer a subsidy or some other economic benefit in return for compliance.

Administrative guidance may also be classified according to the source of its authority.[35] First, a statute may explicitly authorize administrative guidance by providing for the issuance of non-

---

[33] For details of this type of administrative guidance, see Matsushita, "Export Control and Export Cartels in Japan," *Harvard International Law Journal*, Vol. 20, No. 103 (1979), pp. 123–24.

[34] See, e.g., In re Noda Shōyu K.K., *Shinketsushū*, Vol. 4, p. 1 (4 April 1952); In re Tōyō Rayon, *Shinketsushū* Vol. 5, p. 17 (6 Aug. 1953).

[35] K. Yamanouchi, *Gyōsei Shidō no Riron to Jissai* (Theory and Practice of Administrative Guidance), pp. 73–77 (1984).

binding recommendations. Second, a statute may not provide for administrative guidance itself, but may authorize formal action to achieve similar goals. Third, the guidance may lack statutory authority except for the general subject matter competence of the regulatory agency.

Administrative guidance is based on explicit statutory authority when the law in question authorizes the agency to issue "suggestions" (kankoku) or "warnings" (keikoku); both terms refer to administrative guidance. An example of this is the Petroleum Industry Law (PIL), which authorizes MITI to recommend production and price levels so that supply will not exceed predicted demand leading to excessive competition.[36]

Administrative guidance is most frequently exercised, however, as a substitute and in support of existing legal authority. It is issued in lieu of invoking legal sanctions, but the threat of formal action is used to compel compliance. For example, in 1977 MITI used administrative guidance to direct electronics manufacturers to create a cartel to fix prices for television sets exported to the United States. If the Japanese companies had failed to comply with this "direction," MITI would have ordered the practice under the Foreign Exchange and Foreign Trade Control Law.[37]

Administrative guidance is also sometimes exercsed in the absence of specific statutory authority. In the Sumitomo Metals case, MITI "suggested" that steel production be reduced to a level of 90 percent of the previous year's output and that production of steel for export should be specifically approved by an export committee, in order to cope with a decline in the price of iron and steel.[38] Sumitomo Metals Co. applied for approval to produce 47,000 tons, but was told that it could produce only

[36] Sekiyu Gyō Hō, Law 128, 1962.

[37] See Zenith Radio Corp. v. Matsushita Electric Indus. Corp., 513 F. Supp. 1100 (Eastern Dist. Pa. 1981), rev'd, 723 F. 2d 238 (3d Cir. 1983); rev'd and remanded, 475 U.S. 574 (1986).

A similar use of administrative guidance was employed to implement the voluntary export restraint agreement between the United States and Japan to limit Japanese passenger car and steel exports to the United States. See Matsushita, "A Japanese View of United States Trade Laws," Northwestern Journal of International Law and Business, Vol. 8, No. 1 (1987), pp. 30–58.

[38] For details of this case, see Yamanouchi, supra note 35, pp. 29–30; Upham, "The Legal Framework of Japan's Declining Industries Policy: The Problem of Transparency in Administrative Process," Harvard International Law Journal, Vol. 27, pp. 425, 435–43 (1986).

9,300 tons. There was no statutory basis for MITI's suggestion except for the MITI Establishment Law, which bestows general powers and responsibilities on the agency with regard to the industries under its jurisdiction. Sumitomo at first declined to obey the guidance, but gave in when MITI announced that if it did not, its foreign currency allotment to purchase coal from abroad would be reduced.[39]

Administrative guidance also may be contrary to established law. The most infamous examples of this are several cases arising out of price and production cartels created by the oil refining industry in 1973, known collectively as the Oil Cartel cases.[40] The cases arose because the Petroleum Association, whose members had a predominant share of the crude oil refining market, decided to reduce production of petroleum products. As stated before, the PIL authorizes MITI to issue guidelines on price and production levels. Under this law, MITI is authorized to formulate and announce the "petroleum products supply program," which is based on the projected demand and supply of petroleum products for a period of five years. To implement this power, MITI can require crude oil refining companies to report their respective plans for import and refining of crude oil into petroleum products. It can also direct the companies to modify their production plans if they tend to lead to overproduction. In

[39] Yamanouchi, supra note 35, p. 41–42.
[40] The civil cases were Kai v. Nippon Sekiyu, K.K., *Minshū*, Vol. 41, p. 785 (Sup. Ct., 2 July 1987) and Satō v. Sekiyu Remmei, *Hanrei Jihō*, No. 1147, p. 19 (Sendai H. Ct., 26 March 1985). The criminal cases were Japan v. Idemitsu Kōsan, K.K., *Hanrei Jihō*, No. 985, p. 3 (Tokyo H. Ct., 26 Sept. 1980), tr. in Ramseyer, "The Oil Cartel Criminal Cases: Translations and Postscript," *Law in Japan*, Vol. 15, pp. 57, 66 (1982), aff'd in part and rev'd in part, *Hanrei Jihō*, No. 1108, p. 3 (Sup. Ct., 24 Feb. 1984), and Japan v. Sekiyu Remmei, *Hanrei Jihō*, No. 983, p. 22 (Tokyo H. Ct., 26 Sept. 1980), tr. in Ramseyer.
Another important case involving import control by administrative guidance is that of the Lions Oil Company. See *Nihon Keizai Shimbun*, 5 Feb. 1985 (morning ed.), p. 5; Id., 14 Feb. 1985 (evening ed.), p. 14. In 1984, Lions intended to import gasoline from Singapore and filed a report under the PIL with MITI. MITI, of course, objected to it strongly, but Lions also insisted that it would import gasoline. While negotiations were proceeding between Lions and MITI, gasoline was shipped from Singapore to Japan. According to news reports, MITI, having found that it would be difficult to persuade Lions to give up the importation, decided to pressure financial institutions to suspend financing to Lions if the company insisted on importing gasoline. Lions finally gave in and decided to abandon the plan to import gasoline. The gasoline, which had been shipped from Singapore to Japan, was imported not as gasoline, but as "naptha."

actuality, however, MITI has never utilized this formal power. Instead, it has always informally advised the refining companies to limit or stabilize production.

The Petroleum Association had initiated a program to limit the production of petroleum products by allocating quotas to its member companies. Since MITI's policy was to avoid over-production, MITI made use of this program and requested the association through administrative guidance to come up with a production program that MITI regarded as desirable.

Despite MITI's involvement, the FTC objected to the cutbacks of production and price fixing and brought a criminal complaint in the Public Prosecutor's Office. The Public Prosecutor indicted both the Petroleum Association, its member companies, and several top executives, charging them with violating article 8(1) of the Antimonopoly Law (AML), which broadly condemns restraints of competition by trade associations, as well as price fixing, which is prohibited under article 3 (as defined by article 2(6)) of the AML as an "unreasonable restraint of trade." In 1980, the Tokyo High Court handed down two separate decisions. In the Oil Cartel (price fixing) case, the court convicted the twelve oil companies of criminal conduct and sentenced fourteen of their top executives to prison. However, the sentence was suspended. In the Oil Cartel (production restrictions) case, the defendants' conduct was held to be illegal, but they were acquitted on the grounds that they lacked the requisite criminal intent. (The government did not choose to appeal these acquittals, although it could have under the applicable law.)

The Tokyo High Court decision in the Oil Cartel case is a compromise of many conflicting demands and legal theories, and the resulting ambiguity is subject to a multitude of interpretations. The decision consisted of three major parts. In the first part, the court discussed whether or not the conduct of the association satisfied the constituent elements of a crime under article 8(1) of the AML. The court concluded that there was a violation of article 8(1) because the defendant was a trade association comprising all the major oil refineries in Japan, and their joint decision to reduce production was reached in a noncompetitive manner.

In the second part of the decision, the court addressed the

question of whether there was a justifiable reason for the association's conduct. In Japanese criminal law, even if an act meets the required constituent elements of a crime, the defendant may be exculpated if his conduct was justified (for example, the killing of a person in self-defense).[41] The association alleged that the production adjustment was a result of MITI's suggestion, and, therefore, the association's conduct should be regarded as the implementation of government policy. In rejecting this defense, the Court stated that in this particular set of facts, administrative guidance could not be relied upon to immunize otherwise illegal conduct. One reason for this holding, the court explained, was that the defendants' conduct was not totally dependent on MITI's administrative guidance. In support of the conclusion, the court noted that there were differences of opinion between the defendants and MITI as to the question of how much petroleum the industry should produce.

The court also pointed out that the defendants determined the amount of production and other terms of business on their own, without any direction from MITI. The court found that the production amount was initially set by the association to maximize their members' profits, and that MITI's later adoption of their plan did not change the essentially private nature of that decision. Even though the defendants were partly influenced by administrative guidance, the court concluded, the defendants' conduct, taken as a whole, was private and did not constitute simply the implementation of government policy.

The court also stated that a government agency cannot use administrative guidance to direct private persons to act in a way that violates the AML. The court stated in dictum, however, that private conduct that would normally violate the AML may under some circumstances be upheld due to intervening administrative guidance even without explicit statutory exemption. According to this dictum, there are two situations in which private conduct based on administrative guidance may be immune: (1) when such conduct has been directed by the government; and

[41] Arts. 35, 36, and 37 of the Criminal Code (see supra note 4) provide the basis for the requirement for justification. Art. 35 provides that conduct based on a law or conduct which amounts to the exercise of justifiable business shall not be punished.

(2) when such conduct, though not explicitly directed, is regarded as cooperation with government policy. On the facts of this case, however, these considerations were held irrelevant.

The third part of the decision addressed the requirement of criminal intent. There is a difference of opinion as to whether or not criminal intent is necessary for criminal liability; the prevailing opinion holds that it is not.[42] The court, however, took the view that on these particular facts, proof of criminal intent was necessary, thereby leading to the conclusion that the defendants should not be punished. Further, the court pointed out that MITI had not only tacitly approved of the conduct but also had positively utilized it for the purpose of its petroleum policy. The court also noted that the FTC chairman's testimony before the Diet could also be taken to mean that the association's production adjustment program did not violate the AML.

Despite the exoneration of the defendants, the Oil Cartel decisions have cast doubt on the wisdom of using administrative guidance to induce private conduct that runs counter to provisions of the AML. Since that time, administrative agencies are regularly called upon to guarantee that their administrative guidance will not result in antitrust violations.

The Oil Cartel decisions leave unanswered the important question of the antitrust liability in the case of parallel conduct by private enterprises induced by administrative guidance exerted individually on each of the enterprises. MITI maintains that the AML does not come into play as long as the administrative guidance directs each enterprise on an individual basis without requiring agreement among the enterprises involved. The FTC, on the other hand, argues that even if administrative guidance is exerted on each enterprise individually, there is the danger that this may touch off communication among the enterprises involved and lead to the formation of a cartel.

Administrative guidance has played a vital role not only in restricting exports under orderly marketing agreements to which

[42] See also Pape, "Gyōsei Shidō and the Antimonopoly Law," *Law in Japan*, Vol. 15, p. 12 (1982). Compare Sanekata, "Administrative Guidance and the Antimonopoly Law: Another View of the Oil Cartel Criminal Decisions," *Law in Japan*, Vol. 15, p. 95 (1982); Ramseyer, "Japanese Antitrust Enforcement after the Oil Embargo," *The American Journal of Comparative Law*, Vol. 31, p. 395 (1983).

Japan is a party but also in import regulation. For example, naptha is the basic raw material of the Japanese petrochemicals industry. Under the PIL, anyone wishing to import petroleum products, including naptha, must first register with MITI. The PIL, however, requires only registration and notification; it gives MITI no further power to control imports. MITI, nonetheless, used administrative guidance to restrict the right to import naptha to petroleum refining companies, thus forcing petrochemical producers to purchase both imported and domestic naptha from the refiners.

Of course, the petrochemical producers were free at any time to register with MITI and thereafter to import naptha directly. To do so in the face of contrary administrative guidance would have been extremely unusual and difficult within Japanese society. As the widening gap between world and domestic prices for naptha began to threaten their economic survival, however, the petrochemical companies rebelled. After initial negotiations with MITI failed, they threatened to register en masse and to import naptha themselves. At that point, a compromise was reached, and in 1982 MITI changed its policy to allow the importation of naptha by the petrochemicals industry. Nevertheless, this case shows the effectiveness of administrative guidance in regulating imports without the use of formal legal controls and the willingness of the companies affected to regard administrative guidance with almost as much respect as compulsory legal measures.

Although traditionally Japanese courts considered objections to administrative guidance to be nonjusticiable,[43] recently courts have permitted direct challenges to administrative guidance under the Administrative Case Litigation Law.[44] However, the

[43] Young, supra note 31; see also Young, "Judicial Review of Administrative Guidance: Government Encouraged Consensual Dispute Resolution in Japan," *Columbia Law Review*, Vol. 84, p. 923 (1984).

[44] Gyōsei Jiken Soshō Hō, Law 139, 1962; hereinafter Litigation Law. Four different typessof lawsuits are permitted under this law: (1) a complaint lawsuit (*kōkoku soshō*) permits a regulated party to bring an action to revoke an administrative order on the grounds of illegality. Litigation Law, art. 3(2); (2) a regulated party can also bring an action to revoke an administrative order after filing an objection under the Administrative Complaints Inquiry Law, Law 160, 1962. Litigation Law, art. 3(3); (3) an action can be brought to declare an order void. Litigation Law, art. 3(4); and (4) an action may be brought to compel an agency to act. Litigation Law, art. 3(5).

courts apply a standard of judicial review that is conceptually vague and designed to maximize the discretion of the administrative agency: the guidance must advance reasonable and necessary societal goals;[45] and the agency's action must not preclude the possibility of a settlement based on good faith bargaining and mutual consent.[46] As the High Court stated in one of the Oil Cartel decisions,[47] administrative guidance is proper even without explicit legislative authorization, as long as it is reasonable and the methods used are not oppressive.

Administrative guidance can be of a great value both to the government and to citizens and enterprises, and there is nothing inherently sinister about it. Administrative guidance, generally speaking, is more flexible than the formal enforcement of law. In emergencies like the oil crisis of 1973, economic regulation by law may be too inflexible; it may take too long a time before the law is invoked, and the scope of the law may be too limited to cope with changing situations. In contrast to enforcement of a law, administrative guidance is much more flexible, and the response of the government to the situation is much more prompt. This should be regarded as an advantage of administrative guidance. Usually negotiations and persuasion are used before an administrative guidance is invoked, and economic regulation is accomplished in a more amicable way than unilateral imposition of a legal order by the government, which may create tension between the government and business.

However, the advantages of administrative guidance, viewed from a different perspective, are also its shortcomings. The flexibility of administrative guidance may mean that its exercise is not circumscribed by any limits. Since, as explained before, administrative guidance can be an irresistible pressure exerted upon the addressee, the lack of a clearly defined area within which it can operate may lead to an arbitrary and capricious exercise of *de facto* governmental power and to infringement of individual rights.

[45] Yoshida v. Nakano Ward, *Hanrei Jihō*, No. 886, p. 15 (Tokyo Dist. Ct., 21 Sept. 1977).
[46] Gōmei Kaisha Nakatani Honten v. Tokyo, *Hanrei Jihō*, No. 955, p. 73 (Tokyo H. Ct., 24 Dec. 1979).
[47] Japan v. Sekiyu Remmei, *Hanrei Jihō*, No. 983, p. 22 (Tokyo H. Ct., 26 Sept. 1980).

Another shortcoming of administrative guidance is a lack of transparency of the process through which it is executed. In enforcement of a law, the procedures are usually provided for in the law, and everyone can see the process of enforcement. In administrative guidance, however, there is no clearly defined procedure, and even if a compromise reached between the government and the enterprise which has received the administrative guidance injures the interests of outsiders, there is no standard procedure in which they can raise their objections. Also, the general public is deprived of the opportunity of knowing what is under consideration by the government, and of participating in the formulation of policy.

Therefore, administrative guidance should not be without limits; it should be carried out in accordance with a fixed system of rules. Legislation is needed to establish the general framework concerning the range of activities in which guidance may be issued and who may be the object of such guidance. It is not sufficient for MITI to rely only on its Establishment Law as a basis for administrative guidance over the industries subject to its regulatory authority. Moreover, the process by which administrative guidance is carried out should be more transparent. A valid criticism of administrative guidance is the secrecy surrounding it. Not only third persons affected by administrative guidance, but the population in general also has a right to know what kind of regulation is in fact carried out through administrative guidance.

§ 2–7. LEGAL REMEDIES AGAINST GOVERNMENTAL AGENCIES

A foreign enterprise or individual who is affected by the decision of a governmental agency that may be contrary to law or Japanese international obligations has a choice of three different kinds of remedies under Japanese law. First, a lawsuit may be brought in the Japanese courts to obtain judicial review of the governmental decision involved; second, an action for damages and compensation may be filed; and third, a complaint may be deposited with the Office of the Trade and Investment Ombudsman. Each of these remedies will be considered in turn.

Article 3(2) of the Litigation Law permits "any person" to

bring legal action against the government in order to cancel a wrongful governmental determination. Although the Litigation Law makes no provision for a lawsuit filed by a foreign person or enterprise, article 7 of the law states that for matters not explicitly covered, the Code of Civil Procedure will apply. Article 51 of the Code of Civil Procedures states that: "An alien is deemed to possess the power to be party in a litigation according to Japanese law, even though he has no such power according to the law of his home country." It is clear from this provision that a foreigner has the power to bring suit under Japanese law.

In order to have standing as a plaintiff in a suit against the government under article 3(2), a party must have a recognized legal interest in the determination in question.[48] If a foreign enterprise has been denied a license or approval of sale or import, however, there is little doubt that it has a legal interest in requesting a court to cancel the determination.

Article 3(5) of the Litigation Law provides a remedy for a refusal to act by a government agency. For example, if an administrative agency is required by law to decide whether to grant an application for a license within a reasonable time it has a duty to make its decision within that period. Therefore, if a foreign enterprise has applied to an agency for approval to sell a certain type of product, and the agency has not acted for an unduly long period, it could be subject to suit under this provision.

In most cases involving governmental ministries, however, it will be difficult to achieve success under either article 3(2) or 3(5). This is because many categories of administrative decisions are discretionary under Japanese law.[49] If the ministry has discretion over an issue, the courts will usually uphold the action. The government can be forced to act or to cancel a decision only with regard to a ministerial act over which the agency involved has no discretionary authority.

A second category of redress against the government is an

---

[48] Article 9 of the Litigation Law limits standing to parties that have a "legal interest" in an administrative disposition. If a person has no more interest in a matter than the general public, this is held not to be a legal interest but only a factual interest; thus there is no standing. See Sakamoto v. Japan, *Minshū* Vol. 16, p. 57 (Sup. Ct., 19 Jan. 1962), partial tr. in H. Tanaka, *The Japanese Legal System* (1976) p. 689; Shufu Rengōkai v. FTC (The Juice case), *Minshū*, Vol. 32, p. 211 (Sup. Ct., 14 March 1978).

[49] See supra § 2–5.

action for damages. Under article 17 of the Constitution, "any person can ask the state or a public body for compensation in accordance with a provision of law in the event he has sustained damage due to a tort (*fuhō kōi*) of a public official." The applicable law under which an action may be brought is the State Compensation Law,[50] which provides recovery upon proof of negligence. This act explicitly permits a foreign national to recover damages against the government as long as there is reciprocity—if a Japanese national would be able to recover in the foreigner's home country.[51]

Under the State Compensation Law, damages are recoverable not only in the case of a decision negligently made by a government official but also if an official seeks to enforce a law or regulation in conflict with Japan's constitutional obligations.[52] Where a decision is based on government discretion, however, damages are not recoverable.

A case which shows the difficulty of recovering damages under the State Compensation Law for wrongful government exercise of authority is the Model Gun case.[53] In this case, the police issued administrative guidance to a toy gun manufacturer to refrain from importing and selling a certain model gun because of its similarity to a real weapon. As a basis for the guidance, the police cited only the Law to Prohibit the Possession of Guns, Swords, and Weapons.[54] The manufacturer was later indicted for illegally importing weapons but was found not guilty. In a subsequent civil suit under the State Compensation Law, the toy gun importer sought to recover damages suffered due to the wrongful police action. Although the court held that administrative guidance, when it is backed by government au-

[50] Kokka Baishō Hō, Law 125, 1947.

[51] Id., art. 6. There is an argument that since article 6 is more restrictive than article 17 of the Constitution, the reciprocity limitation is invalid. See Hashimoto, *Nihonkoku Kempō* (The Japanese Constitution) (1980), p. 347.

[52] Damages were recovered in a case involving the enforcement of an unconstitutional regulation abolishing home voting for disabled persons. See *Hanrei Jihō*, No. 762, p. 34 (1979).

[53] Kondoru Kōgyō K.K. v. Japan, *Kakyū Minshū*, Vol. 27, p. 498 (Tokyo Dist. Ct., 23 Aug. 1976). See, on this case, Matsushita, "The Legal Framework of Trade and Investment in Japan," *Harvard International Law Journal*, Vol. 27, Special Issue (1967), pp. 361–88, 379.

[54] Jūhō Tōkenrui Shoji Tō Torishimari Hō, Law 125, 1947.

thority, is an exercise of governmental power which may be the subject of a suit under article 1, the plaintiff was denied recovery on the grounds that there was neither malice nor negligence on the part of the police who issued the guidance.

A third and often the best way to challenge a governmental decision in Japan is to file a complaint with the Office of the Trade and Investment Ombudsman (OTO), a high-level interministerial body established in 1982. The OTO is headed by the Deputy Chief Cabinet Secretary and consists of the vice ministers of 15 government ministries and agencies (see Appendix), assisted by two advisory councils whose members are drawn from the private sector and universities.

Complaints are accepted in any understandable form at the Secretariat of the OTO (in the Economic Planning Agency's Coordination Bureau), Japanese governmental ministries and agencies, Japanese diplomatic missions abroad, or at the offices of JETRO (Japan External Trade Organization). A complaint may concern virtually any subject related to trade, such as import procedures, direct investment, or market access problems. A complaint may even be filed anonymously, without revealing the name of the actual complainant.

The processing of the complaint is quite rapid and informal. The complainant is given a status report within ten days, and if processing takes more than one month, a progress report is given monthly. At the end of the process, the complainant is given a detailed report of the reasons for the decision.[55]

The OTO complaint process is a typical example of Japanese dispute settlement procedures. After a complaint is filed, OTO officials consult by telephone or in person with responsible officials. There are no formal hearings, and it is not expected that parties will be represented by attorneys. Most of the disputes so far have involved testing, certification, and customs valuation and classification. An illustrative complaint concerning testing was submitted by a U.S. producer of aerosol products who wished to have its products tested by an independent facility to deter-

---

[55] See Office of Trade Ombudsman, Progress Report on OTO Complaints Processing (29 July 1983).

mine whether Japanese import standards were met. MITI responded to the complaint by allowing the selection of a private test facility.[56] Another example involved silicone dioxide, a common filtering agent for beer, which was not an approved food additive. In response to a complaint, the Ministry of Health and Welfare (MHW) approved the substance, which in turn facilitated the importation of beer.[57] A complaint about the length of time required for the approval of imports of cosmetics prompted MHW to shorten the period.[58] Complaints have also obtained changes in customs classification and valuation; for example, the MOF has reclassified paint roller covers, previously classified as "knitted goods" (16.8 percent duty rate), as "paint rollers" (10 percent duty rate).[59]

[56] Id., p. 12 (OTO Complaint No. 94).
[57] Id., p. 13 (OTO Complaint No. 107).
[58] Id., p. 16 (OTO Complaint No. 100).
[59] Id., p. 13 (OTO Complaint No. 103).

CHAPTER THREE

REGULATION OF IMPORT AND
SALES ACTIVITIES

§ 3–1. Negotiating the Contract

Establishing a business relationship in Japan usually involves
the negotiation of a contract or series of contracts. These can
range from quite simple transactional agreements, such as export
sales, to more complex agreements that establish long-term business relations, such as distributorships, joint ventures, or licensing
agreements. While in some respects the negotiation of a contract
with a Japanese business is the same as other international negotiations, there are unique problems and characteristics that
deserve special treatment. The Japanese approach to contract
negotiations is that they are a kind of courtship intended to cul-
minate, if successful, in the establishment of a long-term cooperation between the parties based not only on legal considerations
but also on a spirit of mutual trust. Since the establishment of
mutual trust requires some time, negotiations with Japanese
companies are often extended and prolonged. Moreover, in Japanese companies decisions are usually the product of extensive
consultations with people and departments throughout the organization, not merely a few top-level executives. Negotiations
will therefore often involve many separate meetings over a
long period of time and endless discussion of points seemingly
already settled. Although the negotiations may be tiresome, the
benefits of such a process are that once an agreement is signed,
implementation will proceed relatively easily because understanding and support have been obtained from the entire organization of the company.

Selling in Japan and negotiating with Japanese companies
requires extensive preparation. First, the character of the Japa-

47

nese market and distribution channels for the product involved should be carefully analyzed. Second, competition in the relevant Japanese market should be carefully examined. Third, demographic and economic trends that will affect purchasing power in the future should be studied. Finally, the company seeking to obtain access to the Japanese market should consider the characteristics and tastes of Japanese consumers. The product involved must be suitable or adaptable to the Japanese market, and service will be very important. The company should take pains to develop a reputation for both quality and reliability.

Great care should be employed in selecting a Japanese business partner. In investigating an appropriate entity, inquiries should be made about long-term business goals, marketing relationships, and pricing policies, as well as potential conflicts of interest. As an alternative to establishing an autonomous sales office in Japan in the form of a branch or subsidiary, other options should be explored, such as agreement with a Japanese import agent who will be responsible for handling customs clearance and making arrangements to put the product into appropriate channels of distribution. It may be also possible to utilize the services of a manufacturer of products in a closely related field or a noncompeting product line in order to take advantage of existing methods of distribution. Another option is to seek out a relationship with one of the Japanese general trading companies (sōgō shōsha).[1] In entering into any business agreement with a Japanese company or distributor, the determination should be made in the agreement whether the relationship is to be exclusive or not.

Once it is signed, the business contract can be regarded as the blueprint or structure of the relationship between the parties.

---

[1] Approximately 8,000 business organizations in Japan are classified as trading companies which are in the business of exporting and importing. The largest of these are the general trading companies. The nine largest general trading companies are: Mitsubishi Corp.; Mitsui & Co., Ltd.; C. Itoh & Co., Ltd.; Marubeni Corp.; Sumitomo Corp.; Nissho-Iwai Corp.; Toyo Menka (Tomen) Kaisha, Ltd.; Nichimen, Corp.; and Kanematsu-Gosho Ltd. Each general trading company has a business relationship with a leading Japanese bank. These companies finance and carry out importing and exporting activities all over the world and have expert knowledge of products, markets, and sources of supplies.

In Japan, the law of contract is governed by the Civil Code and the Commercial Code, which are largely derived from German law. In general, freedom of contract prevails, and contracts are formed by a concurrence of offer and acceptance.[2] Under article 524 of the Civil Code, however, an offer to a person in a "distant place" that does not prescribe a time for acceptance cannot be revoked before the expiration of such time as is reasonably necessary for the offeror to receive notice of acceptance. Under Japanese law, there are extensive provisions governing such issues as the risk of loss, warranties, remedies, and contract formation.

Under article 7 of the Law Concerning the Application of Laws, a choice of law clause whereby the parties to a contract agree on a governing law is valid in Japan.[3] Accordingly, the parties may want to choose the Uniform Commercial Code, the law of a particular state of the United States, or the Vienna Convention on Contracts for the International Sale of Goods[4] as the governing law. The parties may also wish to incorporate *Incoterms* (Publication No. 350), published by the International Chamber of Commerce in Paris. This publication contains detailed definitions and rules concerning the principal terms and conditions inherent in international sales transactions, such as the risk of loss of goods in transit, the passage of title, and the costs of transportation, customs duties, and insurance.

The financial provisions of the contract are obviously of utmost importance. Not only should the price be clearly stated, but when it is payable and if there are any conditions precedent to payment. In international contracts, it is also important to determine how the price is payable and in what currency. The currency may be the home currency of the seller, the buyer, or of a third unrelated country. The parties may want to consider various options to minimize the difficulties caused by unforeseen fluctuations in currency exchange rates. For this purpose, the contract may itself define the exchange rate which will be used when

---

[2] See, generally, Lansing and Wechselblatt, "Doing Business in Japan: The Importance of the Unwritten Law," *The International Lawyer*, Vol. 17, p. 647 (1983).

[3] Hōrei, Law 10, 1898.

[4] U.N. Doc. A/CONF. 97/18, 10 April 1980, reprinted in *International Legal Materials*, Vol. 19, p. 668 (1980). Japan has not yet ratified or acceded to this convention.

payment is made, even though another exchange rate prevails at the time of payment. The parties may also specify that a currency basket, which is a composite index of several different currencies, perhaps on a weighted basis, will be used as the standard of value for the currency used for payment. A possible currency basket might be the International Monetary Fund's Special Drawing Right (SDR), which is composed of the U.S. dollar, the German mark, the Japanese yen, the French franc, and the British pound sterling.

As a payment mechanism, an irrevocable letter of credit may be used, which is an irrevocable promise to pay by the buyer's bank and can be confirmed by a local bank acceptable to the seller. The set of rules generally governing international letters of credit is the *Uniform Customs and Practices for Documentary Credits* (International Chamber of Commerce Publication No. 400). For a longer-term relationship, a "stand-by credit" can be arranged, which operates as a guarantee of performance by one or both parties.

The parties will also want to negotiate an appropriate force majeure clause which specifies unforeseen events to excuse the timeliness of performance. These can include such matters as strikes, work stoppages, and shortages of raw materials.

Warranties should also be negotiated to define the time period during which repair or replacement will be made and to negate inappropriate express and implied warranties. Consequential damages should also be the subject of negotiation as well as possible liability for defective products.

The parties should come to clear understandings regarding industrial property rights such as patents, trademarks, and copyrights. The owner of such rights will want to insist on appropriate protections.

The parties will also want to negotiate concerning provisions for the duration and termination of the agreement. A time period should be provided for withdrawal of the agreement after appropriate notice has been given to the other party. The parties may also wish to define the consequences of major and minor breaches of the agreement and such matters as delay in delivery and nonperformance of part of the agreement.

§ 3–2. AGENCY AND DISTRIBUTORSHIP AGREEMENTS

A common way of marketing goods in Japan is through an exclusive agent, consignee, or distributor. While an agent is a sales representative who sells goods on behalf and for the account of his principal, a distributor purchases goods from his supplier and resells them for a profit. A consignee occupies an intermediary position: he acquires possession of the goods and sells them in his own name, though they remain the property of his consignor.

Agency, consignment, and distributorship agreements are contracts governed by the Civil and Commercial Codes, unless the parties agree on another governing law. In some cases, such agreements also must be reported to the Fair Trade Commission (FTC) under the Antimonopoly Law (AML).[5] An exclusive dealership or agency agreement with a sole Japanese importer is not illegal per se; the AML prohibits only those exclusive arrangements that are likely to impede fair competition.[6] Practices that impede fair competition are retail price maintenance, customer restriction agreements, and restrictions on parallel importation (an attempt to limit importation of the goods by third parties).[7]

Arbitrary or unilateral termination of an agency or distributorship will render the supplier liable for lost profits of the agent or distributor.[8] Accordingly, such agreements should have fixed termination dates, clearly specified grounds for termination, or provisions for calculating compensation in the event of termination. It is a good idea to provide in the agreement that the agent or distributor waives any right to compensation if the agreement is terminated according to its terms.

[5] Arts. 6 and 7.
[6] Id., art. 9.
[7] See "Antimonopoly Act Guidelines for Sole Import Distributorship Agreements," Fair Trade Commission, 22 Nov. 1972; for more extensive discussion see infra § 6–6.
[8] K.K. Hayashiya v. K.K. Yamamoto-Yama, *Hanrei Jihō*, No. 634, p. 50 (Nagoya H. Ct., 29 March 1971); Fujikura Gomu Kōgyō K.K. v. K.K. Wada Shōten, *Hanrei Jihō*, No. 286, p. 25 (Tokyo Dist. Ct., 13 Dec. 1961).

For a general review of this problem, see Herold and Knoll, "Negotiating and Drafting International Distribution, Agency, and Representative Agreements: The United States Exporter's Perspective," *The International Lawyer*, Vol. 21, p. 939 (1987).

§ 3–3. Arbitration and Dispute Resolution

In Japan, there is a distrust of the adversary process and the use of lawyers and litigation to resolve disagreements and disputes. The submission of a dispute to a court is only a last resort. The Japanese way of resolving disputes is discussion, compromise, and conciliation. Conciliation is commenced by making application to the District Court, which will appoint a three-member Conciliation Committee to hear the case. In Japanese contracts, there is frequently a "good faith" clause which provides that in order to settle future dispute between the parties, they will "confer in good faith" (*seii o motte kyōgi suru*). Another version of the same thing is an agreement in which all disputes will be settled "harmoniously by consultation" (*kyōgi ni yori emman ni kaiketsu suru*).

Nevertheless, in most international contracts it will be desirable to have a provision for commercial arbitration as an alternative method for dispute resolution.[9] Arbitration has the advantage that the parties can submit a dispute to a neutral tribunal that is not a part of the governmental structure of any state. Arbitration is also usually, though not always, speedier and less expensive than litigation. The parties may fashion an arbitral procedure to suit their needs as long as minimum due process norms are kept. The parties may choose the substantive law by which they want to resolve the issues involved as well.[10]

There are a variety of arbitral tribunals and regimes. If parties do not want to wholly construct their own rules for arbitration, they can utilize the rules of arbitration of the United Nations Committee on International Trade Law (UNCITRAL) which provide a set of rules that are not tied to any specific arbitral tribunal and can be used for arbitration anywhere in the world.[11] The parties may also choose to utilize the services of

[9] See, generally, Seki, "Effective Dispute Resolution in United States–Japan Commercial Relations," *Northwestern Journal of International Law and Business*, Vol. 6, p. 979 (1985); Kanowitz, "Using the Mini-Trial in U.S.–Japan Business Disputes," *Mercer Law Review*, Vol. 39, p. 641 (1988).

[10] See Perlman and Nelson, "New Approaches to the Resolution of International Commercial Disputes," *The International Lawyer*, Vol. 17, p. 215 (1983); Golsong, "A Guide to Procedural Issues in International Arbitration," *The International Lawyer*, Vol. 18, p. 633 (1984).

[11] 31 U.N. GAOR, Sup. No. 17, Doc. A/31/17 (1976), reprinted in *International*

an arbitration institution, such as the Court of Arbitration of the International Chamber of Commerce (ICC)[12] headquartered in Paris, France, the American Arbitration Association (AAA),[13] and the Hong Kong International Arbitration Center.[14] Although arbitration is a technique for avoiding judicial resolution of a dispute between the parties, and for that reason the arbitration clause should generally be quite broad as well as exclusive, the parties may want to consider allowing the application to a court for certain types of provisional relief, such as an injunction, where necessary to protect important rights, such as intellectual property rights.

Arbitration has gained international acceptance because of the widespread acceptance of the United Nations Convention on the Recognition and Enforcement of Arbitral Awards.[15] The New York Convention, as this is called, has been accepted by Australia, Canada, the United States, Great Britain, and Japan, as well as by 75 other countries. The convention provides that agreements to arbitrate are enforceable before the courts of all the signatories. This means that clauses in international contracts providing for arbitration will be enforced by the courts, which will remit the parties' dispute to the arbitral tribunal.

The Supreme Court of the United States has taken a broadly favorable view of international arbitration. In Bremen v. Zapata Off-Shore Co.,[16] the court approved a forum selection clause in a contract involving international trade stating that "the expansion of American business and industry will hardly be encouraged if notwithstanding solemn contracts would insist on a parochial concept that all disputes must be dissolved under

Legal Materials, Vol. 15, p. 701 (1976).

[12] International Chamber of Commerce, "Rules for the ICC Court of Arbitration," Pub. No. 291 (1980). For a description of the ICC Court of Arbitration, see W. Craig, W. Park, and J. Paulsson, *International Chamber of Commerce Arbitration* (1983).

[13] See Meade, "Arbitration Overview: The AAA's Role in Domestic and International Arbitration," *Journal of International Arbitration*, Vol. 1, p. 263 (1984).

[14] See Williams, "Law Reform: Hong Kong Arbitration," *International Business Lawyer*, Vol. 10, p. 317 (1982).

[15] New York (10 June 1958) 330 U.N.T.S. 38, No. 4739 (1959); [1970] 21 U.S.T. 2517 T.I.A.S. 6997. See, generally, Comment, "Enforcement of Foreign Arbitral Awards under the United Nations Convention of 1958: A Survey of Recent Federal Case Law," *Maryland Journal of International Law and Trade*, Vol. 11, p. 13 (1987).

[16] 407 U.S. 1 (1972).

our laws and in our courts." In Scherk v. Alberto-Culver Co.,[17] the court enforced an arbitration clause in an international agreement holding that a claim under the Security Exchange Act of 1934 was subject to arbitration by an agreement between parties to an international contract. The reasoning of Scherk was confirmed and extended in the case of Mitsubishi Motors Corp. v. Soler Chrysler Plymouth Inc.,[18] holding that there is nothing in the nature of the federal antitrust laws that prohibits parties from agreeing to arbitrate antitrust claims arising out of international commercial transactions. It now appears that there are no restrictions on the scope of international arbitration unless Congress explicitly imposes them.[19]

In Japan, arbitration clauses and choice of law clauses are also broadly upheld for international contracts.[20] Commercial arbitration is available under the auspices of the Japan Commercial Arbitration Association in Tokyo and the National Committee of the International Chamber of Commerce. The Japan Shipping Exchange handles maritime arbitration. Arbitration procedures are set out in Part Eight of the Code of Civil Procedure, which is substantially the same as the German Code of Civil Procedure. Part Eight, entitled "Arbitration Proceedings," deals with such subjects as the scope of arbitration, the appointment of arbitrators, arbitration procedure, awards, and appeals from awards.[21]

In 1952, a private agreement for cooperation was signed between the Japan Commercial Arbitration Association and the American Arbitration Association. In contracts between Japanese and U.S. companies, it is useful to provide for arbitration in Japan if the call for arbitration is made by the U.S. company, and arbitration in the United States if the arbitration is asked by the Japanese company. Under the New York Convention, an arbitration award will be enforced by the courts of all signatory

[17] 417 U.S. 506 (1974).

[18] 473 U.S. 614 (1985). For comment, see McClendon, "Subject-Matter Arbitrability in International Cases: Mitsubishi Motors Closes the Circle," *North Carolina Journal of International Law and Commercial Regulation*, Vol. 11, p. 81 (1986).

[19] See Shearson/American Express, Inc. v. McMahon, 107 Sup. Ct. 2532 (1987).

[20] Kokusan Kinzoku Kōgyō K.K. v. Guard Life Corp., *Hanrei Taimuzu*, No. 308 p. 230 (Tokyo Dist. Ct., 25 Dec. 1973), aff'd Sup. Ct., *Minshū*, Vol. 29, p. 1061 (15 July 1975).

[21] See, generally, T. Hattori and D.F. Henderson, *Civil Procedure in Japan* (1983; looseleaf supplements).

countries. Under the convention, the courts may not look into the merits of the matter for which the award was granted before enforcing it.[22]

§ 3–4. The Distribution System

Many foreign business people consider the distribution system in Japan to be a non-tariff barrier to trade. The channels of distribution are complex and varied; there are perhaps as many distribution channels as there are products, and many products themselves are sold in diverse ways. Nevertheless, these obstacles can be readily overcome by careful advance planning, product-specific research, and the preparation of a marketing strategy tailored to the particular circumstances involved.

The Japanese retail industry is characterized by several million small stores[23]—neighborhood shops, specialty stores, and convenience stores—that coexist with relatively few larger chain stores and department stores. The large retailers, although few in number, have many outlets and account for more than a third of retail sales. Of the larger stores, the department stores, concentrated in larger cities, are trend setters mass-marketing quality goods. They often function as entertainment and cultural centers and hold fairs displaying both imported and domestic products. The chain stores, which are often located in suburban areas, mass-market standard consumer items, such as clothing, household goods, and food.

This pattern presents several difficulties for foreign suppliers. First, smaller stores, because of their limited shelf space, tend to

[22] Article 5 of the 1958 New York Arbitration Convention establishes limited grounds on which recognition and enforcement of an arbitral award may be refused by a national court. These grounds include the absence of a valid agreement, deprival of a fair opportunity to be heard, improper composition of the arbitral tribunal or improper arbitral procedure, and that the award is not binding or has been set aside or suspended in the country of origin. Moreover, an award also may not be enforced on the grounds that the subject matter of the dispute is not capable of settlement by arbitration under the laws of that country or on grounds of public policy.

[23] See supra ch. 2, note 18. The Large Retail Store Law was enacted to preserve the pattern of small neighborhood shops. Under this law, all retail outlets with total floor space of over 500 square meters must register with MITI and are subject to MITI regulations. MITI has a policy of restricting large-scale stores from certain areas and functions.

carry a limited selection of goods. Second, Japanese business-people desire stable, long-term relationships in which a great deal of emphasis is placed upon human relationships. Third, for many products there are several layers of wholesalers or processors between the manufacturer and the retail levels, which tends to drive up the prices of certain goods. Fourth, in Japan it is customary for wholesalers and manufacturers to take back unsold goods. Fifth, marketing goods in Japan usually requires the producer to employ a detail force to call on wholesalers and retailers, establish personal relationships, and provide payments to enable the retailer to display and sell products effectively. Rebates are commonly paid on the basis of the number of goods sold in order to motivate wholesalers and retailers. A producer in pricing his product must also take into consideration the profit margins commonly expected by both wholesalers and retailers.[24]

Japan is also a potentially important market for many types of industrial products. Distribution channels for industrial products tend to have several levels of sales companies or wholesalers before reaching a dealer who sells to the user. A successful marketing strategy for marketing industrial products will usually require the product to be adapted to the specific requirements of the Japanese user; adequate provision for after-sales service; efficient delivery and installation; user training; competitive financing methods; and suitable promotional activities.[25]

A foreign company that desires to sell in Japan must determine an appropriate marketing and distribution strategy.[26] This may take the form of establishing their own importing and marketing subsidiaries; establishing their own production facilities either alone or as a joint venture with a Japanese company; appointing a sole agent for the importation and distribution of its products; tapping into existing channels of distribution using its own employees; or establishing new channels of distribution through direct sales to department and chain stores.

In order to circumvent distribution channels, foreign com-

[24] See, generally, JETRO, *Selling in Japan* (1985), pp. 52–57.

[25] Manufactured Imports Promotion Committee of the International Trade Conference, "An Analysis of and Recommendations Regarding the Japanese Distribution System and Business Practices 5" (1983) (Summary of Report).

[26] See, generally, JETRO, *Japan's Distribution System* (1978).

panies can use department stores, chain stores, and trading companies effectively, since they are able to function as a countervailing force to the powerful Japanese manufacturers and their vertically integrated distribution networks. Because these retail-oriented firms have buying agents both in Japan and abroad, they are able to purchase goods from sources outside the established network of Japanese producers and manufacturers. Franchising is also growing as a method of penetrating the Japanese market.[27]

§ 3–5. TARIFFS AND CUSTOMS PROCEDURES

Customs services in Japan are administered by the Customs and Tariff Bureau of the MOF. Regional custom houses are located in Tokyo, Yokohama, Kobe, Osaka, Nagoya, Moji, Nagasaki, Hakodate, and Okinawa. There are branches at all international airports and port facilities. The Customs and Tariff Bureau administers the Customs and Tariff Law[28] and the Tariff Law.[29]

In order to import any articles to Japan, an import permit is required. In order to obtain an import permit, the importer or his agent (usually a customs house broker) must present to the customs authorities a bill of lading or waybill describing the goods, the invoice for the goods, the certificate of origin, an import declaration, and any other documents necessary in the particular case. The goods must be moved into a bonded area— a designated warehouse and storage area—to await customs clearance upon payment of the prescribed duties. In order to be sure that customs clearance proceeds smoothly, importers should first contact the Customs Clearance Consultation Office, which will provide instructions on how to comply with customs formalities.

Japan is a member of the Custom Cooperation Council (C.C.C.), the major international body established to harmonize tariff nomenclature. As a result, the Japanese tariff is classified

[27] See Nishimura, "Franchising in Japan: The Business and Legal Environment," *International Business Lawyer* (Oct. 1986), p. 312.
[28] Kanzei Teiritsu Hō, Law 54, 1910, as amended.
[29] Kanzei Hō, Law 61, 1954, as amended.

according to the so-called harmonized system (Harmonized Commodity Deception and Coding System), established by the C.C.C. Convention for the Classification of Goods in Customs Tariffs.[30]

Since Japan is a member of the GATT, the basic tariff rate for products from GATT member countries is the GATT bound duty. Article 3 of the Tariff Law provides that tariff rates shall be applied in accordance with any international treaty to which Japan is a party. Japan has fully implemented the tariff reductions mandated at the last GATT negotiating session, the Tokyo Round,[31] and Japan's tariff rates for GATT members are the lowest of any industrialized nation in the world. In addition, Japan applies preferential tariff rates to certain less-developed countries in accordance with the Generalized System of Preferences.[32] An "additional duty" is charged on products imported from countries that are not GATT members and which do not accord "most favored nations" treatment on goods imported from Japan.

Japan has also accepted the Multilateral Trade Negotiation (MTN) agreements concluded during the Tokyo Round. The MTN Codes on tariff reduction, subsidies and countervailing duties, antidumping, import licensing, customs valuation, technical barriers to trade, government procurement, and civil aviation were all approved and promulgated on April 25, 1980;[33] on the other hand, the agreements on dairy products and bovine meat were not introduced in the Diet for approval, but were signed as executive agreements.[34]

Generally speaking, the codes that were submitted to the Diet were those that required some changes in domestic laws or regulations for implementation. However, one exception is the Code

---

[30] 22 U.S.T. 320, T.I.A.S. 7063, 157 U.N.T.S. 129. Under this system, goods are classified into 21 sections with 99 chapters; each tariff classification is given a four-digit number; the first two digits are the chapter, and the last two represent the numeric position in the chapter.

[31] See, generally, J. Jackson, J.-V. Louis, and M. Matsushita, *Implementing the Tokyo Round* (1984).

[32] See GATT Decision of 25 June 1971, GATT Doc. L/3545, GATT, 18th Supp. B.I.S.D. 24 (1972). See also OECD, "Report By the Secretary General, the Generalized System of Preferences: Review of the First Decade" (1983).

[33] See supra § 1–3.

[34] Agreement on Dairy Products, *Kampō*, 25 April 1980 (Special Issue), pp. 1–8; Agreement on Bovine Meat, id. pp. 3–5.

on Import Licensing. Although the government did not think it necessary to change a domestic law or regulation in order to implement it, this code touched on a fundamental principle of the GATT, and it was therefore considered advisable to submit it to the Diet for its consideration and approval.

In order to implement the MTN agreements in Japanese law, some amendments to domestic laws and regulations were considered necessary. This was the case in the areas of: (1) customs valuation, (2) countervailing duties, (3) antidumping duties, and (4) technical standards. The implementation of the Government Procurement Code required some changes in the regulations, but not in the basic law. It was not necessary to amend the existing law to reduce the Japanese tariff in compliance with the Geneva Protocol. However, since this code was approved by the Diet as a treaty, some changes were made in the Tariff Special Measures Law to reduce tariffs from the existing rate.

Customs valuation is provided for in article 4 of the Customs and Tariff Law. According to this provision, the valuation must be based on the "transaction value" of the commodity imported, which means that the tariff rate applied to an imported commodity must be based on the sum of money that has been actually paid by the importer to the exporter when the import transaction occurred. Before the Tokyo Round, the valuation had been based on a kind of constructed value. Under the previous article 4, customs valuation was based on the price of an imported commodity which would exist between the exporter and the importer if the exporter and the importer were independent from each other and if the condition of perfect competition existed. Under this system, there was room for manipulation by the customs appraisers, and there were some complaints that "customs uplift" sometime took place. When the Tokyo Round Agreement on Customs Valuation took effect, the Japanese government amended article 4 to make it conform to the principle incorporated in the agreement.

Under article 4 of the law, customs valuation is based on the transaction value of an imported commodity. The transaction value is defined as the actual price paid or payable by the purchaser of the commodity in question plus the cost of transport and certain other costs to the extent that they are not included in the price actually paid for the goods. If the transaction value is not known, the valuation is based on the transaction value of a similar or the same commodity exported on the same day as the commodity in question was exported or some day close in time. If any of the foregoing methods are not feasible, customs valuation is based on a price arrived at by calculating backward from the domestic sales price or a price arrived at by adding manufacturing costs and other costs. If that is also unworkable, customs valuation will be based on a price determined by procedures provided for in a Cabinet decree.

The amount of tariff calculated for a particular imported commodity on the basis of the above methods is not necessarily lower than that calculated using the methods available before the amendment of article 4. However, under the existing system, there is much less room for discretion on the part of the customs appraisers. This reduces any arbitrariness that may be involved in the customs valuation and that may cause instability in import trade.

Article 9(3) of the Customs and Tariff Law provides for tariff quotas. Under this system, a low tariff is applied to an imported commodity up to a certain level of imports, and when this level is exceeded, then a higher tariff is imposed; the lower rate is called the primary rate, and the higher rate is called the secondary rate. The primary rate is usually applied to the amount of imported product that is equal to that amount obtained by subtracting the amount of domestic production from the amount of total domestic demand, that is to say, the level of imports necessary to satisfy domestic demand for the commodity in question. This tariff system is designed to secure the necessary amount of a product for domestic consumption while protecting domestic producers.

§ 3–6. IMPORT AGREEMENTS

Article 7(2) of the Export and Import Transactions Law[35] permits importers, with the approval of MITI, to enter into an import

[35] Yushutsunyū Torihiki Hō, Law 299, 1952, as amended (1965); tr. in *Japan Foreign Trade News* (spec. ed., 1974); hereinafter Transactions Law.

agreement fixing a purchase price, limiting the maximum quantity to be purchased, setting a minimum standard for quality, or restricting channels of import. Such an agreement will be approved only when one of the following conditions is met: (1) when export competition is substantially restrained or import competition in Japan is excessive; (2) when there is an international agreement providing that Japan import a certain amount of a commodity; or (3) when an import agreement is necessary for the exploitation of natural resources overseas.

An import agreement is allowed when export competition is substantially restrained or when import competition in Japan is excessive. A typical example of this is a state-trading agency in a socialist country. Since, in a non-market economy, a state trading agency has the exclusive power to engage in foreign trade activities, an import cartel is an appropriate counterbalance to the fact that there is no export competition. An import agreement may also be necessary to counteract an export cartel, especially since export agreements are generally exempt from the antitrust laws of many countries. If the export trade in a foreign country is monopolized by one enterprise, the situation would be similar to an export cartel.

An import agreement is also allowed when it is necessary to import a certain amount of a commodity due to an international agreement signed by the Japanese government. In this situation, the price of the commodity exported to Japan from the other party to the agreement may be higher than the price of that commodity available from a third country. Under these circumstances, importers of the commodity can enter into an import agreement in order to offset the disadvantages of the price differential.

The third type of import agreement under the Transactions Law is an agreement for the purpose of promoting the exploitation of natural resources in a foreign country. This is illustrated in the following example. Suppose Japan needs to import a certain amount of a natural resource from country B, but it is very expensive to exploit this natural resource, and country B is unwilling to invest the necessary money unless it is certain that Japanese importers will import a certain amount each year. In this situation, the Japanese importers can agree to purchase a certain amount of the commodity and allocate quotas among themselves. This agreement assures the exporting country of a stable market.

An "outsider regulation" may be imposed by MITI under article 30 of the Transactions Law when it is judged that an import agreement cannot achieve its purpose because of the activities of non-parties. "Outsider regulation," however, is only a nickname. In fact, when such an order is invoked, it binds not only the outsiders but also the parties to the agreement. In order for MITI to invoke outsider regulation, there must be a preexisting import agreement and proof that it has not been effective.

An import agreement can be organized by an import association, that is, an association which determines the conditions of import trade, such as the import price, quantity, and other terms to be observed by member importers. An import association operates in much the same way as an import agreement, since the conditions of trade imposed on the members must be filed with and approved by MITI. The activities of the association are exempted from the application of the AML.

Strictly speaking, whenever importers wish to agree on some terms of import of a commodity, they must do so under the authority of the Transactions Law, and an agreement which is not so authorized is contrary to that law. In actuality, however, import agreements are entered into between enterprises without the authority of the Transactions Law when they have relatively little impact on the market.

There have been relatively few instances in which an import agreement has been used. One of these is the Scrap Iron case,[36] which arose in 1974 due to shortages of scrap iron, which led the United States government to impose an embargo on the export of scrap iron under the authority of the Export Administration Act. MITI, in order to cooperate with this embargo, invoked the import approval system under the Control Law and banned the import of scrap iron. The American embargo was short lived, however, and in a few weeks the export ban was lifted. MITI then lifted the prohibition of the scrap iron imported

[36] *Nihon Keizai Shimbun*, 8 Jan. 1975, p. 4.

from the United States. But because of concern that scrap iron imports might increase dramatically, which might touch off additional export controls in the United States, MITI issued administrative guidance to scrap iron importers, suggesting that they enter into an import agreement restricting the amount of imports from the United States. The Japanese importers complied.

Another is the Chinese Silk case,[37] which arose because of import restrictions on raw silk under the authority of the Silk Price Stabilization Law. Because of these restrictions, the price of raw silk in Japan rose sharply. Then exporters in China and South Korea began to process raw silk into a semi-finished product for export to Japan. This product was technically not raw silk, but it was processed by spinning raw silk very loosely and could easily be converted back to raw silk.

Nevertheless, under the Silk Price Stabilization Law, the power given to the Silk Business Agency was limited to raw silk, and technically the importation of the semifinished product could not be stopped. But MITI advised the trading companies engaged in importing processed silk to enter into an import agreement whereby each participant would be given an import quota. At the same time, MITI issued an "outsider regulation" to make sure that the import agreement would not be disrupted.

Even though the above-mentioned cases are important, they are not typical of import agreements authorized under the Transactions Law. In both cases, the requirements for an import agreement under the law were formally satisfied since there was substantial restraint of export to Japan. In both cases, however, the purpose of the agreement was merely to maintain orderly international trade.

§ 3–7. TECHNICAL BARRIERS TO TRADE: STANDARDS AND TESTING

Japan, like other nations, maintains technical regulations relating to manufactured products, food, and drugs to protect

---

[37] See Ikeda, "Kiito Kinu Seihin no Yunyū Seigen" (Import Adjustment of Raw Silk and Silk Products), *Jurisuto*, No. 623, p. 85 (1976).

human and animal health, to ensure minimum standards of quality for consumers, to protect the environment, and to protect national security. Such standards, however, are often barriers to trade because of lack of standardization and the circumstances of their enforcement.[38] Despite the fact that Japan has adhered to the GATT Agreement on Technical Barriers to Trade,[39] concluded during the Tokyo Round, many difficulties remain. Generally speaking, Japanese standards for product safety, health requirements, inspection practices, and government approval are more stringent than those in other countries. These standards and requirements are designed not to discriminate against foreign products but to meet domestic necessities. However, because Japan and foreign countries establish and enforce such standards in different ways, it is sometimes difficult for foreign products to penetrate the Japanese market. A Special Progress Report of the U.S.–Japan Trade Study Group (TSG) states:[40]

As a general matter, the Japanese government has set very strict (though often ambiguous) basic rules in establishing

[38] For a compilation and guide to standards for leading products, see JETRO, *Outline of Standards and Certification Systems* (1983). See also International Trade Institute, Japan Foreign Trade Council, *Comparison of the U.S. and Japanese Standard and Certification Systems* (1988).

[39] GATT, 26th Supp. B.I.S.D. 8 (1980). Some of the difficulties encountered by foreign exporters with regard to technical standards and inspections are described in Weil and Glick, "Japan: Is the Market Open? A View of the Japanese Market Drawn from U.S. Corporate Experience," *Law and Policy in International Business*, Vol. 11, pp. 845, 865–79 (1979).

The major principles declared in the Standards Agreement are as follows:

(1) International Harmonization of Standards. Each country endeavors to incorporate the contents of international standards into its domestic laws and regulations. However, if a country cannot do so due to some circumstances prevailing in the country, it is not compelled to do so.

(2) Prior Disclosure of Formulation of Standards. When a member country formulates a standard, it must notify the interested parties promptly and also the other member countries through the GATT Secretariat. Each country must offer relevant information upon request and an opportunity for interested parties to express their views.

(3) Testing Procedure. Each country shall not discriminate against products from abroad with respect to testing procedures, fees, and other relevant testing conditions in favor of national products.

(4) Domestic Certificate System. Each country discloses the certification system to foreign suppliers, and, when it establishes a new certification system, there shall be prior disclosure of the process of formulating that system.

[40] United States–Japan Trade Study Group, "A Special Progress Report 17"(1980), pp. 4–5.

technical relations, but has given the administrative officials who deal directly with the public wide discretion to relax regulations in individual cases. This practice has given the bureaucracy a combination of firm control plus the flexibility to deal with changing technology and economic circumstances. Unfortunately, this approach has tended to work to the disadvantage of foreigners, who usually have not had the experience or relationships necessary to take advantage of the system's flexibility.

Let us review some major laws and regulations on technical standards and the agencies that enforce these laws:[41] (1) the Pharmaceutical Affairs Law provides for approval and testing of pharmaceuticals and cosmetics; (2) the Poisonous Substances Control Law provides for the control of poisonous substances; (3) the Food Sanitation Law requires food producers, sellers, and importers to meet various standards in sanitation, safety, and related matters; (4) the Law for the Prevention of Infectious Diseases in Domestic Animals provides for inspection of imported foods; (5) the Law for Standardization of Agricultural Products and the Improvement of Their Representation provides for representation and labeling of the dates of manufacture of imported foodstuffs; (6) the Law to Promote Mechanization of Agriculture authorizes the inspection of tractors for agriculture; (7) the Agricultural Chemicals Control Law provides for registration of agricultural chemicals; (8) the High Pressure Gas Control Law provides certain standards for containers of high pressure gas substances, and for the testing of such containers; (9) the Consumer Product Safety Law provides for safety standards for various consumer products; (10) the Electrical Appliances Control Law provides for approval of products and for various safety standards for them; (11) the Law Concerning the Examination and Regulation of the Manufacture of Chemical Substances provides for testing and approval of chemical substances; (12) the Metric Law provides for representation of weight, length, and other dimensions; (13) the Industrial Standardization Law

---

[41] On the following laws, see The Intra-Governmental Council on Standards and Certification Systems, *Standards and Certification Systems in Japan* (1984).

establishes the JIS (Japan Industrial Standard) mark; and (14) the Road Transportation Vehicles Law provides for approval of models of cars and the inspection of their performance.

These laws are enforced by many different agencies. For example, the MHW enforces the Pharmaceutical Affairs Law, the Food Sanitation Law, and the Poisonous Substances Control Law. The MAFF regulates agricultural products under the Law for the Prevention of Infectious Diseases in Domestic Animals, the Law for Standardization of Agricultural Products and the Improvement of Their Representation, the Law to Promote Mechanization of Agriculture, and the Agricultural Chemicals Control Law. The High Pressure Gas Control Law, the Consumer Product Safety Law, and the Electrical Appliances Control Law are enforced by MITI. The Metric Law and the Industrial Standardization Law are also enforced by MITI. The Road Transportation Vehicles Law is enforced by the Ministry of Transportation.

According to a survey conducted by Nihon Keizai Shimbun,[42] the following five categories of complaints are raised by foreign and domestic enterprises engaged in importing products to Japan: (1) inspection procedures are too cumbersome and too detailed; (2) the results of foreign tests are not very well accepted in Japan; (3) standards are too stringent in comparison with those generally accepted by most countries; (4) the enforcement of standards is arbitrary and capricious; and (5) sometimes foreign manufacturers cannot apply for an import license.

Some of these complaints are frivolous or not based on fact, but others are well founded. In Japan, some improvements are necessary to improve access to the market. Much can be accomplished by changing the internal regulations of the enforcement agencies or by simply changing administrative practices.

First, in order to give foreign enterprises the opportunity to participate in the formulation of standards, a cabinet decision containing the following procedural principles was made on May 22, 1979.[43]

[42] *Nihon Keizai Shimbun*, 4 Jan. 1982 (morning ed.), p. 7.
[43] *Kampō*, 24 May 1979, p. 18.

When adopting or modifying standards, public notification of intention will be made, to the extent possible, sufficiently in advance.

After such notifications are made, opportunity for interested parties, whether domestic or foreign, to submit their views will be provided as much as possible, and views submitted will be given due consideration. For this purpose, improvement in procedures shall be facilitated where necessary.

In addition, the Action Program for Improved Market Access adopted on July 30, 1985, states that foreign representatives will be allowed to participate in the drafting and revising of industry standards.

Second, on April 1, 1979, MITI established a "commissioned testing system for Category A electrical appliances and materials," under which a foreign applicant may submit products for testing by a "designated testing authority" in Japan. After a successful test, he receives a certificate of test results. He then sends this certificate to his importer, who forwards it to the "designated testing authority" to obtain a "type test." After the "type test," the importer receives a successful test certificate and sends it to MITI, which then issues the "type authorization."[44] In short, under this system a foreign manufacturer or exporter can apply for testing and licensing of his product while located in a foreign country.

Third, on May 18, 1983, a law was enacted which amends seventeen existing laws on technical standards of one kind or another to make it easier for foreign enterprises manufacturing products abroad to be exported to Japan to acquire approval from the Japanese government for new models.[45] This legislation amended such laws on technical standards as, inter alia, the Consumer Product Safety Law, the High Pressure Gas Law, the Electrical Appliances Control Law, the Pharmaceutical Affairs Law, and the Road Transportation Vehicles Law. In general, the laws were amended to enable foreign enterprises

[44] "Special Progress Report," supra note 40, p. 13 et seq.
[45] Gaikoku Jigyōsha ni yoru Katashiki Shōnin Tō no Shutoku no Enkatsuka no tame no Kankei Hōritsu no Ichibu o Kaisei suru Hōritsu, Law 57, 1983.

manufacturing products for export to Japan to register themselves in the Japanese ministry in charge and to acquire approval
from the ministry for new models.

Fourth, to comply with the requirements of the Tokyo Round
Standards Code, the Industrial Standardization Law[46] was
amended to permit foreign manufacturers or importers to affix
a JIS mark on goods manufactured in foreign countries. Use of
the JIS mark is voluntary, and it has no legal effect in Japan.
However, because it carries prestige and authority, sometimes it
is imperative for a seller to affix this mark on a product in order
for it to be accepted by customers and government purchasing
agencies. Moreover, some laws require that the products or parts
used for certain purposes meet the requirements for JIS standards,
as for example the Electrical Appliances Control Law and the
Ship Safety Law. In such a case, the use of this mark is essential
for sales in Japan.

The provision of the Industrial Standardization Law most relevant to permitting foreign manufacturers to affix the JIS mark
to products imported to Japan is article 25–2, which provides
in part:

> When an application is made to the minister in charge by a
> manufacturer of a designated commodity which carries on
> business in a foreign country, the minister may grant an ap-
> proval for such foreign manufacturer to affix the mark provided
> for in article 19(1) [the JIS mark] on the designated com-
> modity, package, vessel or invoice thereof manufactured by
> such manufacturer on the basis of an inspection of each factory
> or business located in such foreign country.

The Industrial Standardization Law adopts a factory inspection system rather than a product inspection system, according
to which authorization to use the JIS mark is given after the
factory that manufactures the products in question is examined

---

[46] The most comprehensive work on the Industrial Standardization Law is Kōgyō
Gijutsuin Hyōjunbu Hyōjunka, *Kaisei Kōgyō Hyōjunka Hō: Chikujō Kaisetsu* (The Industrial Standardization Law, as Amended: Article-by-Article Comments) (1980).

and found to have sufficient technical and productive facilities. Under this system, the JIS mark is granted en bloc to products manufactured by a factory that has been inspected and proven to possess such facilities.

However, there is a special problem in applying this inspection system to foreign manufactured goods. Since the Industrial Standardization Law is a domestic law, its scope is in principle limited to products within Japanese territory. Thus it is difficult to prohibit use of the JIS mark in foreign countries. Accordingly, the law adopts a system of controlling imports. An importer cannot sell a product on which the JIS mark is affixed if it was manufactured by someone who has not obtained a license or approval to use the mark from the minister in charge. But it is impossible to enforce penalties for violation against a foreign manufacturer operating in foreign countries. Therefore, if such a violation occurs, approval to use the JIS mark is simply revoked. To enforce this system, Japanese government officials must inspect foreign factories. This, however, involves an extraterritorial application of Japanese domestic law, and is impossible to accomplish if a foreign authority refuses to admit the official in charge of the inspection. So instead of stating that a Japanese government official may carry on an inspection in a factory located in a foreign country, article 25–3 of the law provides that when a foreign manufacturer refuses an inspection, approval to use the JIS mark may be denied or revoked.

Fifth, there have been complaints that Japan has tended not to accept product testing conducted in other countries, and as a result, imported products must also be tested in Japan to determine whether they meet Japanese requirements, a process which in some cases may take several years and involve considerable expense. The complaints have stated that this results in undue delay in getting foreign products ready for sale in Japan. It has been alleged that this problem is compounded by foreign exporters' limited knowledge about the requirements to be met and their resulting difficulty in minimizing the expense of testing in Japan.[47] Although this problem has not been solved completely, the Japa-

---

[47] See "Special Progress Report," supra note 40, p. 13 et seq.

nese government has made some significant moves to mitigate the difficulties by providing that the results of foreign testing will be accepted under some circumstances.

Thus, on May 22, 1979, the Cabinet decided to improve the procedures for adopting standards and test results made in foreign countries in line with the Standards Code. This decision, in relevant part, stated as follows:

Cabinet Decision
RE: Improvement of Procedures Concerning Technical Regulations and Standards (hereinafter "Standards") and Test Methods

As Japan's position in the international community is becoming greater than ever, it is increasingly important for Japan to seek international standardization and simplification of procedures as well as non-discriminatory application of such standards and test methods as are generally employed in various countries.

Japan intends to maintain its efforts to further improve its procedures concerning adoption and modification of standards and in testing procedures concerning imported goods. Thus it is hereby resolved that efforts for procedural improvements will be made in line with the following guidelines.

1. When adopting or modifying standards, conformity with international standards will be sought as much as possible, while taking into account circumstances unique to Japan.

2. When adopting or modifying standards, public notification of such intention will be made, to the extent possible, sufficiently in advance.

3. After such notifications are made, opportunities for interested parties, whether domestic or foreign, to submit their views will be provided as much as possible, and views thus submitted will be given due consideration. For this purpose, improvements in procedures shall be facilitated where necessary.

4. When there is sufficient ground to regard foreign results as meeting in substance the requirements of Japanese standards, testing procedures in Japan should be simplified as much as possible.

Some progress has been made in accepting foreign test results for electric appliances, pharmaceuticals, and agricultural chemicals.[48] For example, the administration of the Pharmaceutical Affairs Law has been changed.

Under article 14 of the law, in order to import pharmaceutical products from abroad, it is necessary to obtain an approval from the Minister of MHW. Also, approval is given only after the effectiveness and other attributes of the pharmaceutical product in question have been examined. Some foreign countries (especially the European countries) had complained that the Japanese government would not approve the import of a foreign-manufactured product approved by the government of the country in which it had been manufactured unless an examination was conducted in Japan under the Pharmaceutical Affairs Law. The position of the government was that pharmaceutical products were examined differently in Japan; that is, most of the foreign governments conducted an examination by a sample test, but Japan examined every unit of the product. The government also believed that foreign countries used more relaxed standards than Japan, and therefore the results of their examinations were not quite acceptable.

There have been several debates on this subject in the Diet,[49] and some Diet members have questioned the wisdom of this treatment of foreign pharmaceutical products. For example, it was alleged that an examination by sample test is not necessarily more relaxed than a test in which every unit is examined.[50] However, government officials testifying in the Diet reiterated the position of the government as explained above.

Finally, a decision was made to change the regulation under the Pharmaceutical Affairs Law and accept the results of the examinations conducted by the foreign authorities under some circumstances. On April 1, 1980, the Director General of the Pharmaceutical Affairs Bureau of the MHW amended this reg-

---

[48] Id.

[49] See, generally, the following report: MITI, Trade and Tariff Section, "Tokushu Kanzei Tō ni kansuru Kokkai Gijiroku" (Records of the Diet on Special Tariff System and Related Matters) (1981). This is a compilation of the Diet debates on tariff and trade matters collected by the Tariff and Trade Section of MITI (hereinafter cited as Record).

[50] Id., pp. 217–72.

ulation, providing that examinations of pharmaceutical products conducted in a foreign country may be accepted by the government as data to be used in conducting examinations in Japan. Under the amendment, the government may accept the results of a stability test conducted by the relevant body of the foreign country concerned as data in conducting its own examination. All test data and supporting documentation, however, must be written in Japanese.

§ 3–8. QUOTAS

Under article 52 of the Foreign Exchange and Foreign Trade Control Law,[51] MITI is authorized to establish an import quota system. This provision states: "In order to promote the sound development of the foreign trade and the national economy, any person who desires to import an article may be required to obtain approval therefore as provided by Cabinet order." The Cabinet order referred to here is the Import Trade Control Order,[52] which sets forth the details of import regulation. The enforcement of this law and order is vested in the Minister of MITI.

Articles 4 and 9 of the Control Order establish the import quota system and an import approval system respectively. According to these provisions, MITI can designate commodities that are subject to the import quota system. When MITI has so designated a commodity, a person who desires to import this commodity must apply for and obtain a quota allocation before applying for an import approval. In the 1950s and 1960s, this import quota system was widely used to control many different categories of imports. There are a few agricultural items which are still controlled.

It is difficult to justify this import quota system as an implementation of article XIX of the GATT (the escape clause). First, there is no requirement in article 52 of the Control Law and articles 4 and 9 of the Control Order that the administering authority find an increase in imports and serious injury to a domestic industry caused by the increase in imports. Nor is there any procedure

[51] Gaikoku Kawase oyobi Gaikoku Bōeki Kanri Hō Law 65, 1979, tr. in *EHS Law Bulletin Series*, Vol. 5, AA; hereinafter Control Law.
[52] Yunyū Bōeki Kanri Rei, Cabinet Decree 414, 1949.

for the agency to find such an injury. Thus the compatibility of these provisions with article XIX and other relevant provisions of the GATT is doubtful at best.

In addition, although there is language in the Export Trade Control Order stating that export will be permitted with the "minimum restrictions," no comparable language is incorporated in the relevant articles of the Control Law or the Control Order with regard to import controls. This incongruity probably stems from the history of the Control Law. Its original legislative purpose was to promote exports and restrict imports together with foreign exchange control. The purposes and functions of the Control Law have changed drastically since the time when it was first enacted, but the language of the law has not been changed.

There has been no court case in which the validity of the import quota and approval system has been challenged either under the Constitution or the GATT. However, the Chinese Silk case,[53] a decision of the Kyoto District Court concerning the import restriction of raw silk, is relevant here. On June 29, 1984, the Kyoto District Court handed down a decision upholding import restrictions under the Silk Price Stabilization Law.[54] This law provides for import restrictions similar to that in the Control Order. Therefore, we can draw an analogy from the decision.

As we have already touched upon, the gist of the decision was that in legislation designed to accomplish some socioeconomic policy matters, courts should refrain from questioning the wisdom of legislation unless it clearly overstepped the boundary of reasonableness, since courts are ill equipped to investigate such questions.

Another question presented in the above case was the incompatibility of the import restriction with the provisions of the GATT. The Kyoto District Court held that even if the import restriction of raw silk was contrary to a provision of the GATT, it would not affect the validity of the law in Japan, although it may trigger

[53] The Nishijin Necktie Case, Kyoto District Court Decision, *Hanrei Taimuzu*, No. 530, pp. 265.

[54] For details, see Matsushita, "The Legal Framework for Import Trade and Investment," in *Dynamics of Japanese-United States Trade Relations* T. J. Schoenbaum et al., eds., (1986), p. 13 et seq.

a request for consultation or even retaliation by another GATT member country. This position, however, seems to ignore article 98(2) of the Constitution which provides that a treaty and the established rules in international law should be accorded due respect as well as the established legal interpretation in Japan that a treaty overrides a contrary domestic law.

In any event, given this case law doctrine, the constitutionality of the import control law is likely to be upheld in Japanese courts, and the only recourse a dissatisfied party would have would be to appeal to the government of an affected country and request the government to initiate a proceeding under article XXIII of the GATT or other relevant international agreements.

One salient feature of the import quota under the Control Law and the Control Order is that no procedure is provided for an individual or a private corporation to petition the government to impose a quota, as is provided for under the Trade Act of 1974 in the United States. This would mean that the determination of whether a quota should be imposed on a product belongs solely to the discretion of the government, and a private party who wishes to have the import quota imposed on a commodity must resort to a "political approach" and try to persuade the relevant agencies to initiate one.

The Control Law is a general law providing for a quota system that can be applied to any item as long as the requirements for its invocation are satisfied. Besides the Control Law, there are several pieces of legislation that are designed to establish import restrictions in specific areas. Most of these laws are in the area of agriculture. Some examples are described below.

In the Agriculture Basic Law,[55] which provides for the basic policies for agriculture, article 13 states that whenever the price of agricultural produce declines due to the importation of some competing product from abroad, and agricultural production is thereby disrupted, the government can put into effect such measures as tariff adjustment, import restriction, and other necessary actions.

The Foodstuff Control Law states that rice, wheat, and barley

---

[55] Nōgyō Kihon Hō, Law 127, 1961.

cannot be imported unless authorized by the government. The import restriction of raw silk under the Silk Price Stabilization Law has been explained already.

In the above laws, restricting imports of agricultural products, the import control is usually combined with domestic measures to stabilize the domestic price. In the Foodstuff Control Law, which restricts importation of rice, wheat, and barley, there is a strong governmental measure to support the domestic price. Under this law, the purchase and sale of rice is concentrated in the hands of the government. The government purchases rice from producers and sells it to distributors, and both the purchase price and selling price are determined by the government. The purpose of this legislation is to guarantee some level of income to rice-producing farmers. In order to maintain this tightly regimented control system, imports of rice and other grains are strictly regulated.

There is a price stabilization program combined with import control under the Silk Price Stabilization Law and the Sugar Price Stabilization Law. Under these laws, the government announces the upper limit and the lower limit of the price of the produce concerned, and when the market price dips below the lower limit, the government purchases the produce to support the price. When it goes above the upper limit, then the government sells the produce from stockpiles it holds to make the price come down again. In this way, the price of the produce concerned is kept within the price range established by the government. Most of the items subject to the import quota under the Control Law are agricultural products, and often there is a similar price stabilization program for those items in the domestic market. For example, beef is one of the items under the import quota system, and a price stabilization program is enforced for the price of beef in the domestic market.

Often, import restriction is linked with the price support system, and the sales price of imported produce under these laws is regulated so that the sale of imported items in the domestic market will not disturb the price stabilization program. For instance, under the Silk Price Stabilization Law, the sales price of imported raw silk should not be below the stabilization price set up for domestic raw silk, and whenever there is the like-lihood that the domestic price tends to go below the stabilization price, the sale of the imported item is prohibited.

There are few items outside the agriculture, forestry, and fish-ery industries for which import quotas are established. One exception may be petroleum products. We have already seen how importation of petroleum products was de facto prohibited by administrative guidance. We have also seen that the govern-ment has enacted a new law providing for the registration of imported petroleum products. This law, however, requires a person who desires to import petroleum products to possess an oil refining facility as well as a facility for selling the products. Since it is costly to build an oil refinery, this requirement operates as a de facto restriction.

As stated earlier, MITI has the general authority to control export and import, and, therefore, even with regard to items whose production is outside the jurisdiction of MITI, it has the authority as long as the control of import is concerned. For ex-ample, even though the import quota established for beef and oranges involves agricultural items, MITI has authority to al-locate quotas and issue import approvals. However, in agricul-tural areas, the authority of MITI is formal, and the actual policy decision as to whether or not an import quota should be added or removed will be made by the ministry which is in charge of the item in question.

In 1987, a GATT panel decision[56] handed down as a result of a complaint filed by the United States found that Japan's quotas on ten agricultural products were in violation of the GATT's article XI, which prohibits quotas with certain exceptions for agricultural products on which domestic production is limited. The ten products covered in the ruling are dairy products, pro-cessed cheese, beef and pork products, fruit purée and paste, fruit pulp and canned pineapple, non-citrus juice and tomato juice, tomato ketchup and sauce, starch, glucose, and miscellane-ous processed foods. A ruling on two other products, beans and peanuts, was deferred. In response to this ruling, the Japanese government decided to eliminate quotas on eight of the products

[56] *International Trade Reporter*, Vol. 4, p. 1382 (11 Nov. 1987).

concerned, but with the exemption of dairy products and starch.

In June 1988, Japan and the United States announced a bilateral agreement to liberalize import quotas on beef and oranges. Under the beef agreement, Japan will increase its beef import quotas by 60,000 tons annually for the next three years and eliminate the quotas entirely by 1991. After removing the quotas, a beef tariff will be levied: 70 percent in fiscal 1991, 60 percent in fiscal 1992, and 50 percent in fiscal 1993. After this time, new tariff levels will be set as a result of talks with beef-exporting countries.

The orange pact calls for the removal of import quotas on fresh oranges on April 1, 1991, and on orange juice on April 1, 1992. The requirement that imported orange juice be blended with juice from domestically grown oranges will be eliminated by July 1, 1990.[57]

It is contemplated that most of the other import quotas on agricultural products will be removed by 1991. The liberalization of rice imports is the most important remaining agricultural issue between Japan and its trading partners. Because rice is regarded as a "staple food," Japan has consistently resisted importing rice despite pressure from abroad. In October 1988, the United States Trade Representative (USTR) rejected a petition under section 301 of the Trade Act of 1974 filed by the U.S. Rice Millers' Association to compel retaliation against Japan, which has refused to negotiate the rice issue except in the context of the multilateral GATT discussions on agricultural trade. The USTR has indicated that the Rice Millers' Association's petition will be reconsidered unless Japan takes positive steps to open its market. Most observers expect that the crisis will be resolved through the GATT process by 1990.[58]

§ 3–9. EMERGENCY TARIFF

Article 9(2) of the Customs and Tariff Law provides for an emergency tariff. Under this provision, when the import of a commodity into Japan has suddenly increased due to a sharp decline

[57] For the text of the beef and citrus agreements, see *International Legal Materials*, Vol. 17, p. 1539 (1988).
[58] *The Japan Economic Journal*, 5 Nov. 1988, p. 3.

of the price of the commodity in the country where it is produced, or because of other unforeseen changes, and the domestic industry in Japan producing the same or similar commodity sustains serious injury or there is a threat thereof, an emergency tariff may be imposed on the import of this product.

This provision, together with the import quota system provided in article 52 of the Control Law, is regarded as the legal instrument to implement article XIX of the GATT. To invoke this provision, several requirements must be satisfied. First, there must be a sudden decline in the price of the imported commodity in the country where it is produced, or some other unforeseeable events must have occurred, causing a sudden increase of import of the commodity in Japan. This would mean that the event that has led to a sudden increase in the importation of the commodity into Japan must have been something that could not have been easily predicted. In light of this, if capacity to produce the commodity in question has been gradually built up in the exporting country, and an increase of import of this commodity has been foreseen, article 9(2) cannot be invoked even though the import of this commodity has suddenly increased. On the other hand, if the discovery of a mine in the country of export, which could not have been foreseen, has caused a sharp drop in the price of the commodity in the country of export and resulted in a sudden increase of import of this commodity in Japan, article 9(2) may be invoked.

Another requirement is that there must be "serious injury" to the domestic industry producing the same or similar commodity. In contrast to antidumping and countervailing duties, the injury requirement incorporated here is "serious injury" rather than "material injury." It is hard to quantify this serious injury criterion and to enumerate the quantitative tests to be used in judging it. However, it is clear that the major portion of the domestic industry must suffer substantial loss of profit, unemployment, and underutilization of production facilities.

Where the requirements of article 9(2) are satisfied, the MOF can impose an emergency tariff on the import of this commodity. The amount of maximum emergency tariff is equal to the difference between the value of the imported commodity in question and the proper wholesale price of the same or similar commodity sold by the domestic industry minus the amount of the regular tariff. Therefore, this tariff is imposed in addition to the regular tariff on the imported commodity. If, therefore, the value of the imported commodity is ¥100, and the wholesale priec of the same or a similar commodity in Japan is ¥150 and the regular tariff is ¥5, then the amount of maximum emergency tariff is ¥45. Under this circumstance, the tariff of ¥50 is imposed the imported commodity.

Under article 9(2), it is also possible to withdraw any concession (tariff concession) that has been granted by the Japanese government in trade negotiations. If the Minister of MOF chooses this alternative, then the tariff imposed on this commodity goes back to the rate or amount of the preconcession stage.

§ 3–10. REMEDIES FOR UNFAIR TRADE:
ANTIDUMPING AND COUNTERVAILING DUTIES

Under article VI of the GATT, contracting parties are authorized to enforce domestic antidumping laws against an import at an export price lower than its price in the country of export. The GATT International Antidumping Code concluded in 1979 also specifies the conditions under which the contracting parties can exercise regulation over dumped imports. Under these agreements, dumping occurs when: (1) the price of an imported product is lower than the price of the same or similar commodity in the home market of the country of export; (2) a domestic industry suffers (or is threatened with) material injury; and (3) there is a linkage between the low-priced import and the injury to the domestic industry.

Under article VI of the GATT, a countervailing duty can be applied when an import coming into the country is subsidized by the government of the country of export, thereby causing a material injury to a domestic industry in the country of import. Moreover, the GATT International Subsidy and Countervailing Duty Code, concluded in 1979, provides certain requirements that must be observed by contracting parties when they invoke countervailing duties under their domestic laws.

Japan is a contracting party to the GATT and the International Antidumping and Subsidy Codes.[59] It has adopted these international agreements as treaties and, therefore, laws in Japan relevant to the enforcement of those provisions must conform to the requirements of these agreements. In 1980, after adopting these international agreement, the government amended the relevant statutes and regulations to conform to them.[60]

As will be explained later, there are only a few cases in which antidumping and countervailing duty regulations are used. It is expected, however, that in the future some of the domestic industries will utilize them to deal with import problems.

1. AN OVERVIEW OF THE ANTIDUMPING REGULATION

Article 9 of the Customs and Tariff Law provides for the imposition of an antidumping duty, and article 8 provides for the imposition of a countervailing duty. The Cabinet Decree on Antidumping Duties and the Cabinet Decree on Countervailing Duties provide additional details.[61]

Article 9 of the Customs and Tariff Law defines "dumping" as "the selling for the exportation of an article at the price which is lower than the price of the same or a similar article for the domestic consumption in the market of the country of export." The price of the commodity for the domestic consumption is called "normal value," and, therefore, dumping is an export of a commodity at an export price which is lower than its normal value. If a domestic industry has sustained a material injury by reason of such dumping, the Japanese government can impose an antidumping duty whose maximum amount is the difference between the export price and the normal value of that commodity, in addition to the regular duty imposed on the commodity.

The 1986 "Guidelines on the Procedure of the Antidump-

---

[59] See supra § 1–3.

[60] For the law before 1980, see Saxonhouse, "Antidumping Law in Japan," in *Antidumping Law: Policy and Implementation*, Michigan Yearbook of International Studies, Vol. 1, p. 245 (1979).

[61] Cabinet Decree 137, 1980, and Cabinet Decree 136, 1980, respectively. For details on antidumping regulations in Japan, see Matsushita, "Economic Regulation" in *CCH Japan Business Law Guide*, M. Matsushita, ed. (1988), paras. 33–600; Hagiwara and Noguchi, "Anti-Dumping Laws," *Japan Business Law Letter*, Vol. 1, No. 3 (1988), pp. 7–11; Hagiwara, Noguchi, and Masui, "Antidumping Laws in Japan," *Journal of World Trade*, Vol. 22, p. 35 (1988).

ing and Countervailing Duties and Related Matters" (hereinafter referred to as "Guidelines") lay out the details of the procedures.

2. INITIATION OF INVESTIGATION

An antidumping investigation can be started in two ways: (1)
by a petition or complaint by an interested party and (2) by
self-initiation by the government. Under the International Antidumping Code, an investigation initiated by a complaint is the
rule and self-initiation by the government the exception.

An interested party can file a complaint with the Ministry of
Finance when he believes that a product from a foreign country
is being imported at a price lower than its domestic price in the
home country and that a Japanese domestic industry is suffering
a material injury caused by such dumping. The complainant must
state the article, the manufacturer, the brand, the model, the
features of the commodity, the exporter and the country of export, and outline the facts of the dumping and of the material
injury and other relevant data. The complainant must produce
evidence of these items that are "reasonably available."

Even though the interested party can be an individual, corporation, or trade association, it is usually a trade association
which represents the industry affected by dumping. Such a trade
association must show that its constitution states that it is authorized to act on behalf of its members.

The Minister of MOF may initiate a formal investigation if he
believes that the complaint is supported by sufficient evidence.
He has two months to decide whether to initiate a formal investigation or not after he receives a complaint. Even though
self-initiation is rare, the Minister can initiate an investigation
when he believes that there is evidence of dumping and of material injury to a domestic industry.

Investigation is carried out by an investigatory group composed of officials of the MOF, MITI, and the ministry in charge
of the product under investigation.

The right of interested parties to produce evidence is guaranteed, and also the Minister may request interested parties to
submit evidence. Information supplied to the Minister can be
held in confidence if the party which submits it so requests. How-

ever, the Minister can request the submitting party to provide a non-confidential summary of the information. The Minister can request foreign exporters and producers to submit information concerning the price and other business matters, and, if the foreign party so requested does not cooperate without a good reason, the Minister can determine the case on the basis of the "best information available."

Upon the request of the parties involved in a case, the Minister holds an adversary hearing in which both parties present their views and a cross-examination of witnesses is permitted.

3. DOMESTIC INDUSTRY

A "domestic industry" is a concept important to the enforcement of the antidumping regulation. Under cabinet decree, a domestic industry is defined as manufacturers who produce a considerable portion of the commodity which is in competition with the dumped commodity. Under the Guidelines, a "considerable portion" is defined as at least a 50-percent share in the production. Also, under the Guidelines, those domestic manufacturers which import the commodity under investigation or which are related to the foreign exporters must be excluded from the scope of domestic industry. (This is due to a "clean hands" principle.) However, if a domestic enterprise ceased importing the commodity under investigation six months prior to the filing of a complaint, it is included within the scope of domestic industry.

4. PROVISIONAL MEASURES AND FINAL MEASURES

Under certain circumstances, a provisional measure can be taken. If it is determined that there has been dumping and an injury to a domestic industry is likely to occur, the Minister can invoke a provisional measure in the form of a provisional duty or a bond or security for an amount equal to the provisional duty. The maximum period of a provisional measure is four months, although this period can be extended to six months upon the request of the interested party.

After the facts of dumping and injury have been established, the Minister of MOF can impose an antidumping duty on the import in question. The maximum amount of an antidumping duty is the difference between the export price and the normal value of the commodity.

5. PRICE UNDERTAKING

An antidumping investigation is lengthy and is burdensome on both the foreign exporters and the government which enforces the antidumping law. Therefore, an antidumping issue can be settled by way of price undertaking. If a foreign exporter proposes to the Minister of MOF to stop exporting the commodity in question or to increase the export price so as to eliminate the dumping margin, the Minister of MOF can suspend the antidumping investigation if he judges that the proposal is appropriate to resolve the issue. This is different, however, from an informal agreement between the foreign exporter and the domestic industry by which the domestic industry will withdraw the complaint if the foreign exporter raises its export price.

6. NORMAL VALUE AND EXPORT PRICE

As explained earlier, "dumping" is the export of a commodity at an export price lower than its normal value of the same or similar commodity sold in the market of the exporting country. Therefore, to determine whether a commodity is dumped or not, it is necessary to examine the export price and the normal value of the commodity in question.

"Normal value," in general terms, is the price of the commodity in question in the home market of the country of export. It is the price charged by the manufacturer/exporter of a commodity in the home market of the country of export to an independent purchaser. If a manufacturer/exporter of a commodity sells a commodity in the home market to a wholesaler who is independent of the manufacturer/exporter, the price charged by the manufacturer/exporter to the wholesaler is considered the normal value of the commodity. If, however, a foreign manufacturer/exporter sells a commodity in the home market to a purchaser who is related to the manufacturer/exporter by reason of stock ownership, interlocking directorate, or some other means, this sale is disregarded, and the price of the commodity charged to the first independent purchaser is used as the normal value of the commodity.

Also, the sale by the manufacturer/exporter in the home market at a price below the production cost of the commodity may be disregarded by the antidumping authority, in which case a constructed value is used for the normal value. "Constructed value" is computed by adding an appropriate estimate of general expenses and a reasonable profit to the cost of producing the commodity in question.

If there is no domestic price of the commodity, then either a third-country export price or the constructed value is used as the normal value. The International Antidumping Code does not provide whether a third-country export price or the constructed value should be used first, and, therefore, either one can be used.

"Export price" is generally the price at which a foreign manufacturer/exporter sells the commodity in question for export. Therefore, if a foreign manufacuturer/exporter sells the commodity to an importer, the price paid by the importer is the export price. If a foreign manufacturer/exporter sells the commodity to a trading company in the country of export which then exports it, the export price is probably computed on the basis of the price paid by the trading company for the purpose of exporting the commodity.

If, however, a foreign manufacturer/exporter sells the commodity to an importer that is a party related to the foreign manufacturer/exporter, the price paid by the importer cannot be relied upon in computing the export price because the price probably does not reflect the market price of the commodity. In this situation, the price charged by the importer to an independent purchaser is used as the export price.

Under the International Antidumping Code, both an export price and a normal value must be computed at the same level of trade and, if possible, at the ex-factory level. Therefore, in arriving at both the export price and the normal value of a commodity in question, expenses incurred on the way are deducted and both their net values are computed. If a foreign manufacturer sells the commodity to an independent purchaser, in computing the export price the transportation charge from the factory of the manufacturer/exporter to the port of departure, the costs of ocean freight and insurance, the tariffs imposed by the Japanese government, the transportation cost from the port of entry to the purchaser's warehouse, and any other costs are deducted from the price paid by the purchaser. Likewise, if the foreign manufacturer/exporter sells the commodity to an unrelated wholesaler, then all the expenses incurred in delivering it to the wholesaler are deducted from the price paid by the wholesaler.

Factors which affect the difference of prices must be taken into consideration. For example, if the foreign manufacturer/exporter gives technical assistance to domestic wholesalers of the country of export with regard to the commodity it sells, while no such technical assistance is given to Japanese importers and distributors, the normal value must be adjusted accordingly; that is, it must be reduced by the amount by which such assistance is given. Likewise, if there is a difference in the methods of payment resulting in a difference of interest, such a difference must be taken into consideration. If, for example, a foreign wholesaler pays the foreign manufacturer/exporter for the commodity it buys in the home market of the country of export by a promissory note whose term is, say, four months, whereas Japanese importers pay the foreign manufacturer/exporter for the commodity by means of a letter of credit payable on sight, then the interest for the period of those four months should be taken into consideration, and the normal value should be reduced by that much.

The above examples are only a few of various factors which should be taken into consideration when arriving at the export price and the normal value.

7. MATERIAL INJURY

If, by reason of a dumping, as explained above, a domestic industry is "materially injured," then the requirements for imposing an antidumping duty are satisfied. Even though in the Japanese law and regulation there is no definition of "material injury," it is generally considered as an injury lighter than a "serious injury," which is necessary for the purpose of invoking the safeguard measure.

Various economic factors are taken into consideration when deciding whether or not there is a material injury due to dumping. First of all, the increase in imports of the commodity under investigation is considered. If the rate of increase is rapid or the quantity of imports is great, this will be an important factor in determining the existence of an injury. Second, the pattern of pricing of the commodity is considered. If, for example, the domestic price in question has been depressed or a rise in the price halted by the influx of the dumped goods, this will be regarded as a contributing factor to an injury sustained by the domestic industry. Third, the effect of the dumping on the domestic industry is considered. This involves an examination of such matters as a decrease in the rate of profits, a decline in the utilization of production facilities, and an increase in unemployment. Although not spelled out clearly in either the law or the regulation, probably all these factors noted above must be present in order to decide whether there is an injury to a domestic industry due to a dumping.

Another question is that of linkage or causation between a dumping and an injury. Under the International Antidumping Code, an injury caused by factors other than dumped imports should not be attributed to the dumping. This language is somewhat vague, but it seems to indicate that a dumping must be an important contributing factor to an injury to a domestic industry. Therefore, if there are several other important factors contributing to an injury and dumping is a negligible cause, it should lead to a finding of no injury to a domestic industry.

8. COUNTERVAILING DUTY

A countervailing duty is imposed if a foreign government provides a subsidy for the export of a commodity, thereby causing an injury to a domestic industry in the country of import. Since Japan has adhered to the International Subsidy and Countervailing Duty Code, items listed in the code as export subsidies are regarded as countervailable subsidies. Under this code, such items as rebates given to exporters in proportion to the amount of exports, tax exemptions, preferential financing by the government or by government-related agencies at a rate of interest more favorable than the prevailing market rate, and government aid afforded to the manufacture of products to be exported are some of the examples of countervailable subsidies.

In addition to export subsidies, "indirect subsidies" can be countervailed. For example, if a foreign government subsidizes the production of parts to be incorporated into a finished product for export to Japan, such a subsidy may be regarded as an "indirect subsidy." Such a subsidy, however, must be a grant given exclusively for the production of parts used in exported products.

The procedure used to investigate and impose a countervailing duty is similar to that for an antidumping duty. A domestic party that believes that it has been injured because of increasing imports aided by subsidies granted by a foreign government can file a complaint with the MOF. In addition, the Minister of MOF can *ex officio* initiate an investigation. The investigation must be completed within one year. If the facts of subsidy, injury, and the linkage between the two are established, the Minister can impose a countervailing duty equal to the amount of the net subsidy in addition to the regular duty.

As in an antidumping investigation, the issue may be settled by undertaking on the part of the foreign government after an investigation has been started with regard to a possible subsidy given to an export. If the foreign government promises to eliminate the subsidy or otherwise take a measure which would eliminate the injurious effect of the subsidy, then the Minister of MOF can suspend the investigation.

9. CASES OF ANTIDUMPING AND COUNTERVAILING DUTIES

So far there have been only a handful of cases in which petitions were made by the Japanese domestic industries on the basis of the antidumping and countervailing duty regulations. At least two reasons are attributable for this dearth of cases: (1) the Japanese economy was shielded from imports until about 1960 by import quotas and other trade restrictions and, in those days, there was little need for such regulations, and (2) after the trade liberalization since the mid-1960s, the Japanese manufacturing industries generally enjoyed a high degree of international competitiveness, and, therefore, there has been little need for the enforcement of antidumping and countervailing duties.

However, some traditional industries are on the way to decline, and enterprises in the NIEs are advancing rapidly. Given this situation, it is easy to predict that there will be an increase in petitions by domestic industries seeking relief against imports through antidumping and countervailing duties.

There have been four cases in which domestic industries petitioned the government for relief under the antidumping and countervailing duty laws. In 1982, the Japanese Cotton Spinners' Association brought a petition to the Minister of MOF alleging that Korean products had been dumped on the market and had caused material injury to the textile industry. It also claimed that the Pakistani government gave an export subsidy in the form of: (1) export financing at a preferential interest rate, (2) a kickback to exporters at the rate of 7.5 percent of the export price, and (3) tax reduction of 0.5 percent of the income derived from export. Because of an increase of import aided by the government, there had been a material injury to the Japanese domestic industry.

With regard to the Korean dumping issue, there was a conference in Korea between the representatives of the Japanese and Korean industries, and the Korean industry decided to effectuate a voluntary export restraint. The Japanese industry accepted this settlement and withdrew its petition.

On the Pakistani subsidy issue, there was a conference between the Japanese and the Pakistani governments, and the Pakistani government promised to abolish the preferential financing and the rebate. The Japanese government, considering that the tax reduction would produce only a *de minimus* effect, decided to terminate the investigation.

The third case is the ferro-silicon case. The ferro-alloy industry, which had been designated by MITI as a "depressed industry" under the Law to Promote Improvement of Industrial Structure in Specific Industries, was in the process of an industrial reform program. Between 1980 and 1983, however, there was a sharp increase in import of this commodity, and foreign imports came to occupy 62 percent of the market. The Ferro-Alloy Association in Japan claimed that the products had been dumped onto the market by France and Norway and that a subsidy had been given by the Brazilian government to export the product to Japan. However, before an investigation was initiated with regard to the dumping and subsidy question, conferences were held between the Japanese government and the governments of the countries in question. The foreign governments promised that they would make sure that there would be no dumping or export subsidy. Also, the market condition in Japan showed a marked improvement. Considering all of these factors together, the Ferro-Alloy Association decided to withdraw its petition.

In 1987, the import of knit textile products surpassed the export of these products from Japan for the first time in history. The major foreign sources of supply were Korea and China. The Japan Knitting Industry Association, considering exports to Japan from Korea had been dumped, filed a petition in 1988 under the antidumping regulation. In early 1989, the Korean exporters announced that they would restrain the export of the products voluntarily, and the Japanese association decided to withdraw its petition.

§ 3–11. RETALIATION FOR UNFAIR TRADE PRACTICES

Article 7 of the Customs and Tariff Law grants the government authority to impose a special supplementary duty on any products imported from a nation that discriminates against Japanese goods, shipping, or airlines. This provision, which has not yet been invoked in Japan, is similar to the U.S. law remedy, section 301 of the Trade Act of 1974.[62]

§ 3–12. GOVERNMENT PROCUREMENT

Government procurement requirements have been progressively liberalized in Japan to allow more purchases from foreign suppliers. Until 1972, Imperial Edict No. 556 of 1964 stated that "in order to promote use of domestically produced articles, the minister of each ministry may use a single tendering procedure in purchasing commodities as designated by the MOF." In 1972, however, this system began to be liberalized. In 1980, Japan adhered .to the Government Procurement Code of the GATT[63] and conformed its law to the principles in that code.[64]

At present, there are one law and several orders concerning

---

[62] 19 U.S.C. 2301. Under this provision, the president has wide powers to retaliate in the case of unfair trade practices directed against the United States.

[63] See supra § 1–3.

[64] See, generally, M. Kadotani, ed., *Seifuchōtatsu ni kansuru Kyōtei to Kanchō Keiyaku Seido* (The Government Procurement Code and the Government Contract System) (1981).

government procurement in Japan. These are: (1) the Accounts Law,[65] (2) the Cabinet Order Concerning the Budget, Auditing, and Accounting,[66] (3) the Special Provisions for the Cabinet Order Concerning the Budget, Auditing, and Accounting,[67] (4) the Cabinet Order stipulating special procedures for government procurement of goods,[68] and (5) the Ministerial Ordinance stipulating special procedures for government procurement of goods.[69]

Because before 1 January 1981, the Order of 1947, the Special Provisions of 1946, and the Accounts Law included some provisions for procedures not identical to those set out in the agreement, some adjustments were required to implement the agreement. The Special Cabinet Order and the Ordinance of 1980 were thus issued to provide for special procedures and for the stipulations necessary in accordance with the Order of 1947 and the Special Provisions of 1946 so that the procedures applicable to the special procurement would be in full compliance with the agreement. In this way, the agreement has been incorporated into domestic law. The essentials of the present procurement system are as follows:

1. Notice or Proposed Purchase and Tender Documentation. The notice of proposed purchase by means of open or selective tendering procedures must be published in the official gazette (*Kampō*) at last 30 days prior to the day for submitting tenders.

2. Open and Selective Tendering Processes. Open and selective tendering procedures are adopted in accordance with the provisions of the [GATT] agreement. Where selective tendering procedures are adopted, the invitation for participation in the tendering shall be issued on the same date as the publication of notice for the tendering.

3. Use of Single-Tendering Procedures. Use of single-tendering procedures is limited to those cases permitted under

---

[65] Kaikei Hō, Law 35, 1947.
[66] Imperial Edict 165, 1947, hereinafter the Order of 1947.
[67] Imperial Edict 558, 1946, hereinafter the Special Provisions of 1946.
[68] Cabinet Order 300, 1980, hereinafter the Special Cabinet Order.
[69] MOF Ordinance 45, 1980, hereinafter the Ordinance of 1980.

the [GATT] agreement (article 29–3 of the Accounts Law, articles 10 and 11 of the Special Cabinet Order).

4. The Lowest Bidder. Purchasing agencies award a contract to the supplier submitting the tender that offers the lowest price within the limits of the provisional value of the contract. Agencies may, because of the nature or objective of a contract, award a contract to the supplier submitting the most advantageous tender in terms of price and other factors.

5. National Treatment and Nondiscrimination. The principle of equal treatment for domestic and foreign suppliers is one of the bases for the new procedures for procurement in Japan, and the principle has been confirmed by the MOF Minister's directive entitled "With Regard to the Implementation of the Cabinet Order Stipulating Special Procedures for Government Procurement of Goods," issued on 27 December 1980.

6. Local Governments. On 23 January 1981, the MFA and the Ministry of Home Affairs sent to all the prefectural governments, the municipal or local governments, and some city authorities a joint letter describing the contents of the [GATT] agreement, with particular reference to paragraph 2 of article I.

Under the present system, the basic principle in government procurement in Japan is open tendering, and if it is impossible to rely on open tendering, selective tendering, which is open to both domestic and foreign persons. As indicated above, the use of a single-tendering procedure is limited to some exceptional cases. Article 29–3 of the Accounts Law provides that single tendering shall be adopted where the circumstances (the nature or purpose of the contract concerned) do not allow the governmental entity concerned to adopt open or selective tendering procedures for a contract for procurement, when open or selective tendering procedures cannot be adopted because of extreme urgency, or when open or selective tendering procedures would be disadvantageous for the agency concerned. However, article 29–3(5) of the Accounts Law provides that, notwithstanding the other provisions, a single-tendering procedure may be adopted in the cases specified by cabinet order. Article 99 of the Order of 1947 provides that a single-tendering procedure may be used when a government agency purchases products directly from cooperatives composed mainly of small and medium-sized enterprises, or associations of such enterprises, in order to protect and foster them. By using this provision, the Japanese government can purchase products exclusively from small domestic enterprises. This is potentially an important leeway for the government agencies to use to avoid purchasing foreign products.

CHAPTER FOUR

EXPORT REGULATIONS

§ 4–1. Export Controls

In Japan, exports are regulated under the Foreign Exchange and Foreign Trade Control Law (Control Law) and through export agreements or cartels created under the Export and Import Transactions Law (Transactions Law). There is a policy difference between the Control Law and the Transactions Law, on the one hand, which are designed to restrict competition, and the Antimonopoly Law,[1] on the other hand, which seeks to promote competition. This conflict and its effects on the regulation of exports is explored in more detail in Chapter 6.

Export restriction under the Control Law is exercised pursuant to the provisions of articles 47 through 51 thereof. The key sections of the Control Law are article 47, which sets forth a general principle of free export, and article 48, which, by providing for approval of exports, restricts that principle. Article 47 provides that the "export of goods will be permitted with such minimum restrictions thereon as are consistent with the purpose of this Law."[2] Article 48 enables the government to find exceptions to the broad mandate of article 47, by providing that "any person desiring to export goods of any designated type, or goods destined for any special areas which have been designated by cabinet

[1] Shiteki Dokusen no Kinshi oyobi Kōsei Torihiki no Kakuho ni Kansuru Hōritsu (Law Concerning the Prohibition of Private Monopolies and the Maintenance of Fair Trade), Law 54, 1947, as amended (1967); tr. in *EHS Law Bulletin Series*, Vol. 2, KA, and in Counselor's Office, FTC, *Antimonopoly Legislation of Japan* (1977); hereinafter AML. See, generally, C.D. Edwards, *Trade Regulations Overseas* (1965); E.M. Hadley, *Antitrust in Japan* (1970); H. Iyori and A. Uesugi, *The Antimonopoly Laws of Japan* (1983); M. Nakagawa, *Antimonopoly Legislation of Japan* (1984); "Antimonopoly Regulation," in *Doing Business in Japan*, Vol. 5, part 9, Z. Kitagawa, ed. (1982).

[2] Control Law, art. 47.

decree as the areas to which the export of the designated goods is likely to threaten the maintenance of international peace and security, shall be required to obtain the approval of MITI as provided for by Cabinet Order."[3]

Article 48(3) continues: "The Minister of MITI may, according to a Cabinet Decree, impose the obligation to obtain an approval on any person desiring to export specified goods or goods to specified areas or goods by means of specified transactions or methods of payment within the limit which the Minister deems necessary to maintain an international balance of payments and a sound development of foreign trade and the national economy."[4]

The Cabinet has issued an Export Trade Control Order[5] which authorizes MITI to institute an export approval system. This order states that "[a]ny person desiring to export goods which fall into [certain categories] shall obtain the written approval of [MITI]" and states that MITI may deny or attach conditions to a license when it deems doing so to be necessary "for the maintenance of the balance of international payment[s] and the sound development of international trade or the national economy."[6]

Export control is used in Japan for a variety of purposes: to preserve supplies of rare materials; to prohibit the export of narcotics, weapons, and pornography; to carry out orderly marketing agreements and voluntary export restraints with foreign governments; and to observe international commitments such as the

---

[3] Id., art 48(1).

[4] Id., art. 48(3).

[5] Yushutsu Bōeki Kanri Rei, Cabinet Order 378, 1949; tr. in *EHS Law Bulletin Series*, Vol. 5, AJ-2.

[6] Export Trade Control Order, art. 1(6). The categories of goods subject to the Export Trade Control Order include:
   (a) items of excess competition (textile goods, binoculars, and other items of excess competition whose export may invoke import restrictions in the foreign countries of destination);
   (b) strategic war materials;
   (c) items which require export restrictions in order to secure a stable supply-and-demand equilibrium in the domestic market (rare materials such as tungsten);
   (d) items of embargo (arms, weapons, counterfeit money, obscene literature, narcotic drugs, national treasures, etc.); and
   (e) items which may infringe upon intangible property rights in the destination country.

Id., sched. (beppyō) 1, 2.

export restrictions on militarily critical equipment and technology required by Japan's membership in the Coordinating Committee (COCOM) for multilateral export controls.[7] Various means of export control may be used, including prohibition, price controls, quotas, and restrictions on channels of distribution.

In 1987, in response to American displeasure over the case of the export of high-tech milling machines to the Soviet Union by Toshiba Machine Co., article 48 of the Control Law was amended to enable MITI to restrict exports for foreign policy reasons. A new Export Control was issued by MITI specifying the products and countries to which trade restrictions apply in order to enforce the trade embargoes set by COCOM.

"Check prices" and quotas have been the primary means used by MITI in the exercise of its powers under article 48 of the Control Law and the Export Trade Control Order. The check price is a minimum export price usually imposed to prevent dumping in the importing country. Quotas on the export volume of each exporter as a proportion of the total export quota for a product have been allocated on the basis of past export volume, on a seniority system founded on the order of application, and on the basis of the good reputation of each applicant. As may be imagined, each of these formulae may be challenged by the various applicants concerned, and adjustments are often made in their actual operation.[8]

---

[7] The Consultative Group Coordinating Committee (COCOM) was established in 1950 as the working committee of the Consultative Group charged with the task of compiling (secret) lists of items subject to strategic controls if destined for export to the European communist bloc. The Consultative Group, established in 1949 under the sponsorship of the United States, was composed initially of export control officials from the United States, Great Britain, France, Italy, the Netherlands, Belgium, and Luxembourg. Norway, Denmark, Canada, West Germany, Portugal, Greece, Turkey, and Japan subsequently joined the COCOM and delegated export control officials to take part in the COCOM's regular meetings in Paris. The COCOM is an informal organization in which nations voluntarily participate. MITI enforced the COCOM in Japan through its general powers to control exports for the "sound development of international trade or the national economy," Control Law, art. 48(1) and Export Trade Control Order, art. 1, but the COCOM does not have the status of a law or treaty under Japanese law.

[8] Other restrictions include transaction alignment by requiring a set route of export; safety and sanitation rules based on certain safety and sanitation standards; design regulation to prevent possible infringement of intangible property rights in the destination countries; and payment terms and recovery of credit by imposing an obligation to comply with certain conditions in order to ensure smooth recovery of credit or to prevent the worsening of payment terms in cases of plant expansions

Two cases have been brought to judgment on the merits concerning the legality of export restrictions issued under the Control Law and the Export Trade Control Order. In one case, 1969 Pekin-Shanhai Nihon Kōgyō Tenrankai v. Japan (the COCOM case),[9] the question was whether or not the disapproval of the export of certain commodities to the People's Republic of China was outside the powers given to MITI by the Control Law and was therefore void and without effect. The plaintiff, the association for the 1969 Peking-Shanghai Japanese Industrial Exhibition, was chosen as the executive organ in carrying out an exhibition of Japanese goods in China in 1969. In 1968, the plaintiff applied to MITI for approval of the export of nearly 3,000 items to be displayed at the exhibition. MITI disapproved the export of nineteen items pursuant to the Export Trade Control Order, claiming that such exports would conflict with the COCOM Agreement to which Japan was a party. Plaintiff sued MITI in the Tokyo District Court (a court of first instance) for cancellation of the ruling and subsequently added a count for recovery of the damages it was alleged to have suffered as a result of being deprived of the opportunity to participate in the exhibition to the extent it desired.

The court held that MITI's disapproval was illegal since it did not fall within one of the limited exceptions to the general principle of free trade specified in the Control Law. The court announced:

The [Control Law] declares the principle of freedom of export by providing in its article 47 that export of goods will be permitted with minimum restrictions so long as such export is consistent with the purpose of the Law. This article should be viewed not merely as providing for the policy objective of free export but also as stating definitively that freedom of export is a right of the people which is part of the freedom of business

---

under deferred payment.

[9] 1969 Pekin-Shanhai Nihon Kōgyō Tenrankai v. Japan, *Gyōsai Reishū*, Vol. 20. p. 842 (Tokyo Dist. Ct., 8 July 1969). The translation of the case is used with the permission of the translators, Messrs. Charles Stevens and Kazunori Takahashi, and may be found among the course materials collection of the East Asian Legal Studies Program of the Harvard Law School.

guaranteed to the people as a fundamental human right under article 22 of the Constitution, although such freedom should be subject to restrictions for the public welfare. . . . The meaning of article I of the Export Control Trade Order is that since the freedom of export is a fundamental human right, its restriction by [MITI] can be permitted only if such restriction is deemed purely and directly necessary for the sound maintenance of the balance of international payments and the sound development of international trade or the national economy.[10]

The government contended that to deviate from the COCOM Agreement would disrupt friendly relations between the United States and Japan and would lead to economic retaliation by the United States and other member nations. Counsel for the government argued that such retaliatory measures would seriously undermine the sound development of Japan's international trade and domestic economy, and, therefore, an export restriction based on the COCOM Agreement was in perfect harmony with the spirit of the Control Law and the Export Trade Control Order. In response, the court replied that if Japan had joined the COCOM for political reasons (as it had), export controls, which are enforced for economic reasons, would have to be based on other domestic laws in the absence of a clear legislative intent that the COCOM be so employed.[11]

In a second case, Japan v. Sekiya Sangyō K.K.,[12] the defendants had exported wool products to Hong Kong. At the time, MITI had adopted a policy of approving exports of wool products if the export price was at or above the check price, i.e., the price determined as necessary to prevent dumping in the destination country. The defendants had obtained approval of their exports

[10] Stevens and Takahashi, id., p. 14.

[11] Id., p. 17–18. The court held: "We must conclude that export restrictions imposed for other than economic reasons are not encompassed by [article 1 of the Export Trade Control Order], even if such restrictions have an indirect economic effect. . . . Consequently, the administrative disposition at issue in this case was outside the scope of the discretionary power which can be exercised by the Minister [of International Trade and Industry] under [article 1 of the Export Trade Control Order]. His disposition must be concluded to have been illegal."

[12] Japan v. Sekiya Sangyō K.K., *Kakyū Keishū* Vol. 3, p. 141 (Kobe Dist. Ct., 25 Feb. 1961).

from MITI by declaring that their export price was above the
check price, but in fact the defendants had agreed illegally with
their importers in Hong Kong that the defendants would pay the
importers a kickback of the difference between the check price
and the actual export price. When MITI discovered this ruse,
the defendants were prosecuted and sentenced to imprisonment
and a fine by the Kobe District Court.

In their defense, the exporters had argued that the check price
established by MITI was unrealistically high, that importers
demanded lower prices, and that, under such circumstances, it
was unreasonable to expect exporters to comply with the check
price. The court replied that the stabilization of free-market swings
in price was one of the purposes of the check price and noted that
their difficulties with the check price did not justify defendants'
illegal actions:

> The check price system is based on a trade policy designed to
> prevent situations where Japanese products are discriminated
> against in foreign markets by charges of dumping, . . . to sta-
> bilize prices, and to promote the sound development of exports
> at proper prices in order to remove the fears of foreign trading
> companies handling Japanese products that they may suffer
> losses due to a decline of prices caused by unstable export
> prices resulting from excessive competition. Therefore, the
> very purpose of this system is to ensure that Japanese trading
> companies will refuse to negotiate transactions with foreign
> traders when they demand prices below the check price. . . .
> The expectation behind this system is that if every Japanese
> company takes this kind of attitude, foreign traders will finally
> give up their demands for transactions at prices below the check
> price. . . . In order to achieve this [end], the check price is
> determined after discussions of the advisory committee in which
> large companies participate, taking into consideration the cost of
> the products, reasonable profit, international market prices, and
> the export prices of the competing countries. Once determined,
> it is not easily changed and is maintained at the level chosen
> for a certain period of time, unless there have been considerable
> changes in the factors mentioned above which would cause the

check price to become unreasonable or would cause the maintenance of the check price to become difficult. Therefore, it is natural that the check price has not been changed from time to time in response to the demands of the industry.

Accordingly, even if a trading company in Hong Kong, a colony famous worldwide for intense market fluctuations, demands transactions at prices below the check price, it is an abuse of the check price system and destroys the national trade policy to utilize an evasive method such as making false statements to the effect that exports have been carried out at a high price . . . while, in fact, exports at prices below the check price were made in accordance with the demands of foreign traders.[13]

Another case, the Textile case, involved a sweeping challenge to the Control Law but did not proceed to judgment on the merits. In 1971, the governments of the United States and Japan signed a declaration that the Japanese government would regulate exports of wool and synthetic textiles to the United States.[14] In order to comply with this agreement, MITI proposed to invoke the Control Law and set up export quotas to be followed by the Japanese textile industry. The plaintiff, Federation of Textile Industries in Japan (Nihon Sen'i Sangyō Remmei), sought an injunction in the Tokyo District Court in December 1971, restraining MITI from implementing the quotas. The federation urged any and all of several findings: (1) that the agreement between the two governments was unreasonable; (2) that the agreement violated the principle of free trade embodied in the GATT;[15] (3) that the quotas proposed by MITI were contrary to the constitutional right of freedom of business activity; and (4) that the export controls proposed by MITI were beyond its statutory powers because MITI had not power to enforce export controls based on a mere memorandum between governments.

[13] Id. Technically, the case arose under the Control Law, art. 30, which provides that "[n]o person may be a party to the creation, modification, liquidation, extinguishment or direct or indirect transfer or other disposition of [assets subject to foreign exchange regulations] . . . unless authorized by Cabinet Order."

[14] Arrangement on Trade in Wool and Man-Made Fiber Textiles, 3 Jan. 1972, United States-Japan, 23 U.S.T. 3167 T.I.A.S. No. 7495.

[15] 30 Oct. 1947, 61 Stat. A3, T.I.A.S. 1700, 55 U.N.T.S. 187.

Scholarly opinion is divided on the plaintiff's chances of success on the merits had the suit been brought to judgment.[16]

In recent years, however, such controls have played a decreasing role in regulating exports. In addition, there are ways of circumventing the check price. For example, if an exporter in Japan and an overseas importer have a sufficient volume of mutual business, the exporter may achieve the same result as would be achieved by lowering the check price by providing the importer with noncontrolled products at a lower price than normal, while making up for the unusually low prices of the noncontrolled goods by exporting controlled goods at or above the check price.

MITI often uses administrative guidance[17] as a means to control exports. This is usually done in the form of an informal request to exporters to set a minimum export price or to restrict the quantity of exports to certain countries. An example of this is the 1981 auto export restraint[18] to implement an informal understanding between the United States and Japan limiting the number of Japanese automobiles to be shipped into the U.S. market.

§ 4–2. EXPORT AGREEMENTS

1. TYPES OF EXPORT AGREEMENTS

1. The Export and Import Transaction Law
Besides the Control Law, the Export and Import Transactions Law is an important instrument for the government to regulate exports and import. Unlike the Control Law, however, the way in which the government exerts its control over exports and imports under the Transactions Law is indirect, rather than direct. Whereas the Control Law authorizes MITI to effectuate the direct control on exports and imports through the compulsory export and import approval system, the Transactions Law

---

[16] Materials on the suit are available in "Nichi-Bei Sen'i Kyōtei ni kansuru Gyōsei Soshō Kiroku" (Record of the Administrative Litigation Concerning the Textile Agreement between Japan and the United States) (1974), a tract published by the plaintiff in the case on 15 Nov. 1974.

[17] See supra § 2–6.

[18] See Fuji, "The Road to the U.S. Japan Auto Clash," in *U.S. Japan Relations: New Attitudes for a New Era*, p. 23 (Center for International Affairs, Harvard University, 1984).

merely authorizes private enterprises to enter into an agreement fixing the price, quantity, and sales outlet of the commodity which is exported or imported or to decide on other terms of business, like sales territories, for example. This section will examine export agreements under the Transactions Law and some related issues.

Formally, the Transactions Law merely authorizes an agreement entered into among private enterprises. Such an agreement is exempted from the application of the AML. As will be touched upon later, MITI can invoke the "outsider regulation" when it is proved that the operation of such an agreement is rendered ineffective due to activities of outsiders. It may thus seem that export agreements entered into under the Transactions Law are private rather than governmental and that the role of MITI is passive rather than active since it merely receives and approves applications filed by private applicants who wish to conclude such agreements.

However, this seeming passivity on the part of the government is deceptive. In actuality, MITI plays an active role in the formation of an export agreement (or export cartels, as they are sometimes called). The details of the way in which MITI plays a role in export agreements will be explained below when we discuss some cases of voluntary export restraint.[19] Here, a general account of the role of the government suffices.

When a trade conflict with regard to a Japanese product breaks out (or threatens to break out) in an importing country, MITI "advises" the private enterprises concerned to form an export agreement. Usually, the price level, the maximum quantity, or other terms of business are suggested by MITI to the export industry. This advice is "administrative guidance" and not a legal measure as such. However, this administrative guidance is generally observed by the private enterprises to which the guidance is directed. There are several reasons for the receptive attitude of Japanese exporters when faced with administrative guidance.

First, the exporters must rely on MITI, at least to a certain

---

[19] On this subject, see, generally, Matsushita, "Export Controls and Export Cartels in Japan," *Harvard International Law Journal*, Vol. 20, No. 1 (1979), pp. 105–25.

degree, for assistance when they are challenged by their competitors or users in a foreign country to which they export under the trade laws of that country. For example, when they are challenged in a foreign country under its antidumping law, they may need advice from the Japanese government in defending their case. Second, if their conduct is challenged under the antitrust laws of a foreign country, they may need a "sovereign compulsion"[20] defense. Third, "outsider regulation," which is issued by MITI and whose purpose is to support an export agreement, means, in effect, that MITI backs up the implementation of an export agreement by an order; therefore, one may say that an export agreement entered into among exporters under the Transactions Law is a semi-governmental cartel in nature. It is therefore advantageous for the exporters to maintain a good relationship with the government so that they can count on the aid of the government when needed.

2. Three Types of Export Agreements

Three types of export agreements are recognized under the Transactions Law. One is an export agreement in which exporters of a commodity agree on the terms of export, such as the export price, quantity, and channels. Such an agreement must specify the commodity and destination to be covered by the agreement. For example, suppose that exporters of television sets wish to enter into an agreement whereby the export price to the United States is fixed or the maximum quantity of the total export is set. Exporters who wish to conclude an export agreement of this type must notify MITI in advance.

In the second type of agreement, the exporters of a commodity agree on the terms of purchase of the commodity in the domestic market. If, for example, exporters of textile products to be exported to the United States agree on the maximum quantity of the products which they purchase from domestic producers,

---

[20] "Sovereign compulsion" or "foreign government compulsion" is a defense frequently raised by foreign defendants in antitrust actions in U.S. courts. Under this doctrine, a foreign defendant is immune from antitrust liability under U.S. antitrust laws if the challenged conduct has been compelled by the foreign government, since, if compelled, the defendant has no choice but to comply. For details, see Department of Justice Guidelines, International Operations: Antitrust Enforcement Policy, *Trade Regulation Reporter*, No. 24 (10 Nov. 1988), pp. 97–105.

then such an agreement belongs to the second type of export agreement. Of course, the ultimate purpose of such an agreement is to limit the quantity of the textile products which will be exported later. This type of export agreement is recognized because, under some circumstances, the restriction of domestic purchases of a commodity to be exported later is more effective than an agreement which fixes the terms of export itself. The second type of export agreement directly affects the domestic market, since it restricts the terms of business in purchasing the products. In this case, therefore, exporters who wish to conclude such an agreement must notify and obtain the approval of MITI in advance.

The third type of agreement is one in which manufacturers of a commodity to be exported later agree on the terms of sale to exporters. For example, if manufacturers of television sets to be exported to the United States agree that the maximum number of television sets to be sold to exporters should not exceed a certain limit or that the floor price for export be set at a certain price level, then such an agreement belongs to the third type. This third type of export agreement has often been utilized since trade problems have occurred with other trading nations mostly in the leading commodity areas, such as electronics, television sets, steel, and autos, in which the manufacturers were called upon to take the initiative in solving trade issues.

This type of export agreement affects the domestic market, since the business terms of domestic transactions are restricted, and, on account of this impact, this type of export agreement is subject to the approval of MITI. Therefore, when manufacturers of a commodity to be exported later wish to enter into this type of agreement, the manufacturers must notify MITI and obtain its approval.

The latter two agreements, i.e., an export agreement to restrict the purchase of a commodity in the domestic market to be exported later and an agreement among manufacturers of a commodity to be exported concerning the terms of the sale in the domestic market, reinforce the effectiveness of export controls through export agreements.

There are no prerequisite conditions for an export agreement, and, therefore, exporters and manufacturers may enter into such an agreement as long as notification has been made or approval been obtained, as the case may be. If an agreement is entered into without notification or approval, then the parties which enter into such an agreement are subject to criminal penalties. There are certain "negative requirements" stipulated in the Transactions Law which state that such an export agreement should guarantee the freedom of entry into and withdrawal from the agreement and should not contain provisions that may impair the international confidence of Japanese enterprises, tend to affect adversely related industries both in Japan and abroad, or hinder the sound development of the national economy and international trade. Export agreements thus entered into among exporters or manufacturers enjoy exemption from the application of the AML. There are, however, some antitrust constraints on the use of export agreements, as will be explained below.

3. Outsider Regulations

The Transactions Law states that MITI can invoke an "outsider regulation" when necessary. There are two types of outsider regulations. In the first, when an export agreement has been concluded, but because of the conduct of "outsiders" (those who are not party to the agreement), e.g., price cutting, the fulfilment of the agreement is prevented. MITI can issue an "export order" that subjects all exporters of the commodity in question to MITI requirements. These can include such requirements as a minimum export price or maximum export quantity. Therefore, if a price-fixing agreement has been rendered ineffective, then MITI can determine that a certain price level be maintained by every exporter of the commodity in question and require every exporter to observe it.

This order is binding on every exporter of the commodity in question including the insiders of the agreement, and, in this sense, the term "outsider regulation" may be a misnomer. However, this order is usually issued when an agreement is rendered ineffective, and it contains the same or similar terms as the agreement. In popular language, therefore, the term "outsider regulation" is often used.

In the second type of outsider regulation, MITI requires that every export of the commodity in question is subject to its approval. When this order is invoked, every exporter intending to export the commodity must obtain approval from MITI, and MITI can then attach such conditions as minimum price or maximum quantity. This order is usually invoked when it is necessary to keep the conditions of export confidential.

4. Export Associations

The Transactions Law authorizes exporters or manufacturers to form an "export association" as an alternative to entering into an export agreement. An export association is a cooperative, and it can issue rules binding on its members. An export association can determine the minimum export price, the maximum export quantity, or any other business terms to which all members must comply, and it can impose conditions on its members. There are in fact probably more export associations than there are export agreements. Export associations must adhere to the same rules as export agreements with regard to notification and approval requirements.

2. EXPORT AGREEMENTS AND VOLUNTARY EXPORT RESTRAINTS

Export agreements under the Transactions Law have been used to implement voluntary export restraint agreements (VER) entered into between Japan and foreign governments.[21] Such agreements are entered into, for example, when a complaint is raised in a foreign country by competitors of a Japanese commodity—that commodity has been dumped, that domestic industries are threatened with injury, or that the export price is too low. Then the Japanese and foreign governments discuss the matter and may conclude that an international agreement should be made, in which case the Japanese government agrees to restrain exports by regulating price, quantity, or the terms of trade. The Japanese government, after concluding such an agreement, will exert "administrative guidance" on the exporters or the manufacturers in Japan, directing them to conclude an export agreement under the Transactions Law. The exporters or manufacturers comply by concluding an agreement as directed, thereby

---

[21] On voluntary export restraint, see Matsushita, "The Legal Framework of Trade and Investment in Japan," *Harvard International Law Journal*, Vol. 27 (Special Issue, 1986), pp. 361–88.

implementing the governmental agreement for the restraint of exports.

MITI is in charge of enforcing the Transactions Law. When MITI directs exporters or manufacturers to conclude an export agreement, it often declares that if the exporters or manufacturers fail to comply with the directive, MITI will promptly take steps to invoke the compulsory export approval system under the Control Law and place the commodity under mandatory control.

This control system has been contrived by MITI to enforce export restraint without violating the antitrust laws of the importing countries. In this way, MITI uses the Control Law to pressure the exporters to comply with its "directive" to form an export agreement. This export scheme is designed as a defense to an antitrust challenge by the importing country that the export agreement in question has been mandated by the Japanese government and, therefore, is immunized under either the act of state doctrine or the "foreign government compulsion" doctrine.

1. The Television Cases

There are two cases involving television receivers in which export agreements were utilized to implement restraints on exports to the United States. In the first case, in 1977, a labor union in the United States brought a claim under Section 201 of the Trade Act of 1974, stating that the domestic television industry had been seriously injured by an increase in imports of television sets. The International Trade Commission determined that the domestic industry was seriously injured due to an increase in imports of television sets and recommended an additional tariff of 20 percent.[22] President Carter, however, decided not to impose the tariff and chose to negotiate with the Japanese government, requesting a voluntary export restraint on television sets exported to the United States.[23]

[22] U.S. International Trade Commission, Publication 808, "Television Receivers Color and Monochrome, Assembled or Not Assembled, Finished or Not Finished, and Subassemblies Thereof," Report to the President on Investigation TA-201-9 under Section 201(b) of the Trade Act of 1974 (March 1977).
[23] President's Memorandum for Special Representative for Trade Negotiations, *Weekly Composition of Presidential Documents*, Vol. 13, p. 761 (27 May 1977).

The Japanese government agreed to issue a "directive" to exporters of television sets limiting the total number of television sets to be exported to the United States. In the agreement between the United States and Japan, it was stated that the latter would take "measures which are mandatory" under the Transactions Law. The phrase "measures which are mandatory" was intended to provide a sovereign compulsion defense in the event the agreement was challenged under the U.S. antitrust laws.

The second case involved an antitrust action in the U.S. federal courts brought by Zenith Radio Corporation and one other American manufacturer of television sets, claiming that certain Japanese manufacturers of consumer electronic products (primarily television sets) had illegally conspired, beginning as early as 1953, to fix and maintain low prices for television receivers exported to the United States in order to drive American firms out of business in the American market.[24] In this case, MITI filed an amicus curiae brief stating that under the authority of the Control Law and the Transactions Law, it had directed the Japanese manufacturers and exporters to adopt and observe regulations concerning the price, quantity, number of customers, and other terms and conditions of the export of television sets and other consumer electronic products to the American and other foreign markets. Although this was in fact "administrative guidance," if the Japanese manufacturers refused to comply or refused to conclude an export agreement reflecting MITI's views, MITI would have promptly invoked a formal export approval system under the Control Law. The Japanese defendants in the antitrust case thus used MITI's indications to invoke the sovereign compulsion defense. A number of foreign governments as well as the Justice Department of the United States filed amicus curiae briefs with the U.S. Supreme Court and supported the Japanese position.

The U.S. Supreme Court, however, chose in favor of the Japanese defendants on different grounds, stating that there was no persusasive evidence to support the predatory pricing conspiracy

---

[24] Matsushita Electric Industrial Co. Ltd. v. Zenith Radio Corp., 475 U.S. 574 (1986).

alleged by the plaintiffs since (1) they had no rational motive to carry out such a conspiracy; (2) the purpose of such a conspiracy had not in fact been attained; and (3) there was no credible evidence of the existence of such a conspiracy. Neither the Supreme Court nor the lower courts that considered this case reached the issue of the sovereign compulsion defense. Thus the appropriateness of this doctrine as a source of antitrust immunity in trade dispute cases remains unsettled.

2. The Automobile Case

The automobile case is another situation in which a voluntary export restraint was employed.[25] In 1980, the Ford Motor Company and the United Auto Workers of America petitioned the International Trade Commission under Section 201 of the Trade Act of 1974, seeking an import relief. They alleged that the American auto industry had been seriously injured by a sudden increase of imported cars from abroad. However, the Commission decided that, even though the American industry was seriously injured, the import of foreign cars had not been the substantial cause of the injury. In the view of the Commission, the injury had been caused by domestic economic factors. Therefore, the petition for import relief was denied.

Nevertheless, due to the high unemployment in the auto industry, it was necessary for the U.S. government to respond in some way, and it discussed with the Japanese government the possibility of alleviating the pressure of imports. In response, the Japanese government promised that it would enforce a voluntary restraint on the export of cars to the United States. On the basis of this informal agreement between the two governments, an elaborate export control scheme for automobiles was established.

MITI did not utilize the Transactions Law in this situation, for in the Zenith case legality of a Japanese export cartel under U.S. law was in doubt. Instead, MITI issued individual

---

[25] See Lochmann, "The Japanese Voluntary Restraint Agreement in Automobile Exports: An Abandonment of the Free Trade Principles of the GATT and the Free Market Principles of the Antitrust Laws," *Harvard International Law Journal*, Vol. 27, No. 99 (1986); Matsushita and Repeta, "Restricting the Supply of Japanese Automobiles: Sovereign Compulsion or Sovereign Collusion," *Case Western Reserve International Law Journal*, Vol. 14, p. 47 (1982).

directives to each automobile exporter and specified the maximum number of automobiles that it could export annually to the United States. It also announced that should the exporters of automobiles fail to comply with the MITI directive, it would create a compulsory export approval system and place the export of automobiles to the United States under control.

MITI asked the U.S. Attorney General if this export scheme would provide an antitrust immunity under U.S. antitrust laws. The Attorney General replied only that "we believe" that such a scheme would be held lawful under U.S. antitrust laws. What is unique about this case is that no export agreement was used, and instead of an agreement, there were individual directives.

3. The Steel Case

There have been several instances involving steel in which export agreements were used, and we will examine the one which is still being enforced today. In 1982, a labor union in the American steel industry brought a claim for import relief under Section 201 of the Trade Act of 1974. The International Trade Commission decided that the industry was seriously injured and recommended relief. However, President Reagan refused to grant relief under Section 201 and negotiated with the Japanese government in order to reach an orderly marketing agreement. In response, the Japanese government agreed to restrain the export of steel products to the United States for a period of five years, that is, from 1984 to 1989.[26]

In order to implement this agreement, MITI directed the steel industy to form an export association and to fix the maximum quantity of steel products to be exported to the United States. MITI also announced that it would invoke a compulsory export approval system immediately should the Japanese steel industry fail to comply with the directive. In this case, MITI reverted to the traditional method of export control by directing exporters to enter into an export agreement and threatening them with a compulsory export approval system in the event of non-compliance.

[26] See U.S. International Trade Commission, Operation of the Trade Agreements Program, 36th Report, 1984, 1985, pp. 19 et seq.

The foregoing cases show that MITI has utilized both of export agreements and export associations to implement a voluntary export restraint. In each case, a compulsory export approval system could have been invoked right away, but MITI chose not to do this because acting on the basis of voluntary cooperation is more effective in the Japanese business environment and the administrative costs are much lower.

3. ANTITRUST CONSTRAINTS ON EXPORT AGREEMENTS

1. The Scope of Permissible Export Agreements

The Transactions Law authorizes export agreements and exempts them from the application of the AML. However, there are limitations to this exemption, and, if an export agreement exceeds them, there will be antitrust scrutiny.

The Transactions Law authorizes export agreements concluded among exporters exporting a commodity to a specified destination and subjects agreements to a notification or approval requirement, as the case may be. Since the Transactions Law grants an exception to the AML, which is a basic economic institution, the scope of exemption should be interpreted restrictively. A strict and narrow reading of the Transactions Law suggests that the scope of permissible export agreements is limited to those entered into among domestic exporters of a commodity destined to a specified area and is not extended to those entered into by domestic exporters and foreign competitors.

This interpretation suggests that an export agreement entered into by Japanese exporters on the basis of another international agreement concluded between Japanese exporters and foreign competitors is outside the scope of the Transactions Law, if the content of the earlier agreement is that the Japanese parties promised to restrain their exports in return for a commitment on the part of the foreign parties that they will refrain from petitioning their government for import relief. From the international trade policy standpoint, this interpretation makes sense, since permitting private parties to agree to terms of export and import without governmental supervision may have an undue "spillover" effect, since restrictions involved may be excessive and unpermitted activities may take place as a result.

2. The Chemical Fiber Cases

The problem of exemption in the case of an export agreement was an issue in the Chemical Fiber cases in 1974.[27] These involved series of international agreements between Japanese chemical fiber companies and their European competitors. Due to the United States and Japanese Textile Agreement, the Japanese textile industry was restrained from exporting chemical fiber to the United States. European producers feared that the surplus of chemical fiber which could not be exported to the United States might be diverted to the European market and thus affect their business.

The European producers accordingly requested that the Japanese producers conclude an "orderly marketing" agreement and impose a restraint on exports to the European market. Negotiations ensued, and the final conclusion was that: (1) Japanese producers would respect the "traditional market" (the European market) of the European producers, and (2) the European producers would respect the traditional market (the Japanese market) of the Japanese producers. In effect, this agreement restricted exports by both parties to each other's traditional market. Even though this agreement was drafted in a way in which both parties assumed mutual responsibility not to export their products to the other's market, the Japanese producers at that time enjoyed higher international competitiveness, and, therefore, this agreement operated in actuality to prevent them from exporting their products to the European market.

The Japanese producers formed a series of export agreements under the Transactions Law to implement the international agreement reached with their European counterparts. In the Chemical Fiber cases, therefore, export agreements under the Transactions Law was the legal basis on which the terms of the earlier international agreement were carried out.

This agreement was subsequently investigated by the German Cartel Authority, the enforcement agency for the German Antitrust Law, which imposed fines on the German participants.

[27] Tōyō Rayon International Cartel Cases, *Shinketsushū*, Vol. 19, p. 124 et seq. (27 Dec. 1972).

The German Authority also notified the FTC in Japan of the existence of the international agreement. The FTC then proceeded against the Japanese parties on the grounds that their conduct was contrary to article 6 of the AML and therefore illegal. The Japanese parties accepted the recommendation of the FTC to cancel the agreement.

The Chemical Fiber cases are significant. First, they show that the scope of export agreements permitted under the Transaction Law should be interpreted narrowly and that, should export agreements be utilized beyond that scope, it may be challenged by the FTC.

Second, the Chemical Fiber cases are a good example of international governmental cooperation in the enforcement of antitrust laws. The German Cartel Authority could have proceeded against the Japanese participants since the German Antitrust Law permits "extraterritorial application." However, it chose not to do so and instead notified the Japanese antitrust authority of the existence of the agreements and expected it to take measures within the scope of the domestic legislation. The result was the elimination of the international cartel agreements. It was not known whether or not the European parties threatened to invoke such European trade laws as the antidumping law and the safeguard measure. It is, however, easy to imagine that such a threat was employed to pressure the Japanese producers to agree to restrain exports to the European market.

4. THE MEMORANDUM OF THE FAIR TRADE COMMISSION

Soon after the Chemical Fiber cases, the FTC issued a memorandum entitled "Concerning the interpretation of the AML in relation to export cartels and international agreements."[28] The memo reads as follows:

* * *

2. (1) Only Japanese enterprises can be parties to (pure) export cartel agreements, and, in accordance with relevant Japanese laws, they should be able to conclude voluntarily a cartel agreement in light of the conditions of export market, modify its contents, or cancel the agreement. Inasmuch as

[28] 9 Aug. 1972. FTC, *Dokusen Kinshi Hō Kankei Hōreishū* (Compilation of the AML and Related Laws and Regulations).

the above conditions exist, an export cartel agreement is exempt from the application of the AML: of the latter provision of article 3 (prohibition of unreasonable restraint of trade) and article 8(1)(1)(prohibition of substantial restraint of competition by trade associations).

(2) On the other hand, if Japanese enterprises enter into an international agreement with foreign enterprises, the content of which is that the Japanese enterprises conclude an export cartel agreement with the consent of the foreign enterprises, such an agreement is different from a pure export cartel in that foreign enterprises participate in the cartel agreement. Furthermore, in such an agreement, Japanese enterprises are restricted from concluding and executing an export cartel agreement or withdrawing from it. Such an agreement amounts to an "international agreement or contract" as stipulated in article 6 of the AML and places an unreasonable restraint of trade on Japanese enterprises or on Japanese and foreign enterprises. Such an agreement is tantamount to an agreement that contains items constituting unreasonable restraint of trade, as prohibited by paragraph (1) of the same article.

3. (1) Therefore, if Japanese and foreign enterprises discuss the amount of export, the export price, and related matters and reach an understanding (international agreement), such an agreement is illegal. It is irrelevant whether the conclusion of the international agreement precedes or succeeds the conclusion of the export cartel agreement. Illegality is recognized when: (1) after an export cartel is concluded, an international agreement containing the same items as the export cartel is concluded; (2) an international agreement is concluded and takes effect when an export cartel, which contains the same items as the international agreement, is concluded; or (3) after an international agreement is concluded and takes effect, an export cartel containing the same items is concluded.

This memo is somewhat ambiguous. One may argue that an export agreement is exempt from the application of the AML and, if the purpose of an international agreement is to allow the Japanese parties to conclude an export agreement under the authority of the Transactions Law—which itself is exempt from the application of the AML—there is no reason to hold this international agreement illegal under article 6 of the law, since the content of the international agreement is identical to the export agreement which is exempted.

The underlying assumption of the memo, however, is probably that when an export agreement is made on the basis of an international agreement concluded between Japanese producers and foreign competitors, one cannot expect that the negative requirement for an export agreement incorporated in the Transactions Law, namely, that the freedom to join and withdraw should be maintained, will be adhered to by the participants. If the freedom of joining and withdrawing from an export agreement were maintained, it would give no assurance and comfort to the foreign competitors which are the members of the international agreement that export competition from Japan would be effectively restricted, since any member of the export agreement would be entitled to withdraw when it wished and engage in active competition. Therefore, it seems that the real intent of the memo is that an export agreement based on an international agreement has generally some features which cannot be permitted under the Transactions Law and the AML and, therefore, is not exempt from the application of the AML.

Interpreted in the above fashion, the memo makes good sense, even though criticism could be raised that it could have been drafted in more precise language.

CHAPTER FIVE

INVESTMENT AND ESTABLISHMENT

§ 5–1. Forms of Establishment

A business enterprise may wish to enter the Japanese market by setting up an establishment in Japan.[1] Unlike export sales, establishing in Japan requires an investment of capital (and frequently technology) as well as compliance with appropriate legal formalities. For ign investment is soaring in manufacturing, commerce, finance, and insurance. Foreign companies increasingly seek a presence not only to gain information about exporting to the Japanese market but also to establish production and sales units in Japan. Often the reason is to take advantage of Japanese engineering and research skills. Many companies are also finding that Japan is an excellent base to sell into other Asian markets.[2]

There are several options for a company desiring to establish in Japan. First, a wholly owned subsidiary may be formed under Japanese law. There are four types of companies[3] under Japanese law: the stock corporation (*kabushiki kaisha*), the limited company (*yūgen kaisha*), the partnership (*gōmei kaisha*), and the limited partnership (*gōshi kaisha*). In most cases, the stock corporation form is most appropriate for foreign direct investment.

Second, an unincorporated branch office may be set up in Japan. Except in certain specialized economic areas, such as banking, insurance, financial services, and transportation, opening a branch office is permitted upon compliance with minimal

---

[1] See, generally, Bank of Tokyo, *Setting Up Enterprises in Japan*, (1984).

[2] See, generally, Reynolds, "Foreign Investment in Japan: The Legal and Social Climate," *Texas International Law Journal*, Vol. 18, p. 175 (1983).

[3] See infra § 5–6.

formalities, commercial registration, and the filing of a Branch Office Establishment Report.[4]

Third, a joint venture[5] may be established in association with a Japanese enterprise. This is generally done by incorporating a new business entity under Japanese law. Fourth, a "liaison" or "representative" office[6] may be established. To establish such an office, there are fewer formalities than in setting up a branch. Fifth, franchising[7] is an increasingly popular method of entering the market.

Sixth, a foreign company may establish a presence by making an equity investment in an existing Japanese company. This is done by purchasing a minority shareholder position for the purpose of strengthening a relationship with a Japanese company and participating in its profits. This may be desirable if the foreign company is selling, transferring technology to, or sourcing from the Japanese company.

Seventh, a foreign company may wish to enter the market by acquiring a majority or control interest in an existing Japanese company. This has not occurred frequently, and there are substantial obstacles to mergers and corporate acquisitions.[8]

§ 5–2. Regulation of Foreign Investment and Capital Movements

Before 1980, Japan applied stringent controls on foreign investment and many capital transactions. Proposed investment was evaluated on a case-by-case basis according to the so-called prohibition principle (*gensoku kinshi*), by which transactions were deemed prohibited unless specifically approved by the competent authorities.

In 1980, however, the Foreign Investment Law[9] was repealed and the Foreign Exchange and Foreign Trade Control Law (Control Law) was thoroughly revised to liberalize foreign investment and exchange transactions. The negative principle was

---

[4] See infra § 5–5.
[5] See infra § 5–7.
[6] See infra § 5–4.
[7] See infra § 5–8.
[8] See infra § 5–9.
[9] Gaishi ni Kansuru Hōritsu, Law 163, 1950.

replaced by a positive principle that transactions are permitted unless specifically forbidden. Nevertheless, a great deal of discretion is vested in the various ministries charged with administering the law.[10]

The revised Control Law is the most basic law in Japan regulating international trade and capital flows. The Control Law covers (1) foreign exchange controls; (2) foreign investment controls; and (3) foreign trade control both in goods and services, including technology transfer. The foreign trade controls are administered by MITI, and the foreign exchange and foreign investment controls are administered by the MOF.[11] Other ministries may become involved as well, if a matter is within their substantive competence.

The exercise of regulatory controls over capital flows is primarily through the authorized foreign exchange banks and authorized foreign money changers who are entities licensed to perform exchange transactions in Japan.[12] Because these exchange dealers report to the Bank of Japan (BOJ), the MOF has delegated to the BOJ the task of receiving any documents required to complete foreign exchange or investment transactions.[13] The authorized exchange dealers will accordingly refer all but the most routine transactions to the BOJ, which in turn will consult the MOF in appropriate cases.[14]

The Control Law reaches four different categories of transactions: (1) export-import transactions;[15] (2) payments;[16] (3) inward direct investment and technology induction;[17] and (4) capital transactions, including service transactions.[18]

---

[10] There is virtually no case of a formal acceptance or rejection of an application to undertake a transaction under the Control Law. Rulings are generally made by means of the technique of administrative guidance. See supra § 2–6.

[11] In general, MITI has authority over export and import transactions and intellectual property rights, while the MOF has power over capital movements and payments. Often, there is concurrent jurisdiction, and MITI and the MOF consult each other and decide questions jointly.

[12] Control Law, arts. 20, 21.

[13] Id., art. 69.

[14] For export or import transactions, however, the documents are transmitted directly to MITI by customs officials. Control Law, art. 54.

[15] Control Law, arts. 47–55.

[16] Id., arts. 16–19.

[17] Id., arts. 26–46.

[18] Id., arts. 26–46.

In keeping with the obligations under article VIII of the Articles of Agreement of the International Monetary Fund, Japan places no controls on current payments (within less than one year) in settlement of import or export transactions. Required documentation by customs authorities is routine and for the purpose of the collection of international trade statistics.[19] MITI, however, places restrictions on imports and exports of certain categories of goods as well as goods originating in specified countries.[20] Exports and imports are also regulated through the Customs and Tariff Law and the Tariff Law.[21] Enforcement is through the customs service and the foreign exchange banks.

Foreign exchange payments and remittances related to larger transactions, such as loans, credits, and repatriation of profits, may also, in principle, be freely carried out. However, the Control Law subjects certain "special methods of payment" to a prior license requirement. These are credit and debit set offs, prepayments for services, exports, or imports in excess of two years, payments in yen sent directly to the payee, and payments to or from resident nominees other than through the exchange banks or the postal system.[22] The MOF also requires a license for contributions and gifts to non-residents in excess of ¥5 million; payments abroad for purposes of certain restricted business activities such as arms trade, narcotics, and trade with South Africa or Namibia; and the import or export of yen-denominated means of payment other than through an authorized foreign exchange bank in the course of its business.[23] These licensing requirements exist in order to police illegal conduct and to enforce Japan's international obligations. The MOF also has the authority to take emergency action to suspend or limit foreign

---

[19] For exports and imports, a declaration must be filed with an authorized foreign exchange bank. MITI has the power to review all import and export documents and may impose sanctions retrospectively. Control Law, art. 53.

[20] These restrictions are detailed in Ch. 3 on imports and in Ch. 4 on exports.

[21] See Ch. 3, notes 28 and 29 (p. 57).

[22] Control Law, art. 17. The foreign exchange cabinet order 260, 1980, designates the MOF and MITI as the competent ministries to administer the licensing requirements for special methods of payment.

[23] MOF ministerial notification no. 117, 28 Nov. 1980, as amended by MOF ministerial modification no. 66, 28 March 1981.

exchange transactions during a balance of payments or foreign currency crisis.[24]

What the Control Law terms "inward direct investment" (*tainai chokusetsu tōshi*) is also subject to regulation. The touchstone of an inward direct investment is the involvement of a "foreign investor," which is defined as a natural person who is a non-resident; an organization which was established under foreign law or which has its principal office abroad; or a company a majority of whose stock is owned or controlled by non-residents.[25]

Inward direct investment is subject to a prior notification requirement. Direct investment includes (1) the acquisition of shares or equity interests in Japanese corporations or other business entities (except acquisitions from another foreign investor or shares listed on a stock exchange); (2) transfers of stock or other equity interests (except listed companies) between non-residents; (3) the purchase of greater than 10 percent of the outstanding shares of a listed company; (4) consent by a foreign investor to a substantial alteration in the business of a company; (5) the establishment of a branch office, factory, or any place of business in Japan by any non-resident individual or foreign corporation; (6) monetary loans greater than ¥200 million for one to five years, or greater than ¥100 million for more than five years, by foreign investors to corporations having a place of business in Japan; and (7) and the acquisition of certain bonds or investment trusts.[26]

The notification requirement for such direct investment transactions may be fulfilled by filing information on the appropriate form supplied by the Bank of Japan, which will consult with the MOF and other concerned ministries. A 30-day waiting period may be imposed before an investment transaction may be carried out, but in most cases this is waived, and the investor may proceed the following day. If the MOF wishes to investigate

---

[24] Control Law, arts. 16, 9.
[25] Control Law, art. 26(1).
[26] Control Law, art. 26(2). Art. 26(3) exempts certain transactions including the acquisition of shares, bonds, or investment certificates to inheritance or bequest, stock splits, mergers, stock dividends, and shares acquired through conversions.

further, the investment can be delayed for up to five months by government order.[27]

Direct investment in several specified industries may not be permitted. These are agriculture, fisheries, and forestry; mining (if 50 percent or more ownership); petroleum refining; and leather manufacturing.[28] In these areas, applications will be scrutinized carefully on a case-by-case basis.[29] In addition, certain industries, such as banking, financial services, utilities, and insurance, are regulated under special statutes.[30]

The government has authority to prohibit or limit any foreign investment transaction on the grounds that (1) national security, the public safety, or public order will be adversely affected; (2) Japanese competitors or the national economy will be adversely affected; or (3) the investment is an attempt to evade controls in a national emergency; or (4) the country concerned does not reciprocate with respect to similar investment by Japanese nationals.[31] The foreign investor should be prepared to consult with the MOF and MITI for administrative guidance for all but the most routine types of direct investment in Japan.

The Control Law also regulates inbound or outbound capital transactions other than "inward direct investment." Several categories of transactions require a prior license from the MOF: (1) monetary deposit contracts and trust agreements between residents and non-residents; (2) the sale of foreign means of payment (such as bills of exchange or bankers acceptances) between residents and non-residents; (3) agreements denominated in foreign security between exchange residents; and (4) the is-

[27] Control Law, art. 26(4).

[28] This is consistent with Japan's reservations to the OECD Code of Liberalization of Capital Movements, 12 Dec. 1961. See "Japanese Reservations to the Code of Liberalization of Capital Movements and Notes Concerning Payments Channels," OECD, June 1978.

[29] See Smith, "The Japanese Foreign Exchange and Foreign Control Law and Administrative Guidance: The Labyrinth and the Castle," *Law and Policy in International Business*, Vol. 16, p. 417 (1984).

[30] Banks are regulated by the Bank Law, Law 59, 1981. Foreign insurers are regulated by the Law Concerning Foreign Insurers, Law 184, 1949. The gas utility business is regulated by the Gas Utility Law, Law 51, 1954. The electric utility business is regulated by the Electric Utility Law, Law 170, 1964. The business of foreign securities dealers is regulated by the Law of Foreign Securities Dealers, Law 5, 1971.

[31] Control Law, art. 27.

suance or offering abroad of yen-denominated securities by a non-resident. Other capital transactions require prior notification and a waiting period of 20 days: (1) loans and loan guarantees between residents and non-residents; (2) direct foreign investment by a resident; (3) issuing or offering foreign denominated securities in Japan by a non-resident; and (4) the acquisition of real property rights by a non-resident.[32] For all of these categories, prior discussion and asking administrative guidance from the authoritie sat the Bank of Japan and the MOF are recommended.

For several categories of capital transactions there is a prior notice requirement but no waiting period: monetary loans from a non-resident to a resident, and the acquisition of securities by a resident from a non-resident or by a non-resident from a resident (except those acquisitions that fall in the category of direct foreign investment).[33]

Both inbound and outbound technology transfer is regulated under the Control Law. Technology induction, the transfer of a non-resident's industrial property rights, know-how, or technical assistance to Japan is treated as a domestic direct investment. Such agreements are subject to a prior notification requirement with a 30-day waiting period which is waived except with respect to certain "designated technologies."[34] Outbound technology transfer is treated as a service contract. While routine

[32] Control Law, arts. 20–21. See Seki, "Major Points in the Revision of the Foreign Exchange and Foreign Trade Control Law," *Japan Business Law Journal*, No. 10 (July 1980). The MOF has the authority to screen potential transactions on the grounds of adverse and qualitative grounds: (1) the potential adverse effects on the international money market or the international currency markets or the international reputation of Japan; (2) the potential adverse effects on Japan's capital markets; (3) potential adverse effects on business activities and Japanese industry; and (4) the potential adverse effects on Japan's treaty obligations and other international obligations. Control Law, art. 22(2). The MOF has the authority to intervene and to order a change or suspension of such capital transactions.

[33] Control Law, art. 22. The latter two categories cover portfolio investments and publicly traded companies as long as the acquisitions are made through authorized securities companies designated by the MOF. See Securities Exchange Law, Law 25, 1948, art. 9.

[34] Control Law, art. 29. The designated technologies are aircraft weapons, gunpowder, nuclear power, space exploration, electronic computers, electronic components of computers, laser processing and optical communication equipment, innovative materials such as superconductor materials, seabed petroleum recovery technology, and leather and leather goods. See Direct Domestic Investment Order, Cabinet Order 261, 11 Oct. 1980. (MITI is the appropriate regulatory ministry.)

prior notification is required,[35] these agreements are not subject to license unless a special payment method is used[36] or unless strategically important technology is being exported.[37]

In emergency situations, the Control Law grants the MOF comprehensive authority to prohibit, restrict, or suspend capital transactions.[38]

§ 5–3. SECURITIES REGULATION

The Securities Exchange Law (SEL),[39] originally enacted in 1948, is similar to the two basic securities laws in the United States: the Securities Act of 1933 and the Securities Exchange Act of 1934. The MOF is responsible for administering this law and has issued numerous regulations concerning the registration of securities,[40] tender offers, and the regulation of securities companies.[41] Advance consultation with the MOF will be indispensable in most cases.

Except for certain specifically exempted types of securities and transactions, the public issuance of securities is permitted only after advance registration and through the use of an offering prospectus. Registration takes effect thirty days after filing the securities registration statement (or its last amendment), but this waiting period may be shortened at the discretion of the MOF. Both new public offerings of securities (*yūkashōken no boshū*) and tender offers (*yūkashōken no uridashi*) are subject to registration.[42]

Many types of securities are exempt from registration, including national government bonds, securities of corporations established by special law, and securities issued by recognized

[35] Control Law, art. 25.

[36] See supra note 23.

[37] Strategically important technology includes technology designated by the Consultative Group Coordinating Committee (COCOM) as well as certain technology designated by MITI. Technology transfer is treated in Ch. 8.

[38] Control Law, art. 21(2).

[39] Shōken Torihiki Hō, Law 25, 1948.

[40] MOF Ordinance 5, 30 Jan. 1973, as amended.

[41] MOF Ordinance 38, 9 June 1971, as amended.

[42] E.g., MOF Ordinance 26, 27 April 1972, concerning foreign securities dealer registration.

international organizations.[43] The most important transactional exemptions are for small issues of securities with an aggregate sales price of less than ¥100 million[44] and private offerings to not more than 50 persons.[45]

§ 5–4. THE REPRESENTATIVE OFFICE

A foreign corporation that desires only to conduct public relations may open what is known as a "representative office." The advantage of operating a representative office is the relatively few formalities that are required. A registered office is exempt from registration requirements under Japanese law and is not subject to Japanese taxation. Remittances of funds for operating purposes may be transmitted to a registered office in Japan without the necessity of obtaining a license under the Control Law. On the other hand, a registered office is restricted to public relations activities that are very limited in scope. A registered office may not conduct any marketing or sales activities. It is limited to advertising, publicity, market research, and public information. It may neither conduct marketing or sales activities nor act as a sales agency.

§ 5–5. THE BRANCH OFFICE

A branch office is an unincorporated wholly owned entity permitted to carry on business activities in Japan on behalf of a foreign corporation. The establishment of a branch office requires numerous formalities, and most companies find that it is more advantageous to form instead a wholly owned subsidiary under Japanese law.

The first step in forming a branch office is to file a "Report Concerning the Establishment of a Branch Office" with the MOF and MITI.[46] This Branch Establishment Report requires

---

[43] SEL, art. 3.

[44] Id., art. 4.

[45] Id., art. 2, requires registration of an offering to or from "unspecified many persons." This is interpreted by the MOF to mean more than 50.

[46] MOF and MITI Joint Order 1, 1 July 1963.

the disclosure of certain information involving the nature of the business and the planned activities of the branch office as well as a financing plan and the scope of its planned business operations. The foreign company involved must also attach a balance sheet and earnings statement.

The Branch Establishment Report is submitted to the Bank of Japan, which consults with the MOF and MITI officials as well as other appropriate ministries. Acceptance of the Branch Establishment Report is informal and oral; there are no formal criteria according to which the proposed business activity is judged, and acceptance of the report is discretionary with ministry officials.

The establishment of a branch office in Japan also triggers article 26 of the Control Law and the requirements for the approval of "inward direct investment" in Japan.[47]

The branch office of a foreign company must also be registered at the local Legal Affairs Bureau of the MOJ in order to comply with article 479 of the Commercial Code. This article provides that any foreign business that intends to "engage in transactions on a continuous basis in Japan" must appoint a person as a representative in Japan as well as maintain a business office. The representative must have complete legal authority to bind the company with respect to any business operations in Japan.

The establishment of a branch office also subjects the foreign corporation to Japanese tax on any income derived from sources in Japan. A branch office must file a notice of establishment with the national tax office within two months of its opening. A certified copy of the articles of incorporation, commercial registration, and a balance sheet must accompany this notice. Remittances of profits from Japan to the home office must also be reported to the BOJ.

§ 5–6. THE SUBSIDIARY

A foreign corporation may establish a wholly owned subsidiary under Japanese law. The establishment of a subsidiary, however,

[47] See supra § 5–2.

is an inward direct investment that requires a license from the MOF through the BOJ.[48]

Four different legal forms of companies exist under Japanese law: the partnership (*gōmei kaisha*); the limited partnership (*gōshi kaisha*); the limited company (*yūgen kaisha*); and the stock corporation (*kabushiki kaisha*). The two types of partnership companies are similar to the general partnership and limited partnership forms under American law.[49] The partnerships are primarily employed by family businesses; they are generally impractical for foreign corporations establishing in Japan.

Both types of partnerships are incorporated entities that must be registered with the local Legal Affairs Office of the MOF.[50] In a partnership company, each partner has an equal right to manage the business and to the profits of the organization, and the transfer of shares requires the consent of all the partners.[51] All the partners are jointly and separately liable for the obligations of a partnership company. A limited partnership differs from a partnership company in that partners with limited liability are permitted as long as at least one partner has unlimited liability.[52] Moreover, in a limited partnership, only the partners with unlimited liability have the right to manage the business; a partner with limited liability cannot take part in the management of the company or represent it. The limited liability partner is liable only to the extent of his contribution to the partnership.[53]

The legal form of business entity that is most frequently employed for the subsidiary of a foreign corporation in Japan is the stock corporation. The first step in forming a stock company is to draft the Articles of Incorporation (Teikan). At least seven promoters or incorporators must prepare a notarized copy of the articles of incorporation. Within two weeks of the first organizational meeting of the corporation, the president or representative director should file an application for registration of incorpora-

---

[48] See supra § 5–2.
[49] There also exists another form of partnership (*tokumei kumiai*) under the Commercial Code.
[50] Commercial Code, arts. 64, 149.
[51] Id., arts. 70–76.
[52] Id., art. 146.
[53] Id., arts. 156–57.

tion with the local commercial registry of the Ministry of Justice. The registration must be accompanied by an authenticated copy of the articles of incorporation, a document certifying the subscription and payment for stock, the minutes of the first organizational meeting, disclosures of the qualifications of the directors and auditors, a document certifying that the officers and auditors have accepted their appointments, a certificate of deposit for money deposited in the bank account, and minutes of the first board of directors meeting.[54]

The articles of incorporation of a stock corporation are normally quite brief. They must contain the company's business purpose, trade name, total shares issued and outstanding, the seat of the principal office, the names of the promoters or incorporators, and the manner by which the stock company will publish notices required by law.[55]

Shares of stock can be either par or no par. The par value of the stock must be stated in the articles of incorporation. There is a requirement of a minimum subscribed capital of ¥50,000. The corporation must immediately issue all the stock specified as issued in the articles of incorporation.[56] Different classes of stock and preferred stock are permitted if stated in the articles of incorporation.[57]

The articles may also include provisions relating to the number of directors, the place of the general shareholders meeting, and provision for dissolution in the event of a deadlock of the shareholders. Shares can be issued either in bearer or registered form; but in Japan, shares are usually issued in registered form and are transferred by endorsement on the books of the corporation.[58] The ability of shareholders to transfer shares can be restricted and made subject to the approval of either the shareholders or the board of directors.[59]

The management of the corporation is in the hands of the

[54] Id., art. 188.
[55] A stock corporation may choose to publish notices either in the official gazette, *Kampō*, or in a specified daily newspaper.
[56] Commercial Code, art. 192.
[57] Id., art. 166.
[58] Id., art. 227.
[59] Id., arts. 204, 348.

board of directors.[60] A minimum of three directors is required, but there is no requirement that they be Japanese or live in Japan.[61] A corporation is permitted to have only one shareholder.[62] Voting of shares is generally one vote per share, but non-voting stock is permitted if specified in the articles of incorporation. Voting at the annual meeting may be either in person or by proxy.[63]

Each stock corporation is required to appoint one or more auditors who may not be directors, officers, or employees.[64] Corporations with a capital of more than ￥500 million must be audited by a chartered public accountant, who also has significant supervisory powers over the performance of the duties of directors. In medium-sized companies with capital from ￥100 million to ￥500 million, the auditor need not be a chartered public accountant, but the auditor appointed has significant advisory and supervisory duties as well. Companies with paid-in capital of less than ￥100 million may employ auditors who are responsible only for accounting functions.[65]

A stock corporation is subject to significant financial disclosure requirements on an annual basis, including the preparation of a balance sheet, a profit and loss statement, a business report, proposals relating to the reserve fund (*junbikin*), and the payment of dividends or interest.[66]

Another form of incorporation available in Japan is the limited company, which corresponds to the close corporation in the United States, the GMBH under German law, and the private company in England. Although not very popular with foreign investors, the limited company is an entity with a separate juristic personality, limited liability, and few formalities with respect to board of director and shareholder meetings. In contrast to a stock company, a limited company may not offer its shares to

[60] Id., arts. 260, 261.
[61] Id., arts. 254, 255.
[62] Id., art. 234.
[63] Id., art. 264.
[64] Id., arts. 254, 280.
[65] Id., art. 281.
[66] Id., arts. 281–83. Law Providing Exceptions to the Commercial Code for Auditing Stock Companies, Law 22, 1974.

the public. Most limited companies are small with a minimum capital of ¥100,000.

A limited company is formed by preparing articles of incorporation and registration with the local commercial registry of the MOJ.[67] It may not have more than 50 members or shareholders.[68] It is also required to have at least one director[69] who has the power to represent the company with respect to third parties. A member of a limited company may not transfer his shares to a non-member without the approval of a general meeting of shareholders.[70] A limited company is not required to publish or disclose its balance sheet; the required accounting documents must be submitted only to the general meeting of shareholders for approval.[71]

§ 5–7. THE JOINT VENTURE

A joint venture is a business entity that is managed jointly by two or more business partners for their mutual profit. A foreign company or investor may desire to form a joint venture with a Japanese company in order to gain the advantages of access to the Japanese market, access to supplies, Japanese management techniques, know-how, and technology. The foreign investor in turn may supply crucial technology, capital, know-how, or intellectual property rights. The resultant entity may achieve success in the domestic market that would be difficult by the foreign company alone. The formation of a joint venture, however, requires a high degree of mutual trust and understanding between the business partners. In Japan, a joint venture is thought of as a cooperative agreement to establish a long-term business relationship and understandings that future differences will be worked out through negotiations. A joint venture is a more permanent arrangement than such alternative agreements as licensing agreements, sales and manufacturing agreements,

---

[67] Limited Company Law, art. 6.
[68] Id., art. 8.
[69] Id., art. 25.
[70] Id., art. 19.
[71] Commercial Code, art. 283.

and distribution agreements. But now that it is possible to form wholly owned subsidiaries under Japanese law, joint ventures between foreign companies and Japanese companies are less frequent than formerly.

A joint venture will almost invariably involve incorporation under Japanese law either as a stock corporation or a limited company. Of these two forms, the stock corporation form is most frequently used.[72] It is also possible to operate a joint venture as an unincorporated association, a general partnership (*kumiai*) under the Civil Code, but this is not recommended for joint ventures involving foreign companies. In addition to incorporation, the formation of a joint venture may involve certain side or subsidiary agreements, such as patent, trademark, or know-how licensing agreements; manufacturing agreements; technical assistance agreements; or distribution agreements.

In a joint venture, the business partners involved are co-owners and must come to an agreement on their proportionate shares of the business. Since share ownership will determine the voting power of all business partners as well as their respective rights to the profits, this should be carefully worked out in advance. Each joint venture partner normally will contribute to the capital of the corporation in proportion to his ownership of the business.

In a joint venture, any contribution to be made by the foreign partner will be "inward direct investment" subject to the Control Law.[73] The share acquisition involved therefore must be registered with the Bank of Japan. Second, any technical assistance agreement involved must also be registered with the Bank of Japan under article 29 of the Control Law. Third, the formation of joint venture may come under article 10 of the AML and a report must be filed with the FTC. The joint venture partners will want to seek administrative guidance regarding these reports and the formation of the joint venture before it is formed.

The joint venture agreement should set out the parties' understanding as to the scope of the business involved.[74] It should also

[72] See supra § 5–7 for the formalities necessary to form a stock corporation.
[73] See supra § 5–2.
[74] See Swisher, "Joint Venture Corporations, Shareholder Contracts and Protection of Minority Shareholders," in *Current Legal Aspects of Doing Business in Japan and*

state the functions of each joint venture partner in connection with the operation of the business. The degree of control should also be decided as well as how to maintain the percentages of control agreed on during the operation of the business. In this regard, the number of directors desired by each party should be set out in the agreement as well as mechanisms to maintain that number in the event of a director's resignation or removal. The transfer of shares should be restricted so that neither joint venture partner can transfer his shares without the consent of the other party involved.[75]

Provision should also be made for resolving any deadlock of the board of directors or shareholders. A deadlock-breaking mechanism could include the appointment of a neutral director or an agreement to submit the disputed issue to arbitration. In the alternative, a more radical solution for deadlock is to permit either party to force the dissolution of the corporation.[76] Adequate provision should also be made for termination of the joint venture after appropriate notice and procedures for the valuation and distribution of the assets involved. Shareholder agreements and other contractual techniques are enforceable under Japanese law.[77]

§ 5–8. FRANCHISING

Franchising has been a notable success in Japan. This method of operation has the blessing of Japanese authorities such as MITI because of the opportunities that are created for small business. Because of the capital requirements for franchise operations in Japan, franchisees are usually corporations or experienced businesspeople.

The central document in a franchise arrangement is the fran-

East Asia, J. Haley, ed., pp. 66 (1978).

[75] A share transfer restriction is upheld under Japanese law. See Takagi v. Sumitomo Shōji K.K., Minshū, Vol. 27, p. 700 (Sup. Ct., 15 June 1973).

[76] Under Japanese law, a 10-percent shareholder has the power to dissolve a corporation on demand if "irreparable injury would otherwise occur." Commercial Code, art. 405–2.

[77] See Swisher, "Use of Shareholder Agreements and Other Control Techniques in Japanese Joint Venture Corporations and Their Validity Under Japanese Corporate Law," The International Lawyer, Vol. 9, p. 159 (1975).

chise agreement which will bind the franchisor to supply management techniques, marketing expertise, and the use of its trademarks and technology. The provisions of this agreement will set the parties' relationship and should be carefully worked out.[78] The franchisor may choose to avoid establishing in Japan and operate through individual franchise agreements or a master franchise agreement with one Japanese franchisee; or the franchisor may wish to establish a branch, subsidiary, or joint venture.[79]

There are several regulatory hurdles to overcome in establishing a franchise operation in Japan. First, a franchise agreement involves trademark licensing and transfer of technology, so the requirements of the Control Law[80] come into play. Thus, within three months prior to the effectiveness of the agreement, a report must be submitted to the Bank of Japan and the MOF. There is a mandatory 30-day waiting period, which is usually shortened to 15 days. This requirement poses little problem, however; franchise agreements are given routine approval.

Second, the Japanese franchisee will typically want to register voluntarily with the Japan Franchise Association (JFA). This involves extensive disclosure of the rights and duties under the franchise agreement.

Third, the foreign franchisor should obtain clearance of the franchise agreement by the FTC. In its September 20, 1983, report, "Application of the Antimonopoly Law to Franchise Systems," the FTC announced that it would examine franchise agreements under the authority of the AML[81] to determine whether the agreement involves anticompetitive restrictions or excessive burdens on the franchisee. The FTC will look carefully at such factors as competition restraints, resale price maintenance, and tying agreements. Considering the vagueness of the FTC's legal mandate and the power of this agency, it is wise to obtain FTC approval in advance.

---

[78] Especially important are the warranty provisions, choice of law, dispute settlement, and termination provisions of the agreement. See supra § 3–1 and § 3–2.

[79] See, generally, Nishimura, "Franchising in Japan: The Business and Legal Environment," *International Business Lawyer*, p. 312 (Oct. 1986).

[80] See the analysis of the Control Law, supra § 5–2.

[81] See Ch. 6.

§ 5–9. Mergers and Acquisitions

Attempts by foreign companies to acquire existing Japanese businesses through mergers and acquisitions are infrequent but are increasing. For example, in 1983, Merck & Company acquired 51 percent of Banyu Pharmaceutical Company, and in 1985, Trafalgar Holding Company unsuccessfully attempted to acquire Minebea Co. Ltd.[82]

There are several advantages to acquiring a company in Japan through a merger or acquisition. First, the acquisition of an existing company is a means of gaining immediate entry into the Japanese market and a ready source of labor and management skills. Second, the acquiring company can step into an existing niche of the complicated Japanese distribution system and gain the advantage of preexisting relationships with both suppliers and customers. Third, the acquiring company may acquire important capital facilities such as land, factories, and equipment in Japan.

From the Japanese perspective, however, acquisitions and mergers, particularly by foreign companies, have been traditionally viewed as intruding upon long-established preexisting business relationships, which in many cases have grown organically over many years. The authorities also tend to view acquisitions and mergers by foreign companies as a potential threat to the domestic economy. Unfriendly takeovers, in particular, are viewed as opposed to the consensual way of doing business in Japan.[83]

Foreign companies will encounter many extralegal and cultural barriers to acquisitions and mergers. A first problem is the degree to which Japanese business is characterized by cross-ownership of shares and interlocking directorates. Large corporations are usually part of industrial groupings, industrial

---

[82] See *Wall Street Journal*, 4 Aug. 1983, p. 6 ("The Merck Acquisition") and *New York Times*, 19 Oct. 1985, p. 33 ("Trafalgar Holding Inc.'s Bid for Minebea Co. Ltd."). See also Crabb, "The Reality of Extralegal Barriers to Mergers and Acquisitions in Japan," *The International Lawyer*, Vol. 21, p. 97 (1987).

[83] The Japanese term sometimes used for corporate takeover, *nottori*, is a term of derogation meaning hijacking. For a review of these problems, see Ames, "Buying a Piece of Japan, Inc.: Foreign Acquisitions in Japan," *Harvard International Law Journal*, Vol. 27, p. 541 (1986).

conglomerates which are often associated with major banks and industrial families which are functional conglomerations that cooperate in marketing, research, servicing, and market development. These business groups are managed not only through a complex system of interlocking personal relations but also through interlocking directorates and cooperative arrangements. These relationships are reflected in cross-shareholding relationships between the corporations involved in an industrial family.[84] This pattern of stable cross-shareholding coupled with close relations with major banks and financing entities tends to prevent the takeover of a target company which is a member of an industrial group.

Second, unlike the United States where corporate democracy is fostered through the regulation of proxies and proxy contests, tender offers, and state laws relating to shareholders, in Japan there are few constraints to management control by the directors of corporations. Although shareholders have the power to elect directors,[85] as a practical matter, members of the board as well as senior personnel are handpicked by the representative director (*daihyō torishimariyaku*), who also has the power to select both the in-house statutory auditors (*jōnin kansayaku*) and independent accounting auditors (*kaikei kansanin*). It is thus virtually impossible to organize a large shareholding group in opposition to management. Even if such a group were formed, the board of a corporation could easily issue new shares at fair market value without shareholder approval to a sympathetic group to prevent an unfriendly takeover.[86]

Third, the financing of a company is often done by the banking member of its industrial group. Although article 2 of the AML forbids a bank from acquiring more than 5 percent of another company, a bank may exert considerable influence through pat-

---

[84] Commercial Code, arts. 211–12, prohibits a subsidiary from owning stock in a parent corporation, but this does not prevent widespread cross-shareholding ownership.

[85] Id., art. 254.

[86] Another defensive tactic, successfully employed by Toyota Motor Company in 1968, was a provision in its articles of incorporation requiring all directors to be Japanese citizens. This nationality requirement was upheld. See Ohba v. Toyota Motor Co., *Kakyū Minshū*, Vol. 22, p. 549 (Nagoya Dist. Ct., 30 April 1971). Later, Toyota dropped the nationality requirement from its articles of incorporation.

terns of cross-shareholding by corporate members of the group to which the bank belongs who tend to hold the debtor company's stock. Therefore, the leading bank and the borrower will have an interdependent relationship, and the lender bank, through its industrial group, will support the target company to resist any unfriendly takeover attempt.

Fourth, in Japanese companies, both management and the labor force will commonly be people who are loyal to the company and look on the company as a source of lifetime employment. Many Japanese companies promote employee shareholding through employee stockholder trusts.[87] The fact that employees either individually or through employee trusts are large shareholder groups tends to inhibit an unfriendly takeover.

There are four basic legal methods of conducting an acquisition of a Japanese company: purchasing its assets; purchasing newly issued shares; purchasing outstanding shares through a tender offer; and merger. Purchasing the assets of a company has the advantage of being able to avoid hidden liabilities and acquiring a stepped-up basis in the assets involved as well as a new depreciation schedule for them. A purchase of assets requires the consent both of the directors and shareholders of the target company.[88] Dissenting shareholders have the right to demand a buyout of their shares at a fair price.[89]

An acquisition can also be carried out by purchasing sufficient newly issued shares in order to obtain working control of the company. This requires the approval of the board of directors. Unless the corporation's charter provides for preemptive rights, the target company can issue any number of new shares at an appropriate market price. If, however, the price is deemed to be "especially favorable," or if the articles of incorporation so provide, the shareholders must approve the sale by a two-thirds vote.[90]

A corporation may also be acquired by purchasing existing

---

[87] In many Japanese companies, employee trusts are among the five largest shareholders. In 1979, 78.1 percent of listed corporations had such programs. See *Tōshō Yōran* (Tokyo Stock Exchange Survey) (1981) p. 55.

[88] Commercial Code, arts. 245, 333.

[89] Id., art. 245.

[90] Commercial Code, arts. 280–82, 343.

shares through a tender offer. The advantage of a tender offer is that the offeror may condition the bid on obtaining a specified minimum number of shares. If this number is not attained, the offeror may revoke its bid.[91] A tender offer combined with the issuance and acquisition of new shares probably is the best method for carrying out the friendly takeover of a Japanese corporation. If management is in favor of the acquisition, such a tender offer would likely be successful unless the articles of the target corporation require shareholder consent for any transfer of shares. Listed corporations, however, are not permitted to have restrictions on share transferability.

A fourth acquisition method is a statutory merger. Japanese law prohibits mergers between a foreign corporation and a Japanese corporation, but the merger can be effected by first setting up a wholly owned Japanese subsidiary of the foreign company. The merger agreement must be approved by the shareholders of both companies by a two-thirds vote.[92] Dissenting shareholders of the target company may demand that their shares be purchased at fair market value.[93] Because of the difficulty of getting the necessary two-thirds vote and the duty to pay dissenting shareholders, a merger is not usually a desirable method for most acquisitions.

There are two principal legal barriers to making an acquisition or merger in Japan. First, article 10 of the AML prohibits acquisitions of shares that result in substantial restraints of trade, and articles 15 and 16 prohibit mergers and asset acquisitions which would have this effect as well.[94] Second, a corporate acquisition or merger is a direct investment, and article 26(3) of the Control Law specifies that a foreign investor desiring to make a direct investment in Japan must first notify the MOF through the BOJ. Article 26(4) of the Control Law further states that the MOF may subject the investor to a waiting period of up to 30 days. And during this 30-day period, the MOF has the authority to extend the waiting period to 120 days in order

---

[91] Shōken Torihiki Hō Shiko Rei (Securities Transactions Law Enforcement Order) art. 13–7 (Cabinet Order 321, 1966).
[92] Commercial Code, arts. 343, 401.
[93] Commercial Code, art. 408–3.
[94] See Ch. 6.

to investigate whether the direct investment has any adverse effect on (1) national security; (2) Japanese business activity; (3) whether there is a lack of reciprocity with the investor's home country; and (4) if the transaction endangers the balance of payments situation in Japan. If the Foreign Exchange Council determines that 120 days is too short a period to issue an opinion, the delay can be extended to five months. At any time during this period, the MOF can recommend that the domestic investment be modified or suspended.[95]

Until 1984, prior notification to the BOJ and the MOF was required for a foreign investor intending to acquire more than 10 percent of the outstanding shares of a listed company or shares exceeding 25 percent of certain designated companies.[96] At the present time, however, the prior notification requirement applies only when a foreign investor seeks to acquire more than 10 percent of the outstanding shares of a listed Japanese company, and it is theoretically possible to acquire even 100 percent of a Japanese company. Despite this, however, the prior notification system interjects government discretion and requires government approval.[97] A potential foreign investor is required to file prior notification 40 days before the actual date of the transaction. Officials may take the full 30-day waiting period to approve the transaction and, even if they do not disapprove it, may exercise their power to delay the transaction for up to five months. This element of government discretion may thus render the acquisition or merger a practical impossibility.

Despite the increased interest in acquisitions and mergers in Japan by foreign companies and the liberalization of the legal requirements, there are still many practical obstacles to widespread merger and acquisition activity in Japan. The foreign investor interested in a merger or acquisition must confront the

[95] See art. 27 of the Control Law.

[96] Until 1984, 11 companies were designated as prohibited for foreign investment beyond this prescribed level. In June 1984, however, the Control Law was amended, and the prior reporting requirements concerning designated companies were eliminated.

[97] See the story of the attempted acquisition of Katakura Industries Ltd. by a group of Hong Kong investors in Crampe and Benes, "Majority Ownership Strategies for Japan," *Pacific Basin Law Journal*, Vol. 1, p. 41 (1986). For additional case studies of mergers in Japan, see Misawa, "Merger and Acquisition Activities in Japan: The Present and Future," *Vanderbilt Journal of Transnational Law*, Vol. 19, p. 785 (1986).

extralegal, cultural, and government discretionary barriers and surmount them in order to be successful. An acquisition or a merger will be successful only if first a relationship of mutual trust and understanding is established with the target company and if there are preliminary contacts and favorable administrative guidance from government authorities. Despite the removal of formal legal barriers, unfriendly acquisitions or mergers are unlikely in Japan.

CHAPTER SIX

ANTITRUST LAW

§ 6–1. A History and Overview of the Japanese Antitrust Law

In the period before World War II, there existed in Japan no legislation to prohibit the formation of monopolies and cartels. In fact, a great deal of prewar legislation permitted—indeed encouraged—a monopolistic system. During the occupation of Japan by Allied forces following the war, the notion of a system of free enterprise was introduced, and accordingly the Japanese Antimonopoly Law was enacted in 1947, a fundamental piece of legislation for the regulation and development of industry.

The development of the law in the years following its enactment in 1947 has been marked by considerable fluctuation in the degree of rigidity in its enforcement. The early period—to which we may set as boundaries the years from 1947 to 1952—was marked by energetic enforcement of the terms of the law. This was in large part due to the support of the Occupation Forces, a vigorous proponent of strict enforcement. In the following years, however, from 1952 to the middle of the next decade, enforcement of the law was significantly relaxed. In 1952, the law was amended, resulting in the elimination of several important provisions, such as the provision which held cartels to be illegal per se and the provision which provided for the dissolution of a large business simply because of its size. Furthermore, provisions were added which exempted certain cartels (specifically, depressed-industry cartels and rationalization cartels) and allowed resale price maintenance.[1]

---

[1] See Yamamura, "The Development of Antimonopoly Policy in Japan: The

Beginning in the mid-1960s, the law was enforced with re-newed vigor. Among the factors contributing to this resurgence must be numbered the continuous inflation during this period, the rise of consumerism, the liberalization of trade and capital transactions, and a shift in the goals of economic policy from high growth to welfare. The year 1977 was a landmark in the history of the AML. In that year, the law was again amended, but this time with an eye toward strengthening its provisions and tougher enforcement.

American ideology and ideas of free enterprise exercised a con-siderable influence during the formative period of Japan's AML; to a great extent the law was modeled after the United States's antitrust laws. However, the history of the law in the 30 years since its enactment demonstrates that there is some difference in the manner of its enforcement as compared with its American counterpart. For example, in Japan private suits for damages on the basis of the AML have yet to play a large role, despite the fact that there have been a few criminal prosecutions against violators. In the main, the AML has been enforced by an ad-ministrative agency, the Fair Trade Commission.

Differences of opinion, and sometimes conflict, have arisen be-tween the administration of antimonopoly policy by the FTC and the industrial policy of MITI. During the 1960s, it was the policy of MITI to encourage mergers in order to build up enter-prises large enough to compete with those of the United States and Europe, while at the same time the FTC was making an effort to control mergers by means of the AML. Excessive concentra-tion of industries, according to the FTC, would result in oligopoly and thereby deprive the economy of viable competition. How-ever, as was made clear by the Yawata-Fuji Merger case,[2] this attempt on the part of the FTC was often futile.

Erosion of Japanese Antimonopoly Policy, 1947–67," *Studies in Law and Economic Devel-opment*, Vol. 2, pp. 1–22(1967); K. Yamamura, *Economic Policy in Postwar Japan*(1967).

[2] In re Yawata Seitetsu, *Shinketsushū*, Vol. 16, p. 46 (30 Oct. 1969). The major part of this decision has been translated in *Antitrust Bulletin*, Vol. 15, pp. 803–27 (1969). On merger control in general, see Ariga, "Merger Regulation in Japan," *Texas In-ternational Law Reform*, Vol. 5, p. 112–26 (1969) and Kanazawa, "Firm Behaviour and Policy on Mergers in Japan," in *International Conference on Monopolies, Mergers and Re-strictive Practices*(Cambridge Conference, 1969), J.B. Heath, ed., pp.117–22(1971). For a businessman's point of view on merger control, see Suzuki, "Big Business Mergers

In the future, business interests in Japan may anticipate continued regulation in the three main areas covered by the law: unreasonable restraints of trade, private monopolization, and unfair business practices. The principles and practices relevant to these areas which have evolved since the law came into force in 1947 form the basis for future developments. In the following sections, the major features of the law governing these three areas will be discussed; we will begin, however, with an analysis of the enforcement procedures available to the FTC.

§ 6–2. ENFORCEMENT PROCEDURES

1. THE FAIR TRADE COMMISSION (KŌSEI TORIHIKI IINKAI)

The AML is enforced by the FTC, an independent regulatory commission consisting of five commissioners, including the chairperson. The FTC is technically a part of the Prime Minister's Office. Its decisions, however, are made independently of the authority of any other administrative body, including the prime minister. The members of the FTC are nominated by the prime minister and must be approved by both houses of the Diet. The FTC has a staff of about 400 persons. The FTC is authorized to investigate suspected violations and to enforce the AML; more often, however, the FTC acts on the basis of advanced consultations or administrative guidance.

A proceeding before the FTC is begun either by a complaint filed by an individual, on the request of the public prosecutor general or of the director of MITI's Small and Medium Enterprise Agency or on its own authority. Whether a proceeding will be instituted is left to the discretion of the FTC.[3]

If the results of an investigation indicate that a violation has been committed, the FTC has two options: (1) it may recommend to the violator that he refrain from the illegal course of action he has taken, and if this recommendation is accepted, a decision is then handed down without a trial; or (2) it may in-

---

and Antitrust Laws: A Businessman's Point of View," in Heath, ed., id., p. 155.

[3] An individual does not have the right to initiate an action before the FTC. Zenkoku Shōhisha Dantai Renrakukai v. FTC, *Gyōsai Reishū*, Vol. 12, p. 933 (Tokyo H. Ct., 26 April 1961).

stitute formal proceedings against the violator. In the latter case, a formal complaint is brought against the respondent by the FTC, and a trial is conducted in which the investigators and the respondent are adversaries, and administrative law judges, or the FTC, preside. At the conclusion of the trial, a formal decision is handed down. In the course of the trial, the respondent can file a document in which the facts in the application of the law as stated in the complaint are accepted and measures are proposed to eliminate the illegality. If this is accepted by the FTC, the trial is then terminated, and a "consent decision" is handed down.

There are then three types of decisions: (1) a recommendation decision; (2) a formal decision; and (3) a consent decision. In legal effect, however, there is no difference among the three, and refusal to comply with any decision is punishable by law. All final FTC decisions are self-enforcing and do not require court approval.

Depending upon the nature of the violation in question, the content of a decision may take various forms. The FTC has authority to enter an injunction against a violation; this can take the form of a cease-and-desist order or affirmative relief. An administrative fine may also be imposed. A corporation may be ordered to take action against company officials by compelling their resignation, and a business association may even be dissolved by FTC order.

The Tokyo High Court has exclusive jurisdiction to review a decision of the FTC. The scope of judicial review of an FTC decision is whether the decision is supported by substantial evidence. The function of judicial review is thus limited to an examination of the correctness of the legal holdings made by the FTC in the particular case on the basis of facts which the FTC has found present.

Foreign companies, however, may have difficulty obtaining standing to sue the FTC and to obtain a review of an FTC decision. With respect to international contracts, the AML requires that copies of agreements between foreign companies and companies in Japan must be filed with the FTC within 30 days of execution. This requirement, which is not made of domestic agreements, ensures that FTC attention will be paid to international contracts. If the FTC decides to act with respect to an international contract, it will bring a proceeding against only the Japanese company involved and not against a foreign company. This is because in many cases the foreign company will not be engaged in business in Japan. In the case of Novo Industri v. FTC, for example, Novo, a Danish company, ´entered into an exclusive dealership agreement with a Japanese company, Amano.[4] After Novo terminated the contract, Amano submitted it to the FTC for the first time, in effect turning itself in. The FTC advised Amano that the non-competition provisions of the agreement as well as certain other provisions violated the AML. Amano was named as a violator of the AML and accepted a recommendation that the violating clauses be deleted. Of course it was happy to do so. When Novo filed suit against the FTC to challenge the recommendation decision, the Tokyo High Court and the Supreme Court held that Novo had no standing to sue on the grounds that Novo's legal interest had not been affected even if its factual interest had been disturbed. The court's ruling leaves little opportunity for someone other than the respondent in an FTC decision to bring an action seeking annulment of an FTC decision.[5]

2. PRIVATE ENFORCEMENT

A private party who is injured by a violation of the AML may bring an action for damages in the Tokyo High Court. In most cases, a private action will not be brought until after the FTC has investigated a charge and handed down a final decision. After an FTC decision has become final, however, a plaintiff may bring a damage suit under articles 25 and 26 of the AML. The plaintiff may recover without proving negligence or intentional conduct. The plaintiff needs only to prove the amount of damage and the causal link between the damage and the illegal conduct. In a civil action, however, multiple damage recoveries are not permitted. If there is no FTC decision, the plaintiff must bring the suit for damages under article 709 of the Civil Code, the general tort provision.

---

[4] *Hanrei Jihō*, No. 800, p. 35 (1975).
[5] For another example of this narrow interpretation as to standing, see In re Shufu

Illegality under the AML is used not only as a sword but also as a shield. In a breach of contract suit, the defense of the party charged may be that the provision in question violated the AML. For example, a dealer who is sued by a manufacturer on account of a breach of a tie-in clause may claim that the clause is a violation of the AML and is therefore not enforceable. The court has the power to decide this question on the basis of the provisions of the AML.

3. CRIMINAL ENFORCEMENT

In the case of egregious or intentional conduct, a criminal proceeding may be brought for violation of the AML by public prosecutors acting on the basis of a complaint filed by the FTC. Criminal enforcement of the AML is rare, although this was done in the Oil Cartel case.[6] A criminal violation is punishable by imprisonment of up to three years and a fine of up to ¥5 million.

§ 6–3. UNREASONABLE RESTRAINTS OF TRADE: CARTELS AND TRADE ASSOCATIONS

Article 3 states that "no entrepreneur shall effect . . . any unreasonable restraint of trade" (*futō na torihiki seigen*). Article 2(6) of the AML defines "unreasonable restraint of trade" as "such business activities by which en trepreneurs by contract, agreement, or any other concerted actions mutually restrict or conduct their business activities in such manner as to fix, maintain, or enhance prices; or limit production, technology, products, or customers or suppliers, thereby causing, contrary to the public interest, a substantial restraint of competition in any particular field of trade."

According to this definition, then, an unreasonable restraint of trade consists of collusion on the part of entrepreneurs resulting in a substantial restraint of trade contrary to the interests of the public. The term "unreasonable restraint of trade" is therefore synonymous with "cartel."

In the AML, there is a distinction between restrictive activities

---

Rengōkai, *Shinketsushū*, Vol. 19, p. 159 (14 March 1973); Shufu Rengōkai v. FTC, *Hanrei Jihō*, No. 746, p. 6 (19 July 1974).

6 Idemistu Kōsan K.K. v. Japan (Oil Cartel Price-Fixing case), *Hanrei Jihō*, No.

by a cartel, which is an agreement entered into among enterprises, and restrictive activities engaged in by a trade association, even though the economic consequences produced by those two types of restrictive activities are similar.

1. PROOF OF THE EXISTENCE OF A CARTEL

Proving the existence of a cartel is fundamental to the application of this part of the AML. A cartel—an agreement which puts an end to competition among the participants in it—may involve various horizontal or vertical restraints. An early case which is still controversial, but which has never been overruled, seems to place limits on finding that a cartel exists in certain cases of vertical restraints. In the Asahi Shinbun case[7] in 1953, the FTC condemned an agreement between several newspaper publishers and 430 retail newspaper dealers in which the dealers were assigned exclusive territories for sales activities. The Tokyo High Court, however, held that only the dealers—not the publishers—were guilty. Although the dealers who were in competition with each other engaged in concerted activities, the publishers, which did not have retail sales, were only "participants" in the illegal activity, not "principals." The publishers, it was found, did not act jointly, but only individually; neither did they deal with the dealers on the condition that they enter into a territorial agreement to avoid competition.

There are also frequently problems of proof of the existence of a cartel, especially where there is no formal agreement between the parties. In the case of parallel conduct between enterprises, two elements of proof are necessary: (1) evidence that the parties at least communicated their intentions, and (2) that the conduct of the participating enterprises is uniform. Thus, for example, if the representatives of competing enterprises "discussed" prices of their products and the prices were raised simultaneously, this is sufficient even though there is no explicit evidence that the enterprises "agreed" to fix prices.

Circumstantial evidence is acceptable proof of the existence of a cartel. For example, if there is evidence indicating that talks have been held or letters exchanged among a group of entre-

---

1108, p. 3 (Sup. Ct., 24 Feb. 1984).

[7] Asahi Shinbunsha v. FTC, *Kōsai Minshū*, Vol. 6, p. 435 (1953).

preneurs concerning prices or other terms of business, such evidence may be used to support the contention that an agreement has been reached to enter into a cartel, so long as the conduct of the entrepreneurs after the agreement has taken effect can be shown to be uniform.

In the Yuasa Mokuzai case, the representatives of enterprises met before a bid where the government was to purchase plywood products and discussed the bid price.[8] There was no evidence to prove that they had explicitly "agreed" to fix the bid price, and the only evidence available was that one of the representatives indicated a specific price level and the rest of the participants stated that it was a "good price." The FTC ruled that the evidence of these "discussions" was sufficient proof of the existence of a cartel.

However, the parallel conduct of enterprises does not as such constitute a cartel unless there is some evidence of communication of the intentions among the participating enterprises. In the National Liaison Committee of Consumer's Organizations case, the Liaison Committee asked the FTC to initiate an investigation into parallel price increases engaged in by the major newspaper companies.[9] However, the FTC, after a preliminary investigation, decided that there was no cartel since no evidence was produced to show that there had been any exchange of intentions among the newspaper companies as to the parallel price increases.

In oligopolistic markets, it is especially difficult to uncover the existence of cartel agreements. In 1977, the FTC received new authority to order entrepreneurs to report the reasons for a price increase when prices for products are increased simultaneously by all the major enterprises in an industry in which the total value of the commodities or services supplied exceeds ¥30 billion.

2. AT WHAT POINT IS A CARTEL ILLEGAL?

Article 2(6) of the AML defines a cartel or unreasonable restraint of trade as an agreement or understanding entered into among enterprises which substantially restrains competition. Under this

---

[8] In re Yuasa Mokuzai Kōgyō K.K., *Shinketsushū*, Vol. 1, p. 62 (30 Aug. 1949). A very similar situation existed in Nihon Sekiyu K.K. v. FTC, *Gyōsai Reishū*, Vol. 7, p. 2849 (Tokyo H. Ct., 9 Nov. 1956).

[9] See supra note 3.

definition, there are two necessary elements: there must be (1) an agreement or understanding among enterprises and (2) substantially restrained competition. This raises the question as to whether a cartel is illegal as soon as it is agreed upon or only when the terms of the cartel are put into effect and competition in the relevant market is substantially restrained.

There are two theories as to when a cartel becomes illegal. The first maintains that as soon as enterprises agree that they will eliminate competition, effective competition is ended, and the requirement that there be substantial restraint of competition is satisfied.

The second theory is that a cartel is basically unstable and often breaks down before it is put into effect. Therefore, the mere fact that a cartel has been agreed on does not necessarily lead to a substantial restraint of competition. Under this reasoning, a cartel becomes illegal only when it is proven that an agreement among enterprises t) restrain competition has been put into practice.

With some exceptions, the FTC has taken a middle-of-the-road approach and has declared a cartel illegal when the participants take the first steps to put it into practice, even though the terms of the cartel are not yet fully in effect. Thus, if several enterprises agree that they will raise their prices in six months, and before this time send notices to dealers and print out new price tags, the FTC will consider the cartel as challengeable. In the Oil Cartel case, the Supreme Court held that it is not necessary to wait for the time when the participants in a cartel have put their agreement into practice if competition in a market is substantially restrained.[10] This indicates that when the participants in fact have ceased to compete with one another and their conduct has become collaborative, an illegal restraint of competition exists.

3. CONTRARY TO PUBLIC INTEREST

Article 2(6) of the AML also requires that the cartel in question be contrary to the public interest. There are sharp differences of views as to the meaning of "public interest" in this article.

The FTC and the majority of commentators maintain that

---

[10] See supra note 6.

"public interest" as stated in article 2(6) means only free competition. Under this theory, if competition is substantially restrained by a cartel, the public interest is injured. The reasoning here is that the AML was passed to foster competition and that the AML was modeled after the United States antitrust laws under which cartels are per se illegal.

On the other hand, the Keidanren (Keizai Dantai Rengōkai, Federation of Economic Organizations) claims that the term "public interest" in article 2(6) should be interpreted broadly to include such matters as the balanced development of the national economy, the protection of consumers, the prevention of economic depression, and the mitigation of trade conflicts. Therefore, if a cartel is useful in solving these problems, it should be upheld as lawful, even if it substantially restrains competition.

The position of MITI on this issue is not clear. However, some MITI officials have expressed, as their personal views, the view that the words "public interest" should be given a meaning broader than mere free competition.

In the Oil Cartel case, however, the Supreme Court announced a new interpretation of "public interest" under article 2(6).[11] The court stated that the term "public interest" should in principle be interpreted to mean free competition, and an agreement which substantially restrains competition therefore should be regarded as contrary to public interest. However, in exceptional situations, where an agreement which substantially restrains competition promotes some social good, this should be weighed against the value of maintaining competition. After weighing the relative advantages and disadvantages of upholding an agreement and maintaining competition, if it is recognized that the merit of the agreement outweighs the advantage of maintaining competition, then such a cartel should be declared lawful.

The Supreme Court did not give any example of such exceptional situations, but one example may be an agreement entered into among the manufacturers of a product that they will not produce and sell a substance which causes environmental pollution. Another example might be a joint undertaking by publishers that they will not sell obscene materials. In those instances, the

[11] Id.

agreements in question restrain competition but promote other important social values.

4. EXEMPTIONS

The AML and other laws contain provisions which permit cartels under certain circumstances. In the AML itself, there are two such provisions, articles 24–3 and 24–4. Article 24–3 provides an exception for a depression cartel agreement arrived at by manufacturers when the price of their product drops below the average production cost and it would be hard to overcome this difficulty through rationalization. Those entrepreneurs who want to enter into a depression cartel are obliged first to resort to limiting the quantity of production. Only after a limitation of the quantity of production has been shown to be incapable of overcoming the depression will permission be granted to fix the price.

Article 24–4 permits rationalization cartels. If a group of entrepreneurs wishes to agree on terms for rationalization (e.g., a specialization agreement or an agreement to build a common transportation facility), they may file a request with the FTC for permission, and, once it is granted, they may proceed to put it into effect.

There are a considerable number of laws that permit certain types of cartels. The Export and Import Transactions Law authorizes the creation of export or import cartels under the supervision of MITI. The Marine Transportation Law authorizes tariff agreements entered into by shipping companies.[12] Shipping conferences are also permitted under this legislation, which confers the power of authorization upon the Ministry of Transportation. The Small Business Organization Law authorizes agreements entered into by small and medium enterprises, and the Insurance Business Law permits the standardization of insurance policy contracts.[13] An agreement is exempted from the provisions of the AML if it is specifically authorized by one of these statutes.

In 1988, a law was passed to introduce a new consumption tax. There are provisions in the tax reform law which exempt

[12] Kaijō Unsō Hō, Law 187, 1949, as amended. A part of the law has been translated in the Appendix in Counselor's Office of the Fair Trade Commission of Japan, *Antimonopoly Legislation of Japan* (1977).

[13] Hokengyō Hō, Law 41, 1939, as amended.

certain agreements among enterprises for the purpose of "passing on" the consumption tax in the form of higher prices.

5. TRADE ASSOCIATIONS

Article 8(1) of the law bars certain restrictive activities of trade associations, which exist in most of the major industries in Japan. If a program establishing restrictive terms of business which are to be observed by the members is adopted by an association following a resolution of the executive committee, then the members cease to compete among themselves. Consider, for example, the case of an association which adopts a resolution establishing specific limits in the quantity of the commodity to be produced by the members of the association. In such a situation, the activity of the association is scarcely distinguishable from that of a cartel.

In the Nihon Yōmōbōsekikai case, the FTC proceeded against a trade association in the field of woolen textiles after it established a program for forecasting the demand for the members' products three months in advance, thus in effect determining both the amount to be produced by the industry as well as the amount to be produced by each individual manufacturer.[14] The FTC ruled that this was a violation of article 8(1) of the law.

§ 6-4. PRIVATE MONOPOLIZATION: MONOPOLIES, MERGERS, AND ACQUISITIONS

"Private monopolization" (shiteki dokusen) is prohibited under article 3 of the AML. This term is defined in the law in article 2(5) as follows: "The term 'private monopolization' as used in this law shall mean such business activities by which any entrepreneur, individually, by combination or conspiracy with other entrepreneurs, or in any other manner, excludes or controls the business activities of other entrepreneurs, thereby causing, contrary to the public interest, a substantial restraint of competition in any particular field of trade."[15]

---

[14] In re Nihon Yōmōbōsekikai, Shinketsushū, Vol. 21, p. 127 (6 Nov. 1974).

[15] In the AML, an "entrepreneur" is subject to regulation. In article 2(1), an "entrepreneur" is defined as "a person who carries on a business that is commercial, industrial, financial, or any other kind."

Even though there are only a handful of cases in this area, meager precedents suggest that large economic power possessed by an enterprise will be necessary for conduct to be held to be private monopolization. For example, in the Tōyō Seikan case, Tōyō, which already had a market share of more than 50 percent, acquired the majority of stock in four companies, giving it a market share of 75 percent.[16] The FTC ordered Tōyō to divest itself of one of the enterprises which it had acquired.

1. EXCLUSION OR CONTROL

The exclusion or control of the business activities of other entrepreneurs may take various forms. Consider for example the case of an entrepreneur who maintains a policy of predatory pricing which discriminates on the basis of geographic distribution or the kinds of customers; or a dominant entrepreneur who sells below cost so as to drive out competitors. Such actions may be held to constitute "exclusion" under the definition of private monopolization if the net result is the creation of a situation where competition has effectively ceased to exist. Certain forms of restrictive contracts which deny access to market channels or sources of raw materials or other entrepreneurs may be held to be exclusion if competition is substantially restrained. To give an example, if a dominant manufacturer enters into a series of agreements with several distributors and imposes upon them restrictions of such a kind that these distributors can no longer purchase and resell the products of competing manufacturers, then the dominant manufacturer may be accused of engaging in the exclusion of the business activities of other entrepreneurs.

In the Snow Brand case, two dominant manufacturers of dairy products conspired with a dominant financial institution and a federation of farmers' cooperatives in the Hokkaido area.[17] The financial institution was persuaded to issue loans to dairy farmers on the condition that they agreed not to supply milk to the competitors of the two manufacturers. Those dairy farmers who borrowed money were thus obligated to refuse to supply milk to

---

[16] In re Tōyō Seikan K.K., *Shinketsushū*, Vol. 19, p. 87 (8 Sept. 1972).

[17] In re Yukijirushi K.K., *Shinketsushū*, Vol. 8, p. 12 (28 July 1956). This decision has been translated in English in *Fair Trade*, Vol. 1, No. 1, pp. 36–37 (1956) as the Snow Brand Dairy Company case.

the manufacturers' competitors, whose business was thereby badly damaged. After the FTC had decided that this constituted a private monopolization, it proceeded to take action against the four parties to the conspiracy and held that the two manufacturers had committed an act of private monopolization.[18]

"Control" of the business activities of an entrepreneur by another entrepreneur encompasses a wide variety of conduct. It can include an acquisition of stock as well as an interlocking directorate. The concept also includes situations where an entrepreneur controls subcontractors or distributors. For instance, suppose a manufacturer of automobiles or electronics deals with subcontractors who are the only producers of key components of the end product. If the manufacturer prohibits the subcontractor from supplying these components to other manufacturers, competition will be restrained.

Control of the business activities of other entrepreneurs may be both direct and indirect. Any exertion of power by a strong entrepreneur against a weaker entrepreneur which directs, restricts, or prohibits the activities of the weaker party is considered direct control. Stockholding, restrictive covenants, and financial pressure are some of the means by which pressure is exerted, but there are others. In the Tōyō Seikan case, the stocks of Hokkai Seikan, a manufacturer of cans, and three other can manufacturers were held by Tōyō, which is the leading manufacturer of cans in Japan. Interlocking directorates were also involved. Tōyō worked to restrict the geographic territory of Hokkai's business to Hokkaido Island and, in some cases, prevented Hokkai from producing certain types of cans. These activities were deemed to constitute direct control over another entrepreneur.

Indirect control is less easy to define. In the Noda Soy Sauce case, the leading manufacturer of soy sauce in Japan directed

---

[18] The other well-known decision on "exclusion" is In re Saitama Ginkō, *Shinketsushū*, Vol. 2, p. 74 (13 July 1950). In this case, the Saitama Bank conspired with its subsidiary, Marusa Silk Company, and imposed upon some manufacturers of silk, which were borrowers of money from the bank, a condition that they must consign their export business to Marusa and thereby excluded other export agents which had handled the manufacturers' export business. The imposition of this condition in loan arrangements effectively drove out other export agents. This restrictive loan arrangement was held to be an "exclusion" in the sense of private monopolization.

retailers to charge a certain "suggested" retail price so as to bring about resale price maintenance at the retail level.[19] In fact, the manufacturer used coercive measures to maintain this price level. Because of the tightly regimented oligopolistic structure of the industry and the problem of product differentiation, the smaller manufacturers were left with no choice but to enforce retail prices at the same level. As a result, on each occasion that Noda raised the retail prices of its own products, the other manufacturers were compelled to follow suit. The FTC and the courts held that maintenance of retail prices by Noda in this way had the effect of giving Noda "indirect control" over the pricing decisions of competing entrepreneurs and constituted a private monopolization.

At this point, it must be noted that smaller businesses operating in some types of oligopolistic markets cannot possibly conduct their business activities (especially pricing decisions) in a manner different from the leading manufacturer. When the leading firm sets its price, its competitors in the market have little choice but to adjust their prices accordingly. In this way, the pricing decisions of the leading firm in an oligopolistic market often set off a chain reaction of parallel pricing moves by other firms, which inevitably results in uniformity of price in the market.

The decision in the Noda case does not necessarily mean that conduct on the part of a leading firm which is paralleled by the conduct of others always will be held to constitute "indirect control." In other words, the simple fact that the pricing procedures adopted by a leading firm are mimicked by smaller firms in the industry should not automatically be considered as indirect control of the business activities of the smaller entrepreneurs, even if the net result is parallel price settings.

The holding in the Noda case does, however, indicate that if a leading firm in the industry has enforced resale price maintenance through coercion applied to the pricing decisions of its distributors and retailers, thereby causing its competitors to

[19] In re Noda Shōyu K.K., *Shinketsushū*, Vol. 7, p. 108 (27 Dec. 1950) and Noda Shōyu K.K. v. FTC, *Kōsai Minshū*, Vol. 10, p. 743 (Tokyo H. Ct., 25 Dec. 1957). The FTC decision has been translated into English in *Fair Trade*, Vol. 1, No. 4, pp. 18–27.

follow similar resale price-maintenance practices, its pricing policy will be held to constitute indirect control of the pricing decisions of the competing manufacturers.

Control of the business activities of other entrepreneurs is therefore not solely limited to conduct of an entrepreneur which directly dictates to other entrepreneurs, thus restricting their activities. The definition of control includes any conduct of an entrepreneur which indirectly causes other entrepreneurs to take similar action due to the rigid structure of the industry, without necessarily involving direct compulsion.

It should be pointed out that from the standpoint of the AML, any evaluation of conduct depends upon the condition of the market in which the conduct takes place. For example, had the soy sauce market not been oligopolistic and had there not been a product differentiation such as there was in the soy sauce industry at that time, then the maintenance of the resale price by Noda would not have been held to be control of the market and private monopolization. Taken in this sense, the question of whether or not the conduct of any given leading firm constitutes private monopolization is entirely relative to the circumstances of the individual case.

2. SUBSTANTIAL RESTRAINT OF COMPETITION IN A PARTICULAR FIELD OF TRADE

According to article 2(5) of the law, private monopolization exists if the conduct of an entrepreneur either in excluding or controlling the business activities of other entrepreneurs is the cause of a substantial restraint of competition in a particular field of trade. Three concepts are central to this provision. The first, that the restraint be "contrary to the public interest," has already been explained;[20] the second is that it must be a "substantial restraint of competition"; and the third is that it must involve "a particular field of trade."

The notion of substantial restraint of competition is a qualitative, rather than a quantitative, concept. Competition in a given market is said to be substantially restrained if a dominant firm, or firms, is able to manipulate prices and other transactions

[20] Supra p. 147.

in the market. That is to say, a situation is created in which competition has effectively ceased to exist in the market.[21] Although this concept is essentially qualitative, not quantitative, it is nonetheless useful to employ some quantitative measures in order to decide whether or not competition has been substantially restrained in a particular field of trade. The market share of an entrepreneur is in all likelihood the most important quantitative measure in making this determination. The dividing line should probably be drawn at a 25 percent share of the market. If the market share of an entrepreneur engaging in exclusion or control exceeds this limit of 25 percent, it would then run the risk of facing an antitrust action.

A "particular field of trade" is defined as a market in which competition takes place. The most important criteria used in defining this slippery term are geographic area,[22] kinds of customers,[23] and the nature of the product in question.[24] In any case it must be a flexible definition suited to the peculiarities of each particular situation. In separating and defining a particular field of trade, such factors as product differentiation and interchangeability of products or services should be taken into consideration.

The third concept in the definition of private monopolization—"contrary to the public interest"—has previously been discussed.[25]

3. MONOPOLISTIC SITUATIONS (DOKUSENTEKI JŌTEI)

Under the definition of "private monopolization," an entrepreneur must engage in "exclusion" or "control" of the business activities of another enterprise in order to be guilty of an offense. Mere size or dominance will not be enough to establish the violation.

The 1977 amendments included a provision for the dissolution of large enterprises. A company with a large share of the mar-

---

[21] Tōhō K.K. v. FTC, *Gyōsai Reishū*, Vol. 2, p. 1562 (Tokyo H. Ct., 19 Sept. 1951).

[22] Tōhō K.K. v. FTC, *Minshū* Vol. 8, p. 950 (Sup. Ct., 25 May 1954).

[23] Nihon Sekiyu K.K. v. FTC, *Gyōsai Reishū*, Vol. 7, p. 2849 (Tokyo H. Ct., 9 Nov. 1956).

[24] In re Nihon Sekiyu Unsō K.K., *Shinketsushū*, Vol. 3, p. 73 (25 June 1951); In re Nihon Gakki K.K., *Shinketsushū*, Vol. 8, p. 51 (30 Jan. 1957); In re Daiwa Ginkō, *Shinketsushū*, Vol. 10, p. 36 (26 June 1961). The FTC decision in In re Nihon Gakki, K.K., tr. in *Fair Trade*, Vol. 1, pp. 32–33 (1959).

[25] See p. 147.

ket is subject to dissolution if it can be proved that the company has engaged in undesirable economic activities. Dissolution is then effected when both requirements of market share and undesirable activities are satisfied.

The requirement with regard to structure is satisfied if a company occupies a 50 percent share of the market, or greater, or if two companies combined occupy a share of 75 percent or greater. The requirements of undesirable activity are met (1), if new entry is excessively difficult, (2) if there has been a conspicuous rise in price or if prices have declined very little over a long period of time in spite of fluctuations in supply and demand and cost of supplies, and (3) if the company in question has acquired a profit which conspicuously exceeds the usual sales and overhead costs in the field of business to which the company belongs. The amended law declares that, if the above requirements are satisfied, a "monopoly situation" exists in the industry, and any entrepreneur which satisfies these requirements may be compelled to divest a percentage of its business. However, if divestiture causes a loss of international competitiveness, an increase in costs, or unsound financial conditions, or if competition can be restored by some other means, then the FTC may not order divestiture even if a "monopoly situation" does exist. The act also provides for procedural safeguards to prevent easy recourse to divestiture.[26]

4. MERGERS AND ACQUISITIONS

Article 10 of the AML prohibits the acquisition of stock or assets of a corporation if, as the result of such acquisition, competition in a market may be substantially restrained. Article 15 of the

---

[26] Under art. 8–4, when the FTC has decided to begin an investigation, it must notify the minister in charge of the industry in question that an investigation will be conducted, and the minister can express his view as to whether or not there exists a monopoly situation and, even if a monopoly situation exists, whether or not some other measures than a transfer of business can be taken. Also, in initiating a formal proceeding, the FTC must again consult with the minister in charge. In ordering a dissolution, at least three commissioners and the chairman must agree. In regular proceedings of the FTC, a simply majority rule prevails, and so the FTC can issue an order as long as two commissioners and the chairman, or three commissioners, agree. Therefore, in dissolution cases, the voting requirement for issuing an order is made more stringent than in regular proceedings.

AML prohibits a merger between corporations if, as the result of such merger, competition in a market may be substantially restrained. Article 15(2) of the AML establishes a pre-merger notification system, according to which the parties that intend to merge must notify the FTC at least 30 days prior to the effective date. During this waiting period, the FTC will examine the proposed merger to determine whether competition may be substantially restrained. Under articles 10 and 15, an acquisition or merger is prohibited only if competition in a market "may be" substantially restrained. The words "may be" are considered to mean the probability that competition will be substantially restrained, even if competition is not yet substantially restrained. Thus, articles 10 and 15 may be used to reach private monopolization in its incipiency as well as upon its completion.

An important question in interpreting both articles 10 and 15 is whether, in determining the relevant market in which the restraint of competition would occur, the domestic market alone should be considered or international market should be taken into account as well. This question has not been fully answered yet either by the FTC or court interpretations. However, it would seem that both domestic and international markets should be considered as long as the goods or services in question are supplied to domestic purchasers.

Case law has not developed well in this area yet. However, there are several guidelines published by the FTC with regard to the enforcement of articles 10 and 15 that provide the general enforcement policy of the FTC with regard to merger control under article 15. These guidelines contain a great many provisions, and only some of the more significant ones will be explained.

According to the guidelines, if the total value of the assets owned by the companies intending to merge is less than ¥5 billion, the merger is usually not questioned. This affords a "safe harbor" for those mergers in which the value of assets involved is relatively small. On the other hand, if because of a merger, (1) the market share of the merged company attains 25 percent or (2) it becomes first in market share with at least 15 percent of the relevant market, or (3) it becomes first and the gap in market share between that company and the second and third companies is great, then the merger will be closely scrutinized. Several other similar criteria are set out in the guidelines.

These market shares and ranking tests do not mean that mergers and acquisitions in which greater figures are involved are automatically struck down. Rather, they are rules of thumb to be considered by the FTC. If there are some redeeming factors, a merger in which the market share and ranking criteria are surpassed may pass FTC scrutiny. It is important to bear in mind, however, that the FTC will closely scrutinize a merger or acquisition in which the market share and rankings exceed the above criteria unless the parties effecting a merger can show that there are reasons to believe that competition in the relevant market will not be hurt.

5. PROHIBITION OF HOLDING COMPANIES

Article 9 of the AML prohibits holding companies, regardless of their impact on competition. This provision has a special significance to foreign enterprises contemplating entry into the Japanese market. This "per se illegality" of a holding company stems from the experience before and during World War II when large industrial combines (zaibatsu) were controlled by holding companies. Article 9 defines a holding company as a company whose main business is to own stocks of other corporations and to control them. Thus, if a company has its own business and holds stocks of another company as well, it is not a holding company under article 9.

If, therefore, a foreign company has no business either in Japan or in its home country other than owing stock in other companies and it owns the stock of Japanese companies in Japan, it will be regarded as a prohibited holding company. But if the foreign company is engaged in business either in its home country or in Japan, then such a foreign company is not regarded as a prohibited holding company, since its main business is not to own stocks of other companies. If a foreign company is engaged in business in its home country but owns a subsidiary which has no business but owning stocks of Japanese companies in Japan, will the subsidiary be regarded as a prohibited holding company? The answer to this question depends upon the relationship between the parent company and subsidiary company. If the subsidiary is wholly owned by the parent company, the two companies probably will be regarded as one economic entity, and therefore, the subsidiary will probably not be regarded as a prohibited holding company.

In view of the fact that holding companies are allowed in many countries, including the United States, and that holding companies are often utilized by foreign companies when they establish businesses in foreign countries, the FTC has taken the policy of giving leeway to foreign companies so that, when a foreign holding company owns only one Japanese company, it will not be regarded as a prohibited holding company.

§ 6–5. UNFAIR BUSINESS PRACTICES
(FUKŌSEI NA TORHIKI HŌHŌ)

Unfair business practices are prohibited under article 19 of the AML. They are defined in article 2(9) of the law as follows:

The term "unfair business practices" as used in this law shall mean any act that comes within any of the following provisions that tend to impede fair competition and is so designated by the FTC:

(i) Unjustly discriminating against other entrepreneurs;

(ii) Dealing at unreasonable prices;

(iii) Unreasonably inducing or coercing customers or a competitor to deal with oneself;

(iv) Trading with another party on conditions that unjustly restrict such party's business activities;

(v) Unreasonable use of one's bargaining position in dealing with another party;

(vi) Unjustly interfering in a transaction between an entrepreneur who competes with oneself in Japan, or between a company of which one is a shareholder or an officer and its customers, or, in the event of such entrepreneur in a company, unjustly inducing, instigating, or coercing a shareholder or an officer of such company to act against the interests of the company.

One of the requirements for an unfair business practice is that

the conduct "tends to impede fair competition." It is not necessary to show, therefore, that competition has been actually impeded or is likely to be impeded by a conduct. As long as there
is a possibility for such impediment, the requirement is satisfied.
Thus the law reaches anticipated or incipient conduct as well
as completed actions. In this sense, the prohibition of unfair
business practices is designed as a precautionary measure in relation to the offense of private monopolization.

An important policy of the AML's prohibition of unfair business practices is to protect consumers. Included in prohibition of
unfair business practices are such matters as resale price maintenance, tie-in requirements, misrepresentation, and control of
sale premiums, all of which are important in consumer protection. There is also a special law entitled Law to Prevent Excessive Premiums and Unreasonable Representation that provides
more specific regulation regarding the prohibition of unreasonable sales premiums and misrepresentation.[27]

Another important policy in prohibiting unfair business practices is to protect small business. Abuse of economic power is
considered to be an unfair business practice, and if a disparity
in bargaining power between a large enterprise and a small enterprise leads to unreasonable conditions in a contract, the FTC may
intervene to correct the imbalance. Opinion is divided regarding
whether the FTC should intervene in such matters. This part of
the AML has become socially so important, however, that it is
an integral part of the protection of small business.

1. DESIGNATION OF UNFAIR BUSINESS PRACTICES BY THE FTC

Article 2(9) delegates authority to the FTC to designate unfair
business practices within the framework of the law. The FTC
has designated two types of unfair business practices: (1) general unfair business practices which apply to all industries and
(2) particular unfair business practices which apply only to
specified industries. Only the former will be briefly commented
upon.

FTC announced its "General Designation of Unfair Business

---

[27] Futō Keihinrui oyobi Futō Hyōji Bōshi Hō, Law 134, 1962, as amended.

Practices" in 1982, a list of the following 16 prohibited practices; the more important of these for international transactions are explained below.

1. Concerted refusal to deal with a particular entrepreneur without good reason.

2. Undue refusal to deal with a particular entrepreneur.

3. Unduly discriminating between customers concerning prices.

4. Unduly allowing certain entrepreneurs favorable or unfavorable terms without good cause.

5. Unduly excluding specific entrepreneurs from a business association or from a concerted activity, or unduly discriminating against specific entrepreneurs in a business association or a concerted activity.

6. Continually supplying a commodity or service at markedly low prices or otherwise unreasonably supplying a commodity or service at low prices.

7. Unduly purcha sing a commodity or service at high prices.

8. Unduly inducing customers of a competitor to deal with oneself.

9. Inducing customers of a competitor to deal with oneself by offering undue benefits in the light of normal business practices.

10. Unduly causing a customer to purchase a commodity or service from oneself or from another entrepreneur designated by oneself by tying it to the supply of another commodity or service, or otherwise coercing the said customer to deal with oneself or with an entrepreneur designated by oneself.

11. Unduly restricting the freedom of a customer to deal with other entrepreneurs.

12. Resale price maintenance without good reason.

13. Any other act which unduly restricts any transaction between a customer and another transacting party, or other business activities of a customer.

14. Engaging in certain acts which unduly, in the light of normal business practices, take advantage of customers by making use of one's dominant bargaining position over a customer.

15. Unjustly interfering in transactions of competitors in Japan.

16. Unjustly influencing a corporate insider to act against the interests of his corporation.

2. REFUSAL TO DEAL

General Designation Nos. 1 and 2 cover refusals to deal and boycotts, stating that an agreement entered into among competing enterprises compelling all the participants to refuse to deal with a person is illegal in principle. An example of this would be a case in which participating manufacturers agree that all of them will stop selling to a distributor who cuts the wholesale price below an agreed level.

A question here is: under what circumstances is an agreement to collectively refuse to deal lawful? There must be a persuasive reason that a refusal would serve some justifiable cause. One case, for example, would be the situation where manufacturers of perishable foodstuffs agree to require the retailers to install a refrigerator which meets the standards set by the manufacturers in order to avoid food poisoning and refuse to deal with retailers who do not comply.

A refusal to deal exercised by a single enterprise is in principle lawful. It becomes unlawful only when an enterprise with a great economic power refuses to deal or when it is used to achieve an illegal purpose. An example of the former would be a case in which an enterprise which occupies a large portion, for example, 80 percent, of the market engages in a refusal to deal. In such a case, the party to whom the refusal has been applied has no alternative and, for this reason, the refusal is held to be illegal. An example of the latter would be a refusal to deal exercised by a manufacturer to a retailer who did not comply with the resale price maintenance imposed by the manufacturer. In this case, a refusal to deal is used to support resale price maintenance which is also illegal.

3. PREDATORY PRICING

General Designation No. 3 deals with price discrimination. If a seller sells the same product to two or more different customers or in different areas with different prices, lessening competition in the seller's market or in the purchaser's market, price discrimination may be held illegal.

General Designation No. 6 states that a sale with a predatory price is illegal. The question here is the meaning of predation.

The designation provides that if a seller "continually" sells a product at a price which is "markedly" below the cost of production or purchase (an unreasonably low price), such a sale is illegal in principle. The terms "continually" and "markedly" obviously allow some latitude for interpretation, and precise definitions have not been worked out. We can only provide an example to illustrate how these terms may be interpreted.

In the Milk Retail case, bottles of milk were sold for several months at the price of ¥100 per bottle even though the cost of purchasing it was ¥160.[28] Several small stores specializing in selling bottled milk complained to the FTC, which rendered a decision holding these sales illegal.

Thus, in order for a sales price to be held unreasonable, it must be far below the cost of production or purchase, be exercised for a considerable period of time (for several months), and be below the prevailing market price. There must also be an injury to competition in the seller's market, e.g., injury inflicted upon a large portion of sellers who are competing with the seller who is engaged in below-cost selling.

General Designation No. 6 states that a sale which is also "otherwise unreasonable" is illegal. "Otherwise unreasonable" probably means that a sale at a price below the cost (even though not "markedly" below cost) which occurs sporadically (not "continually") may be held illegal under special circumstances such as the injury to competition is extremely great.

4. UNREASONABLE REPRESENTATION AND UNREASONABLE PREMIUM

General Designation Nos. 8 and 9 declare that it is illegal for an entrepreneur to unreasonably coerce or offer unreasonable inducements to customers in an attempt to compel them to deal with him. Of the two activities—inducement and coercion—the former appears to be a great deal more important than the latter. What is meant by offering unreasonable inducements to customers is any inappropriate method used by an entrepreneur in the promotion of sales.

This may be divided into two categories: (1) the offer of an

[28] In re Maruetsu K.K., *Shinketsushū*, Vol. 29, p. 13 (28 May 1981); In re K.K. Harōmaato, *Shinketsushū*, Vol. 29, p. 18 (28 May 1981).

excessively large premium during the process of the sale of a commodity to a purchaser and (2) sales or misleading advertisements and representations. The offer of excessive premiums, and false or misleading advertising are prohibited in some cases under this designation.[29]

In 1962, the Law to Prevent Excessive Premiums and Unreasonable Representations was enacted and, in fact, the majority of cases involving excessive premiums or false or misleading advertising are handled under this law and not under General Designation Nos. 8 and 9. This law was enacted because of the lack of clarity in the standards set out in General Designation Nos. 8 and 9 by reference to which a judgment must be reached as to whether the conduct of an entrepreneur constitutes unreasonable inducement. In addition, it was considered necessary to establish more precise and predictable tests. Although in the regulation of sales promotion activities, speedy action on the part of the FTC is essential, the procedures outlined in the AML are still somewhat too involved.

Under the Unreasonable Premiums Law, the FTC is authorized to announce the maximum value and amount of premium which can be offered with the sale of a particular commodity. There are many rules based on commodity lines. In the area of unreasonable representation, the criteria are less certain, and whether an advertisement is "unreasonable" depends on interpretation. Some of the important rules will be briefly summarized.

If a representation or advertisement is false, it is clearly an unreasonable representation. Even if a representation is not false, it can be held unreasonable if an expression used in an advertisement has more than one meaning and one of the meanings is contrary to the truth. In the Bentley case, a seller of sweaters imported a machine to produce sweaters from an English company called "Bentley."[30] The seller manufactured sweaters with this machine and sold them in Japan under the name "Bentley." It was not made clear whether the sweaters were manufactured by an English company, or were made in Japan. From the name, the general public could have the impression that they were

---

[29] See, for example, FTC v. Chūbu Yomiuri Shinbunsha, *Hanrei Jihō*, No. 776, p. 30 (Tokyo H. Ct., 30 April 1975).
[30] *Haijo Meireishū*, p. 3 (1968).

manufactured and imported from England to Japan; therefore, the FTC held that use of the name "Bentley" was unreasonable.

This legislation, however, deals with premium and representation insofar as the retail consumers and the general public are concerned. If a sale with a premium or a misrepresentation is made toward business enterprises (for example, if manufacturers use premium sales when they sell to distributors), this legislation does not apply. In such cases, General Designations Nos. 6, 8, and 9 must be utilized.

5. TIE-IN CLAUSES AND EXCLUSIVE DEALING

General Designation No. 10 prohibits tie-in clauses in which a seller of a commodity conditions the sale on the purchase by a purchaser of another commodity. A tie-in clause is not illegal per se; however, if it is used by a powerful seller to coerce purchasers to buy other products, it may be held illegal. In the Textbook case, a distributor which had a monopolistic position in the sale of textbooks in an area licensed retailers on the condition that they handle other regular books as well.[31] The FTC held this illegal.

In an exclusive dealing arrangement, a supplier supplies a commodity to purchasers only on the condition that the latter not handle commodities supplied by competitors of the former, or a purchaser purchases a commodity from sellers only on the condition that the latter not sell the commodity to competitors of the former. An exclusive dealing arrangement is not illegal in principle. It creates a problem only when it is exercised by a powerful enterprise.

There are several cases in which exclusive dealing was held to be illegal. However, in all of those cases, powerful suppliers or purchasers were involved. In the Mutō Kōgyō case, a manufacturer of stationeries which held the market share of 75 percent required dealers to refrain from handling competitors' products. The FTC stated that this was illegal.[32]

---

[31] In re Nagano Ken Kyōkasho Kyōkyūsho K.K., *Shinketsushū*, Vol. 12, p. 100 (11 Feb. 1964).

[32] In re Mutō Kōgyō K.K., *Shinketsushū*, Vol. 21, p. 148 (22 Nov. 1974). The latest exclusive dealing case was remanded to the FTC by the Tokyo High Court. Tōyō Seimaiki v. FTC, *Hanrei Jihō*, No. 1106, pp. 48, 49 (17 Feb. 1984). Tr. and discussed by Radcliffe, *Law in Japan*, Vol. 18, p. 76 (1986).

It is unclear as to how much economic power possessed by a party engaged in an exclusive dealing arrangement is necessary in order for the exclusive dealing arrangement to be held illegal. It seems certain, however, that a market share of less than 25 percent would be insufficient for this purpose. If an enterprise had a market share of above 50 percent, it seems almost certain that an exclusive dealing arrangement exercised by such a party would be held illegal. If it is between 25 and 50 percent, validity or invalidity probably depends upon the situation.

6. RESALE PRICE MAINTENANCE

General Designation No. 12 designates resale price maintenance as unfair business practice. In resale price maintenance, a manufacturer (or a party designated by it) sells a commodity to dealers on the condition that they observe the price designated when they resell it. Designation 12 states that resale price maintenance is generally illegal. It is held lawful only in an exceptional case where a parent company is selling a commodity through a subsidiary.

Resale price maintenance should be distinguished from a suggested price or recommended price in which a manufacturer merely "suggests" or "recommends" a price to be charged by dealers without coercing them. A genuine recommended or suggested price is lawful as long as dealers are under no contractual or de facto obligation to observe it. However, even if the term "recommended" or "suggested" price is used, it may be held illegal if the manufacturer using these terms is actually engaged in coercion. In the Noda Soy Sauce case, the producer "recommended" that dealers raise their resale prices.[33] However, when it was discovered that a dealer did not comply with this recommendation, supply to that dealer was terminated. In such a case, there is a resale price maintenance.

There are some exemptions from the prohibition of resale price maintenance. Books and other items which are objects of copyrights are exempted by article 24–4 of the AML. Article 24–4 also provides that the FTC can designate a commodity to be exempted from the prohibition. At present, there are two items

[33] See supra note 19.

of commodity designated by the FTC to be exempted from the prohibition: pharmaceuticals and cosmetics.

7. VERTICAL TERRITORIAL ALLOCATION AND CUSTOMER RESTRICTION

A vertical territorial allocation in which a manufacturer designates a specific geographic territory to each dealer is judged on a case-by-case basis. If it is used by a powerful supplier, it may cause a problem. In the Fuji X-Ray Film case, a supplier which supplied 70 percent of the market allocated territory to dealers.[34] The FTC proceeded against it and held it illegal.

In customer restriction, a manufacturer designates retailers with whom wholesalers can engage in transaction. For example, a manufacturer designates retailers A, B, and C whom wholesaler X can supply, and retailers D, E, and F are allocated to wholesaler Y. Even though such a practice is not illegal per se, it may be risky if it is engaged in by a manufacturer who enjoys a powerful position in the market.

8. ABUSE OF DOMINANT POSITION

General Designation No. 14 states that an abuse of a dominant position by a powerful enterprise is unlawful. There are several questions to be considered here. What is "dominant" position? In the Miyagawa case, the Supreme Court held that dominant position did not mean market domination but rather referred to dominance in a particular transaction.[35] Thus, even if a party is a small enterprise, it has a dominant position if the other party with whom it is engaged in a transaction is even smaller.

"Abuse" is a troublesome concept. It is not unusual that there exists a difference in terms of bargaining positions between two or more parties to a transaction and, as the consequence, one of the parties must accept somewhat disadvantageous contractual terms. If the AML interferes too much in this area, it would be too interventionistic. On the other hand, to allow duly unbalanced contractual terms to be enforced may be contrary to the sense of social justice.

[34] In re Fuji Shashin Film K.K., *Shinketsushū*, Vol. 28, p. 10 (11 May 1981).
[35] K.K. Miyagawa v. Gifu Shōkō Shin'yō Kumiai, *Minshū*, Vol. 31, p. 449 (Sup. Ct., 20 June 1977).

There is no clear-cut answer as to what is abuse, but the meager case law and comments suggest that, if a party to a transaction imposes a condition which is contrary to accepted business customs, coercive, and repugnant, it will be held an abuse of dominant position.

§ 6–6. REGULATION OF INTERNATIONAL CONTRACTS

1. ARTICLE 6 OF THE ANTIMONOPOLY LAW

There is a special provision in the AML for the regulation of international contracts. Article 6 of the AML states that enterprises shall not conclude an international agreement or contract which constitutes an unreasonable restraint of trade or unfair business practice.[36]

A feature of article 6 is that it prohibits enterprises from "entering into" international contracts which constitute an unreasonable restraint of trade or unfair business practice rather than prohibiting unreasonable restraints of trade or unfair business practices. This is a device to effectively prohibit international agreements containing anticompetitive provisions even though the FTC may have no jurisdiction over the foreign party to the international contract.

The way this provision is applied is shown in the following hypothetical case. Suppose Company A, a foreign company, and Company B, a domestic company, enter into an international agreement in which A licenses technology to B and B is obligated to assign to A all the patents on improvement technology which B will develop in the future. This is the so-called grant-back provision and is a type of unfair business practice. Suppose further that A has no branch, subsidiary, or any other business establishment in Japan. In this instance, A is a perpetrator of an unfair business practice, but it is impossible to apply law on A if the FTC or courts in Japan have no personal jurisdiction over A.

Article 6 of the AML, however, states that an enterprise shall

---

[36] There are two sets of guidelines for international licensing agreements announced by the FTC: (1) on patent and know-how licensing agreements and (2) on sole import distributorship agreements.

not "enter into" an agreement containing items constituting unfair business practice, and the domestic company B has "entered into" an international agreement which constitutes unfair business practice. In this way, the FTC in a sense avoids extra-territorial application of the AML, but may effectively enforce the AML in international transactions.

2. WHAT IS INTERNATIONAL AGREEMENT OR INTERNATIONAL CONTRACT?

This question is important in two ways. First, article 6(2) of the AML requires that certain types of international agreements or contracts as designated by the FTC be filed with the FTC within 30 days after they are concluded. Secondly, the prohibition of international agreements or contracts as provided for in article 6 applies only to international agreements or contracts. Thus, it is important to determine the meaning of international agreements or contracts.

Even though there is no definition of these terms in article 6, it is generally understood that an international agreement or contract is an agreement in which one of the parties belongs to Japan and the other belongs to a foreign country. Although this seems self-evident, it requires some elaboration. An agreement between a Japanese company's foreign branch and a foreign company is an international agreement, since the Japanese company and its branch are one corporate entity. An agreement between a Japanese company's foreign subsidiary and a foreign company is generally not an international agreement, since the Japanese company's foreign subsidiary is a foreign company and, therefore, an agreement entered into between this company and a foreign company is an agreement entered into between a foreign company and a foreign company.

However, this distinction may be too formalistic, and in those cases where a Japanese company and that company's foreign subsidiary are functionally one economic unit, they may be regarded as one; accordingly, an agreement between the subsidiary and a foreign company may be regarded as an international agreement.

Similarly, a foreign company's Japanese branch is regarded as a part of the foreign company, and an agreement between this branch and a Japanese company is regarded as an international agreement. A Japanese subsidiary of a foreign company is generally regarded as a domestic company, and an agreement between this company and a foreign company is an international agreement.

3. ARTICLE 6 OF THE AML AND THE STANDING OF A FOREIGN COMPANY

As explained above, article 6 of the AML is applicable to a domestic party to an international agreement in which items constituting unfair business practices are involved. The FTC may apply article 6 to the domestic party by ordering it to cancel the agreement. Often, however, it is the foreign party whose interest is adversely affected by such cancellation, since sometimes the accused provision restricts activities of the domestic party for the benefit of the foreign party, and its elimination would be disadvantageous to the foreign party.

In the Novo case, a contract between a foreign company and a domestic company stipulated that the domestic party would be given an exclusive distributorship for a product in Japan and was under an obligation to: (1) maintain the resale price of the product supplied, (2) refrain from handling competing products supplied by competing companies during the term of the contract and three years after its termination, and (3) refrain from producing competing products during the term of the contract and after its termination. The FTC proceeded against the domestic party and recommended that the domestic party cancel all three of the provisions. The domestic party accepted the recommendation, and a decision was handed down addressed to the domestic party ordering it to cancel the offending provisions of the contract.

The foreign party brought suit in the Tokyo High Court challenging the FTC decision. The Tokyo High Court rejected the contention of the foreign party and held that the foreign party had no standing to challenge the FTC decision, since an international contract which violated the AML was not necessarily invalid as a matter of private law for that reason alone, and, therefore, the FTC decision did not necessarily deprive the foreign party of its contractual interests under the contract.

On appeal, the Supreme Court upheld the decision of the Tokyo High Court on the ground that the decision by the FTC was binding only on the domestic party, and, therefore, the foreign party's legal interest was not necessarily injured.

It seems, therefore, that the standing of a foreign party to challenge an FTC decision is quite restricted unless the foreign party is the addressee of the decision (in which case the standing to challenge will be allowed). In light of the unfairness to the foreign party, the FTC usually makes the foreign party a respondent in an international case, and, instead of issuing a recommendation, initiates a formal hearing.[37]

4. INTERNATIONAL CARTEL CASES

As touched upon before, article 6 of the AML prohibits both international cartel agreements and those containing unfair business practices. There are relatively few cases in which international cartels were held illegal. However, the Chemical Fiber cases decided in 1974 were landmark cases involving a series of international agreements between Japanese textile producers and European textile producers, whereby the Japanese parties promised to refrain from exporting products to Europe and the European parties promised to refrain from exporting products to Japan.[38] The German Cartel Authority discovered the agreements, prohibited them vis-à-vis their German participants, and imposed fines. The Cartel Authority then notified the FTC of the existence of the cartel and the measures taken.

The FTC thereafter proceeded against the Japanese participants and ordered them to cancel the agreements. In this case, the Cartel Authority probably could have proceeded against the Japanese participants also. However, the Cartel Authority preferred to notify the FTC so that it could take action against the Japanese participants. This is one way to avoid extraterritorial application of domestic law and to solve international problems by means of international governmental cooperation.

---

[37] See, e.g., The Komatsu-Bucyrus case, *Shinketsushū*, Vol. 28, p. 79 (26 Oct. 1981).
[38] In re Asahi Kasei, *Shinketsushū*, Vol. 19, p. 124 (27 Dec. 1972); In re Tōyōbō, *Shinketsushū*, Vol. 19, p. 140 (27 Dec. 1972).

CHAPTER SEVEN

FOREIGN SERVICES IN JAPAN

§ 7–1. SERVICES IN GENERAL

International trade in services is of growing importance.[1] Services have become a major component of economic activity both in themselves and in association with the sale of goods. The issue of international trade in services is presently the subject of negotiation in the Uruguay Round of the GATT trade talks.[2]

Barriers to international trade in services generally include a complex of issues relating to licensing and immigration requirements. Japan is committed to national treatment with respect to citizens of its trading partners rendering services in Japan. The Action Program for Improved Market Access announced on July 30, 1985, adopted a policy of removal or relaxation of barriers in service industries such as transportation, insurance, and data and information services. As a result of pressure brought to bear by Japan's principal trading partners, especially the United States, Japan has adopted specific reforms relating to financial services, legal services, and construction activity.

§ 7–2. FINANCIAL SERVICES

In the 1980s, Japan began a thoroughgoing liberalization of its

---

[1] The term "services" includes virtually any economic activity that is not a physical unit or goods. For purposes of international trade, the services of chief importance include primarily banking, insurance, accounting, law, education, entertainment, transport, information services, engineering, data processing, construction, and financial services.

[2] See Berg, "Trade in Services: Toward a 'Development Round' of GATT Negotiations Benefiting Both Developing and Industrialized States," *Harvard International Law Journal*, Vol. 28, p. 1 (1987). The GATT presently regulates only trade in goods.

financial markets and the financial services industry that has markedly and rapidly improved access for foreign firms. This new policy has concentrated on achieving (1) the internationalization of the yen as one of the major currencies of the world; (2) the liberalization of interest rates; (3) greater access for foreign companies to Japanese money markets; (4) greater ease of establishment by foreign banks and securities companies; and (5) the introduction of a greater variety of investment vehicles and opportunities.[3]

The Japanese financial system includes several different types of institutions:

1. Commercial banks. There are 13 city banks, all of which rank among the largest in the world, as well as 63 local banks. Both categories of banks are permitted to have branches. The primary business of commercial banks is short-term lending, typically for less than one year, although rollover credit and renewals of loans are common. Loans to industry are the major assets of commercial banks as well as their primary source of income.

2. Special banks. There are special banks to fulfill specialized financial needs. Three long-term credit banks, the Industrial Bank of Japan, the Nippon Credit Bank, and the Long Term Credit Bank of Japan, specialize in long-term credit. These banks are allowed to raise money through the issuance of bank debentures.[4] Trust banks, another specialized category, have as their main function the management of money and securities investment trusts, pension funds, and loan trusts.[5] There are also foreign

[3] See, generally, Tahiro, "Legal Restrictions on Financial Operations and Recent Trends," *Japan Business Law Letter*, Volume 1, No. 5, pp. 1–5 (1989); Kawamura, "Recent Legal Issues under Japanese Securities Regulations," *Japan Business Law Letter*, Vol. 1, No. 5, pp. 6–12 (1989); Yagi, "Liberalization of Japanese Financial Markets," in *U.S.-Japan Relations: New Attitudes for a New Era* (Harvard University Annual Review 1983–84), p. 85. See also B. Robins, *Tokyo, A World Financial Center* (1987).

[4] The activities of these banks is regulated by the MOF under the authority of the Long Term Credit Bank Law (Chōki Shin'yō Ginkō Hō), Law 187, 1952.

[5] These banks are subject to regulation under the Trust Business Law (Shintaku-gyō Hō), Law 65, 1922; the Trust Law (Shintaku Hō), Law 62, 1923; the Law on Trust Business of Ordinary Banks (Futsū Ginkō no Shintaku Gyōmu no Ken'ei Tō ni kansuru Hōritsu), Law 43, 1943; and the Loan Trust Law (Kashitsuke Shintaku Hō), Law 195, 1952.

exchange banks that specialize in international commerce, such as the Bank of Tokyo.[6]

3. Specialized financial and regional institutions. A variety of specialized institutions serve medium and small business and a range of needs. These are mutual savings and loan banks (*sōgō ginkō*), credit associations, and credit cooperatives.

4. Financial institutions to serve agriculture, forestry, and fisheries. These are specialized banks to serve the needs of the principal rural industries of Japan.

5. Securities companies. These are joint stock corporations licensed by the MOF to engage in several different activities: (a) the underwriting of securities; (b) distribution of securities to the public; (c) brokerage activities; and (d) dealing and trading in securities for one's own account (*jikobaibai*). Securities companies are regulated under the Securities Exchange Law (SEL) of 1948,[7] which is modeled on the federal securities laws of the United States[8] and embraces both securities registration and the licensing of broker-dealers and exchanges. Securities finance companies (*shōken kin'yū kaisha*), also regulated under the SEL, provide securities companies with necessary funds through loans.

6. Insurance companies. These companies, regulated under the Insurance Business Law of 1939, are important sources of investment funds for long- and short-term lending and the purchase of government bonds.

7. Government financial institutions. These entities provide loans to supplement private lending institutions in certain areas of economic activity. Important examples are the Export-Import Bank of Japan and the Japan Development Bank.

8. The postal savings (*yūbin chokin*) system. This system is a government-owned financial institution catering to small savers controlled by the Ministry of Posts and Telecommunications.

Formerly rigidly compartmentalized, the distinctions between

---

[6] The Bank of Tokyo is regulated under the Foreign Exchange Bank Law (Gaikoku Kawase Ginkō Hō), Law 67, 1954. Article 11 of the Control Law permits the MOF to license other banks to engage in the foreign exchange business as well. See supra § 5–2.

[7] Foreign securities firms are regulated by the Law of Foreign Securities Dealers as well as cabinet orders and ministerial decrees promulgated thereunder.

[8] The Securities Act, 1933, 15 U.S.C. § 77a et seq.; The Securities Exchange Act, 1934, 15 U.S.C. 78a et seq.

the categories of financial intermediaries have broken down in recent years with the liberalization of the economy. As a result, commercial banks now engage in specialized banking activities, such as trust banking and dealing in foreign exchange. A distinction that still remains, however, is the separation of banking and securities businesses. Inspired by the Glass-Steagall Act in the United States, article 65 of the SEL generally prohibits banks and other financial institutions from engaging in the securities business.[9] However, as in the United States,[10] this prohibition has been loosened in recent years. In Japan, banks may engage in the trading of commercial paper, certificates of deposit, and other short-term debt;[11] may underwrite, purchase, and sell government bonds; and may purchase and sell securities for investment purposes, for the account of a truster, or upon the written order of a customer.[12] Moreover, at present the artificial separation between banking and securities business is considered an anachronism and contrary to the spirit of liberalization of the financial markets in Japan. This separation operates less to the benefit of shareholders of banks than it does to guarantee a monopoly to securities firms. The prohibition is expected to be repealed soon, leading to increased competition in the financial services industry.

The MOF is the principal government agency involved in overseeing and regulating Japan's financial system. It has seven bureaus (kyoku): (1) the Banking Bureau (Ginkō Kyoku); (2) the International Finance Bureau (Kokusai Kin'yū Kyoku); (3) the Securities Bureau (Shōken Kyoku); (4) the Budget Bureau (Shukei Kyoku); (5) the Tax Bureau (Shuzei Kyoku); (6) the Finance Bureau (Rizai Kyoku), which administers the central government's borrowing and issuance of government bonds and short-term government bills; and (7) the Customs Tariff Bureau (Kanzei Kyoku).

[9] Banking Act, 1933, § 15, 12 U.S.C. § 24(7).

[10] See, e.g., Securities Indus. Assn. v. Board of Governors of the Federal Reserve System, 468 U.S. 207 (1984).

[11] This is permitted because under the SEL art. 2(1) they fall outside the definition of a "security."

[12] These activities are specifically exempt from the prohibition of art. 65. SEL 65(2). See Whitener, "The Steady Erosion of Japan's Glass-Steagall," International Financial Law Review, Vol. 11 (May 1988).

The Banking Bureau is divided into nine divisions *(ka)*. The Coordination Division oversees the Bank of Japan (BOJ) and supervises interest rates. The Commercial Bank Division licenses and supervises banks, including branches of foreign banks.

The Bank of Japan, Japan's central bank, is a public corporation, the majority of whose stock is owned by the government.[13] The BOJ, which administers Japanese monetary and exchange rate policy, has sixteen departments, the most important of which is the Foreign Department's Foreign Exchange Division, which monitors all international banking transactions by receiving notifications required under the Foreign Exchange and Foreign Trade Control Law (Control Law).[14] The BOJ often acts informally through "administrative guidance" known as "window guidance" *(madoguchi shidō)*.

The liberalization of Japan's financial and capital markets accelerated in 1979 with the passage of the Control Law. This law removed the presumption that all external capital transactions were prohibited; now government regulators must affirmatively intervene based on objective principles to prohibit external transactions.[15] A second important liberalization law was the Bank Law of 1981, which placed foreign banks on an equal regulatory footing with domestic banks and gave banks the right to sell government securities to the public.[16]

The pace of liberalization increased when on May 29, 1984, the Yen/Dollar Agreement was signed by Japan and the United States under which Japan committed itself to liberalize its domestic capital markets and to remove barriers to foreign entry into the domestic financial services industry.[17]

As a result of this agreement and domestic decisions to internationalize the financial markets, the following measures have been taken:

[13] The BOJ is controlled under the Bank of Japan Law, Law 67, 1942.

[14] See supra §5–2.

[15] See supra Id.

[16] See Shimojo, "The New Banking Law of Japan: Securities Business by Banks," *UCLA Pacific Basin Law Journal*, Vol. 1, p. 83 (1982); Semkow, "Japanese Banking Law: Current Deregulation and Liberalization of Domestic and External Financial Transactions," *Law and Policy in International Business*, Vol. 17, p. 81 (1985).

[17] Report by the Working Group of the Joint Japan-U.S. Ad Hoc Group on Yen/Dollar Exchange Rate, 29 May 1984, reprinted in *Oriental Economist*, July 1984, p. 22.

1. Interest rate liberalization. In order to develop domestic capital markets, interest rate regulation was eliminated on large denomination certificates of deposit (¥10 billion or greater) as well as money market certificates greater than ¥10 million with a maturity of two years or more. Smaller deposits comprising about 50 percent of savings deposits are still subject to interest rate regulation, but in 1987 the government eliminated the tax exemption for small-denomination deposits.

2. Foreign financial institutions access to Japanese markets. Great progress has been made in opening Japanese financial markets to foreign firms. In compliance with the 1984 Yen/Dollar Agreement, national treatment has been accorded to such firms. As a result, foreign banks and securities companies have been licensed to do business in Japan; foreign banks were licensed to perform trust banking functions in Japan, including six U.S. banks; foreign firms were licensed to perform investment advisory functions in Japan; U.S. and other foreign-owned securities companies were admitted to the Tokyo Stock Exchange; and the affiliates of seven U.S. banks were licensed to engage in securities activities. In the latter case foreign banks were permitted to perform operations barred to Japanese banks under article 65 of the SEL. In order to avoid this prohibition, each U.S. bank operates through a branch of an offshore subsidiary that is at most 50 percent owned by the banking concern; the remaining interest in the subsidiary must be owned by a nonfinancial company. Several European so-called universal banks—institutions that can both underwrite securities and conduct commercial banking in their home countries—are also permitted to operate in this manner. Several foreign banks now participate in three aspects of Japanese financial markets: they conduct commercial and trust banking as well as securities operations.

3. The development of new financial markets. As a result of the yen/dollar accord, a great many new financial markets have been created in Japan:

(1) New markets for yen-based bankers' acceptances, short-term government debt, and commercial paper.

(2) Swap limits on converting foreign currencies into yen for branches of foreign and Japanese banks have been abolished.

(3) Non-Japanese banks are permitted to deal in government

securities in the secondary bond markets. The MOF is studying the admission of foreign banks to primary dealer status for government securities.

(4) The MOF has abolished restrictions on so-called Samurai bonds, yen-quoted debt securities issued in Japan by offshore borrowers. This allows yen loans to be made abroad by Japanese and non-Japanese banks.

(5) Restrictions have been lifted for foreign issuers of "shōgun" bonds, foreign currency denominated bonds sold in Japan.

(6) The Euroyen market (yen-denominated bonds sold offshore) has been liberalized and is of growing importance, allowing issuers to raise yen funds deposited outside Japan.

(7) The market for foreign currency futures was liberalized in April 1984.

(8) The domestic straight bond market has been liberalized to allow shelf registration and to eliminate restrictive trading rules.

(9) In May 1988, the Financial Futures Trading Bill was passed to permit the trading in Japan of financial futures similar to those traded on international markets.

(10) In 1988, the MOF announced liberalized rules on Euroyen certificates of deposit (CD) that will permit extended maturities of up to two years.[18]

(11) In response to objections from the United States, Japan has adopted a new rule improving foreign access to underwriting and distributing ten-year government bonds. A 40-percent portion of ten-year government bond issues will be offered for competitive price tenders by members of underwriting syndicates. The remaining 60 percent will be determined by the competitive bidding process.

As a result of these measures, Japan has accomplished the almost complete deregulation of its formerly restrictive policy concerning international financial regulations. Tokyo has taken its place with London and New York as a leading center of international finance. As a result, "internationalization" of the yen—promotion of its use in international trade finance—is

---

[18] The issuer of a Euroyen CD must be either a foreign bank or an offshore branch of a Japanese bank. The sale of a Euroyen CD in Japan is prohibited.

proceeding apace. Further liberalization in coming years is inevitable.[19]

§ 7–3. LEGAL SERVICES

From 1949 to 1955 under the Attorney Law[20] of 1949 foreign lawyers were permitted to qualify and practice law.[21] In 1955, however, the special position of foreign attorneys was repealed, and unless they fully qualify to practice law by fulfilling the requirements applicable to Japanese citizens, they were prohibited from performing most legal functions.[22] Because of the 1 to 2 percent pass rate on the bar examination and the difficulty of the written language, virtually no foreign attorneys were able to qualify to practice law in Japan after 1955.

In 1986, however, in response to American and foreign pressure,[23] the Japanese Diet passed the Special Measures Law Concerning the Handling of Legal Business by Foreign Lawyers, which recognized a limited role for foreign lawyers (*gaikokuhō jimu-bengoshi*).[24]

The Special Measures Law requires a foreign attorney who desires admission to practice as a foreign law *jimu-bengoshi* to file an application with the Minister of Justice.[25] An applicant

---

[19] See Current Plans for the Liberalization and Internationalization of Japanese Financial and Capital Markets, announced by the MOF on 4 June 1987, *The Japan Economic Journal*, 13 June 1987, p. 5.

[20] Bengoshi Hō, Law 205, 1949, Art. 7.

[21] There were two levels of practice recognized. First, foreign attorneys who passed a special examination were permitted to practice Japanese law. Second, foreign attorneys in good standing in their home countries could advise home country citizens on Japanese law and citizens not of their home country on the law of the home country.

[22] Article 7 was repealed. Law Concerning the Partial Amendment of the Attorney Law (Bengoshi Hō no Ichibu Kaisei), Law 155, 1955. Under section 72 of the Attorney Law, non-lawyers cannot present legal opinions or provide representation with respect to lawsuits or non-contentious legal matters. Attorneys who qualified in Japan prior to 1955, however, were permitted to continue under a grandfather clause in the law.

Under the Japan-U.S. FCN Treaty, American attorneys may handle specific legal tasks for their American clients in Japan. Treaty of Friendship, Commerce, and Navigation, 2 April 1953, U.S.-Japan, art. VIII para. 1, 2 U.S.T. 2063, T.I.A.S. No. 2863.

[23] See Ramseyer, "Lawyers, Foreign Lawyer, and Lawyer Substitutes: The Market for Regulation in Japan, *Harvard International Law Journal*, Volume 27, No. 499 (1986).

[24] Gaikoku Bengoshi ni yoru Hōritsu Jimu no Toriatsukai ni kansuru Tokubetsu Sochi Hō. Law 66, 1986.

[25] Id., art. 9(1) and (2).

can be denied admission to practice on several grounds, including lack of good standing in the applicant's home country and lack of an adequate financial basis.[26] Moreover, the application will not be approved unless the attorney has practiced for at least five years in his home country and if the applicant's home country does not extend to Japanese attorneys "substantially equivalent treatment."[27] For American attorneys, this reciprocity requirement means that an attorney may receive approval only if the state in which he is admitted to practice accepts foreign lawyers as legal consultants.

Once approved to practice, an applicant must apply for a requisite "designation" as to the foreign country on whose laws he or she is qualified to give advice and also must register with Nichibenren (Nihon Bengoshi Rengōkai), the Japan Federation of Bar Associations, and comes under its supervision.[28]

Once admitted to practice, foreign lawyers must reside in Japan at least 180 days per year, must not open more than one office in Japan, and cannot employ or enter into partnership with a *bengoshi*.[29]

Foreign lawyers admitted to practice may give advice relating only to their own countries. Attorneys from federal countries like the United States may give advice only on federal law and the laws of their home state unless other states are specifically designated by the Ministry of Justice.[30] The discipline of foreign lawyers admitted to practice is in the hands of Nichibenren.[31]

Despite some criticism,[32] the Special Measures Law is an important liberalization measure that has made it possible for foreign lawyers to establish permanent offices in Japan.

§ 7–4. PUBLIC WORKS

On May 25, 1988, after two years of negotiations, Japan and

---

[26] Id., art. 10.

[27] Id.

[28] Id., arts. 24, 25.

[29] Id., arts. 45, 48, 49.

[30] Id., art. 3. All the states of the United States are in fact so designated.

[31] Id., art. 55.

[32] See Comment, "Japan's New Foreign Lawyer Law," *Law and Policy in International Business*, Vol. 19, p. 361 (1987); Comment, *Columbia Journal of Transnational Law*, Vol. 26, p. 220 (1987).

the United States signed an agreement to give foreign construction firms access to 15 major public works projects to be constructed in Japan over the next 15 years (Table 1). This is the first step in giving foreign construction firms the experience to enter the Japanese public market on a non-discriminatory basis.

TABLE 1 PROJECTS COVERED BY THE JAPAN–U.S. AGREEMENT ON CONSTRUCTION WORK

Project	Time Period	Total Value (Excludes land cost) (¥)	Estimated U.S. Commercial Opportunity (¥)
Kansai Int'l. Airport	1987–93	300 billion	300 billion
Tokyo Bay Bridge	1987–95	750 billion	750 billion
Haneda Airport		Overall value unknown	230 billion
Phase II	1987–95	Terminal 120 billion	
Phase III	1990–95	Phase III 110 billion	
Hiroshima Airport	1980–93	Overall value unknown	44.5 billion
Kitakyushu Airport	To start in 10 years		0
Chūbū Airport	Not yet approved		0
Narita Airport Expansion	1986–90	600 billion	?
Akashi Straits Bridge	1986–98	393 billion	325 billion
Tokyo Port Redevelopment	From 1984	3.4 trillion (teleport 1.9 trillion)	66 billion
Minato Mirai 21 (Yokohama)	1988–93	230.8 billion	58.9 billion
Kansai Science & Cultural Center	1988–93	713 billion	270 billion
Ise Bay Bridge	1987–96	88 billion	88 billion
Osaka Technoport	Completed by 1989		0
Rokko Island	Completed by 1990		0
NTT Intelligent Building		26 billion	26 billion
Total available			2198.4 billion (US $16.9 billion)

Source: "New Agreement Gives U.S. Firms Access to Fourteen Major Japanese Projects," *Business America*, 6 June 1988, p. 8.

Foreign firms are expected to concentrate on high-technology aspects of construction projects in Japan.

The agreement provides for agreed-upon time limits to submit bids after publication of bid opportunities, appeal procedures, and the monitoring of contracts awarded. International experience in construction activities would be considered equivalent to Japanese experience for purposes of qualification for contracts.

Firms desiring to win construction contracts in Japan are required to obtain contractors' licenses as specified in the Construction Business Law. Both branch offices and subsidiary companies of foreign construction firms are eligible to apply. The application and bidding procedures are described in detail in *A Guide to Construction in Japan*, compiled by the Ministry of Construction and the Research Institutes of Construction and Economy (1988).

CHAPTER EIGHT

INTELLECTUAL PROPERTY

§ 8–1. Introduction: Trade in Technology

International technology transfer is a multifaceted process that encompasses a wide range of sales and licensing of intellectual property, equipment, technical services, training programs, and exchanges of information and personnel.

Trade in technology, whether in the form of a licensing agreement, a joint venture, or a technical assistance agreement, is subject to several regulatory constraints in Japan. The negotiation of such agreements requires familiarity with not only the applicable commercial and contract laws but also the Foreign Exchange and Foreign Trade Control Law (Control Law), the Antimonopoly Law (AML), and the intellectual property laws of Japan.

In negotiating a licensing or technology transfer agreement, the parties are in principle free to choose the applicable governing law.[1] Despite this, however, if intellectual property rights registered in Japan are the subject of the license, the substance of the rights transferred will be determined by the Japanese intellectual property statutes. Foreign-registered intellectual property rights must be registered in Japan to be recognized and protected. As a member of the 1883 Paris Convention on Protection of Industrial Property,[2] Japan extends to foreign owners of industrial property from countries that have reciprocal rights with Japan a priority period of six months in which to apply for registration of industrial designs and trademarks and

---

[1] Act Concerning the Application of Laws (Hōrei), art. 7(1).
[2] Jōyaku (Treaty) No. 2, 1975.

twelve months in which to apply for registration of patents and utility models. Foreign firms are advised to seek broad protection of intellectual property rights through early compliance with Japanese registration requirements. Disputes between Japanese and foreign companies over intellectual property rights have arisen primarily because of the lengthy processing time for patent applications in Japan and their narrow scope of coverage. Reforms should be undertaken to harmonize the difference between intellectual property rights in Japan and other industrialized countries.

§ 8–2. The Administrative Regulation of Technology Transfer Contracts

Before 1980, the old Control Law and the Foreign Investment Law[3] was used by governmental authorities both to restrict international technology transfers and to effect the most beneficial terms possible for the Japanese parties involved. At the present time, however, with the enactment in 1979 of the new Control Law,[4] Japan no longer exercises any significant degree of substantive restraint on technology transfer except with respect to export controls on weapon, nuclear, and certain other technologies for national security purposes.[5] Nevertheless, there are significant reporting provisions that must be complied with in concluding any technology transfer contract. These reporting requirements have been greatly simplified and rationalized.

First, the new Control Law requires any technology induction contract to be reported in advance of concluding the contract to the Bank of Japan (BOJ) and the appropriate governmental ministry.[6] This reporting requirement is normally carried out by filing an appropriate form with the Foreign Department of the BOJ.

---

[3] Gaishi ni kansuru Hōritsu, Law 163, 1950.

[4] In 1979, the Diet combined the function of both laws into the new Control Law.

[5] See Comment, "The Administrative Regulation of Technology Induction Contracts in Japan," *Northwestern Journal of International Law and Business*, Vol. 8, p. 197 (1987); Shibuya, "The Administrative Regulation of Transfer of Technology in Japan," *European Intellectual Property Review*, Vol. 1, p. 18 (1982); Sharp, "The Japanese Licensing Environment," *Technology Licensing*, pp. 235–65 (1985).

[6] New Control Law, art. 29.

The notification forms require the following information: (1) the names, addresses, and type of business of the reporting parties; (2) the type of technology; (3) the period of the contract; (4) the payment scheme; (5) an outline of the agreement; (6) the content of the technology; (7) the purpose of the agreement; (8) a summary of the industrial property rights involved; and (9) the production plans. In addition, for twelve especially designated technologies—aircraft, arms, gunpowder, atomic energy, space development, electronic computers, electronic parts for electronic computers of the next generation, appliances for laser processing and light communication, innovative materials technology, salt electrolysis by non-mercurial methods, offshore petroleum production, and leather or leather products[7]—the BOJ will generally request a complete copy of the technology transfer contract. Especially with respect to the designated technologies, the applicants should consult beforehand with officials of the BOJ in order to submit information and prepare for later formal notification.

The purpose of this reporting requirement is primarily information gathering, although the government has authority to restrict or suspend transactions that imperil the national security, disturb the public order, or adversely affect domestic business.[8] In most cases with respect to undesignated technology, an application filled with the BOJ is likely to be accepted at once, and the parties, will be free to conclude the contract the very next day. With respect to designated technologies, however, a waiting period of two weeks after formal acceptance of the application is normally imposed. Administrative guidance—informal advice and instruction—may be used by the BOJ or ministry officials in connection with the approval process, especially with respect to the designated technologies.

Outbound technology transfer is also subject to a notification requirement.[9] Licensing is not required, however, unless the technology falls within the scope of those strategic items that

---

[7] Id. and MOF Notification No. 118 of 28 Nov. 1980.

[8] New Control Law, arts. 29, 30.

[9] Id., art. 251. Outbound technology transfer or cross-licensing arrangements are regarded as service contracts.

MITI has designated as subject to export controls.[10] Those are primarily nuclear and defense technologies and other important high-technology systems.[11]

A second notification requirement placed upon technology induction contracts in Japan is the filing of a report concerning the agreement with the FTC under the AML.[12] This report, which must be filed within 30 days of concluding the agreement by the Japanese party, allows the FTC to review the contract to determine whether it complies with the AML. If the FTC determines that there is an "unreasonable restraint of trade" or an "unfair trade practice," it will usually request voluntary deletion of the offending provision through administrative guidance. If the administrative guidance is not accepted, the FTC may issue an official recommendation or begin formal administrative proceedings.[13]

§ 8–3. Patents and Utility Models

The Patent Office (Tokkyochō) is a division of MITI. Patent applications are examined by officials according to standards promulgated by the Patent Office.[14] Under the Patent Law,[15] "inventions" (*hatsumei*) are patentable, including both new and improved products and processes.[16] In order to be patentable,

---

[10] The New Control Law, art. 25, requires prior licensing of service transactions "considered to be obstructive to the faithful performance of treaties . . . or the maintenance of peace and international security."

[11] See Export Trade Control Order, Cabinet Order 387 (1 Dec. 1984).

[12] Article 6(1) of the AML prohibits businesses from entering into international agreements containing terms constituting an unreasonable restraint of trade or an unfair trade practice. Article 6(2) requires a report of any international agreement to be filed with the FTC within 30 days. For a complete discussion of the AML, see Ch. 6.

[13] E.g., Novo Industri v. FTC, *Gyōsai Reishū*, Vol. 22, p. 761 (Tokyo H. Ct., 19 May 1971); Novo Industri v. FTC, *Hanrei Jihō*, No. 800, p. 35 (Sup. Ct., 28 Nov. 1975).

[14] See *Shinsa Kijun no Tebiki* (Guidelines for Examination Standards) (Patent Office, 1980).

[15] Tokkyo Hō, Law 121, 1959; tr. in R. Foster and M. Ono, *The Patent and Trademark Laws of Japan* (1970). For commentary, see T. Doi, *The Intellectual Property Law of Japan* (1980); A. Kukimoto, *Summary of Japanese Patent Law* (1971). See also Note, "The Role of the Patent System in Technology Transfer: The Japanese Experience," *Columbia Journal of Transnational Law*, Vol. 26, p. 131 (1987).

[16] Id., art. 2. Pharmaceuticals, food and beverage products, and chemical compounds were excluded before 1976, when these limitations were removed. Art. 32

an invention must meet the legal criteria of (1) novelty, (2) utility, and (3) inventiveness.[17] The requirement of novelty means
that an invention goes beyond the "prior art." Utility requires
a showing that the product or process is capable of being
utilized in industry. The requirement of an inventive step
means that the patent office examiner will compare the applicant's invention with the prior art in purpose, construction,
and effect and determine if it is a real advance in all three
respects. The Patent Law of Japan is supplemented by the
Utility Model Law, which protects new products and processes
that may fall short of meeting the requirements under the Patent
Law.[18] The Utility Model Law, which is also administered by the
Patent Office, provides that an invention may be registered if
it meets the requirements of novelty, utility, and inventiveness,
but the inventiveness requirement is satisfied "when a device
is such that it could have quite easily been made by a person
having ordinary knowledge in the technical field to which such
device pertains."

An application for a patent or utility model may be filed by
any person who has made an invention or is the assignee of the
right to obtain a patent. A foreign national may apply for a
patent if he is a resident, or in the case of a corporation, is established in Japan. A non-resident is not entitled to a patent unless
his country gives Japanese nationals the right to apply for patents on the basis of reciprocity. Japan maintains reciprocity
with most nations of the world under the International Convention for the Protection of Industrial Property (the Paris Convention)[19] as well as many treaties of friendship, commerce, and
navigation. Japan has accepted the Patent Cooperation Treaty
of 1970, and the Patent Office employs the International Patent
Classification System under the Strassbourg Agreement of March
24, 1971.

Once a patent is granted by the Patent Office, it is effective

now excludes only invention spertaining to the transformation of atomic nuclei and
inventions likely to harm the public order, good morals, or public hygiene.

[17] Id., art. 29.

[18] Jitsuyō Shin'an Hō, Law 123, 1959.

[19] Paris Convention of 20 March 1883, 25 Stat. 1372, T.S. No. 379, 161 Parry's
T.S. 409.

for 15 years from the date of publication of the application. Utility model rights confer an exclusive right to work the registered device for ten years from the date of publication of the application. Patent and utility model rights are assignable under an exclusive or non-exclusive basis. The assignment must be registered with the Patent Office in order to be effective against a third party and to allow the assignee to bring an infringement action in his own name.[20]

The Patent Law gives priority to the first filer, not to the first inventor. Nevertheless, a person who first invented and used the invention independently of the patentee may continue to use it in his business on a non-exclusive basis.[21] The Patent Office may require a compulsory license of a patented invention if the invention has not been properly worked for more than three years[22] or if there is a strong need to satisfy the public interest.[23]

Unpatentable know-how, trade secrets, and technology may be protected in Japan through the conclusion of contractual arrangements and restrictive covenants between a licensor and a licensee. An agreement or covenant not to disclose trade secrets or know-how is enforceable despite the fact that the matters involved are not patentable.[24]

The patent system poses problems for foreign firms wishing to enter the Japanese market and to protect their patent rights against infringement. First, under the Japanese system it is possible to patent a relatively minor change in existing technology. Thus it is often not possible to protect an invention from imitation by competitors. Second, under the Japanese system patent applications must be accompanied by detailed dossiers disclosing all "prior art." This material is available for public inspection. Third, a patent application may take up to six years to be approved, an inordinately long time. The time has come to har-

---

[20] Patent Law, art. 98.
[21] Id., arts. 72 and 79.
[22] Id., art. 83.
[23] Id., art. 93.
[24] Deutsche Werft Aktiengesellschaft v. Cheutsu-Waukesha Yugen Kaisha, *Kakyū Minshū*, Vol. 17, p. 769 (Tokyo H. Ct., 5 Sept. 1966); Yugen Kaisha Foreco Japan Ltd. v. Okuno and Daimatsu, *Hanrei Jihō*, No. 624, p. 78 (Nara Dist. Ct., 23 Oct. 1970). See Doi, "The Role of Intellectual Property Law in Bilateral Licensing Transactions Between Japan and the United States," in *Law and Trade Issues of the Japanese Economy*, G. Saxonhouse and K. Yamamura, eds., p. 157 (1986).

monize Japanese laws with those of its trading partners, especially with the United States and European countries.

§ 8–4. UNFAIR BUSINESS PRACTICES IN PATENT AND KNOW-HOW LICENSING AGREEMENTS

In 1968, the FTC first announced guidelines on patent and know-how licensing agreements concluded between foreign and Japanese enterprises. In the two decades after the announcement of these guidelines, the circumstances surrounding technology transfer between Japanese and foreign enterprises have changed dramatically. Whereas, in the former days, Japanese enterprises were primarily receivers of technology from abroad, they are now in the position to license technology to foreign enterprises as well as receive it. Also, the weight of transfer of technology among enterprises in the domestic market has increased tremendously. Due to these changes, the old guidelines became somewhat obsolete. In light of this changed business environment, the FTC drafted a new set of guidelines, which were published on February 15, 1989.

The guidelines are entitled "Guidelines on the Regulation of Unfair Business Practices in Patent and Know-How Licensing Agreements" (hereafter referred to as Guidelines) and have some distinct features in comparison with the old guidelines.

The guidelines enumerate the major items in patent and know-how licensing agreements which the FTC considers as falling under unfair business practices as provided for in article 2(9) of the AML and as designated by the FTC. The Guidelines are divided into two parts: (1) unfair business practices in patent licensing agreements and (2) unfair business practices in know-how licensing agreements. The Guidelines are designed to be applied to both domestic and international patent and know-how licensing agreements in which unfair business practices are involved. It should be emphasized that the Guidelines provide for only typical items which frequently appear in patent and know-how licensing agreements and which constitute unfair business practices. They are by no means an exhaustive list of items which may be held liable under the AML.

Under the AML, three basic categories of conduct are held

unlawful: (1) private monopolization, (2) unreasonable restraint of trade, and (3) unfair business practices. The Guidelines deal only with typical items in patent and know-how licensing agreements which may possibly fall under the category of unfair business practices. There may be additional problems of private monopolization and unreasonable restraint of trade, which are considered separately in Chapter 6.

1. THE STRUCTURE OF THE GUIDELINES

The Guidelines classify the items contained in patent and know-how licensing agreements into three categories. In the first category are those items which are lawful in principle. Contract terms which fall into this category are usually lawful unless there are special circumstances which would make them unreasonable. In the second category, there are items which may be held unlawful depending on the circumstances. In this category, there is no presumption of legality or illegality. The legality or illegality of each item in this category is determined after various factors have been weighed, such as the relative powers of the parties, the condition of competition in the relevant market, the conditions of the market in question, and the length of the contract in question. Items falling into this category are judged by a "rule of reason."

In the third category, the items which are likely to be held unlawful are enumerated. Those items are unlawful in principle (if not illegal per se), unless there are some special reasons which exonerate them. The items contained in this category are presumed to be unlawful.

It is mentioned in the Preamble that the Guidelines are applied to contractual terms as long as they affect the Japanese market. Therefore, even if in an international patent and know-how licensing agreement a restrictive condition is imposed on a foreign party amounting to unfair business practice, such a condition may be held illegal by the FTC if it produces some effect on the Japanese market. For example, if a Japanese licensor imposes a condition on a foreign licensee of a patent that the latter must purchase parts and components from the licensor in producing a product in which a licensed technology is utilized, other Japanese suppliers of parts and components will be excluded from supplying the foreign licensee, and there is an impact on the Japanese market. In this situation, the Guidelines will apply.

The old guidelines were applicable only to those agreements in which Japanese parties were the licensees and restrictive conditions were imposed on the Japanese parties. The old guidelines were, in a way, employed to protect domestic enterprises vis-à-vis the abusive conduct of powerful foreign enterprises. However, the Guidelines make it clear that foreign and domestic enterprises are treated equally.

2. PATENT LICENSING AGREEMENTS

In this section, various items which are contained in patent licensing agreements are examined and the enforcement policy is shown. Although an item-by-item analysis in the Guidelines refers only to "patent" licensing, it is mentioned also that the term "patent" inclur es "utility model right" as well.

1. Items That Are Lawful in Principle

1. To grant the license of a patent only for manufacture, use, or sale.

2. To grant the license only for a certain time within the period in which the patent is valid.

3. To grant the license only within a limited territory within an area in which the patent is valid.

4. To grant the license only in a certain area of technology.

5. To set a minimum quantity on the manufacture or sale of the patented product or a minimum frequency of the use of a process patent.

6. To impose on the licensee the obligation to inform the licensor of the knowledge and experience which the licensee has acquired with respect to the licensed technology or the obligation to grant to the licensor a non-exclusive license of the improvement inventions or applied inventions, provided that the rights and obligations of the parties are balanced.

7. To require, within the necessary limit, the licensee to maintain a certain level of quality of the patented products, raw materials, or components in order to guarantee the usefulness of the licensed patent (that is, when the licensor has guaranteed the

licensee a certain degree of usefulness of the licensed patent) or the good will of the trademark or other representations (on the condition that the licensor has granted a licensee the use of a mark).

8. To impose an obligation on the licensee to purchase raw materials, parts, and related items from the licensor or a party designated by the licensor when it is difficult to maintain the good will of the trademark or other representations or the use of the licensed technology by the standards set for the quality of raw materials, components, or related items.

9. To restrict the export by the licensee of the patented products to one of the following areas: (a) where the licensor has registered the patent that covers the patented product, (b) where the licensor is constantly engaged in the sales activity of the patented product, or (c) where the licensor has granted the exclusive right to sell the patented product to a third party.

10. To impose on the licensee a restriction of export price or quantity or an obligation to export through the licensor or a party designated by the licensor when the export area falls within area (a), (b), or (c) as specified above, provided that the restrictions and obligations are reasonable.

11. To use, for the sake of convenience in computing royalties, the quantities of manufacture/sale of the finished product or the value thereof as the basis for computation when the licensed patent relates to a part of the manufacturing process or to components or to use the amount or frequency of use of raw materials or components necessary to manufacture the patented product as the basis for computation.

12. To require the licensee to accept a license of a plural number of patents en bloc to the extent necessary to guarantee the usefulness of the licensed patent.

13. To stipulate that the obligation of the licensee to pay royalties shall continue after the expiration of the patent to the extent that such payment is recognized as installment payment or deferred payment of royalties on the patent.

14. To provide that the license agreement can be canceled when the licensee contests the validity of the licensed patent.

15. To oblige licensees to exert their best efforts in utilizing the licensed technology.

2. Items That May Be Held Unlawful

1. To prohibit, during the term of the license agreement, the licensee from handling competing products or adopting the competing technology.

Note: This item is held unlawful when the business opportunity of competing enterprises or the freedom of the licensee to choose products and technology is unduly restricted and thereby competition is lessened.

2. To impose on the licensee the condition that the licensee sell the patented product through the licensor or a party designated by the licensor or not to sell to a party designated by the licensor.

Note: This item is held unlawful when it unduly deprives the licensee of the freedom to choose sales outlets and thereby reduces competition in the market of the patented product.

3. To impose on the licensee the obligation to inform the licensor of knowledge or experiences which the licensee has acquired with respect to the licensed technology or to grant to the licensor a non-exclusive license of the improvement inventions or applied inventions which the licensee has accomplished, except for cases in which the licensor's obligations are similar in kind and the obligations of both of the parties are balanced.

Note: This item is held unlawful if the licensor has not assumed similar obligations as those imposed on the licensee or the contents are unbalanced and unduly disadvantageous conditions are thereby imposed on the licensee.

4. To impose on the licensee an obligation to use the trademark or other representations designated by the licensor on the patented product.

Note: This item is held unlawful when the freedom of the licensee to choose the trademark or other representations is unduly restricted. Also, by this item, the licensee may have to keep using the trademark designated by the licensor after the patent has expired, and this may be regarded as an unreasonable condition attached to the license agreement.

5. To set the standard for the quality of raw materials, components, or the patented product, except for cases in which such a restriction is necessary to maintain the good will of the trademark or the usefulness of the licensed technology.

Note: This restriction is held unlawful when competition in

the market for raw materials and components or that of the patented product is unduly restrained.

6. To impose on the licensee an obligation to purchase raw materials or parts from the licensor or a party designated by the licensor, except for cases in which the maintenance of the good will of the trademark or the effective use of the licensed technology without restrictions on the quality of raw materials or components is difficult.

Note: This restriction is held unlawful when the freedom of the licensee to choose raw materials or components is unduly restricted or competition in the market for raw materials or components is unreasonably impaired.

7. To restrict the areas to which the licensee can export, except for cases in which the restricted areas are: (a) where the licensor has registered the patent, (b) where the licensor is continuously engaged in sales activities of the patented product, or (c) where the licensor has granted the exclusive right to sell to a third party.

8. To set the export price or quantity of the licensee or to obligate the licensee to export through the licensor or the party designated by the licensor, except for the cases in which the export area falls under (a), (b), or (c) listed above and in which the restriction or obligation is reasonable.

9. To require the licensee to pay royalties on products other than the patented product, except for cases in which the quantity of manufacture/sale of the finished product or the value of manufacture/sale thereof is used for the sake of convenience as the basis for computing royalties when the licensed patent relates to a part of the manufacturing process or to components or in which the quantity or frequency of the use of raw materials or components necessary to manufacture the patented product is used as the basis for computing royalties.

10. To require the licensee to accept a license of a plural number of patents en bloc, except for cases in which such a restriction is imposed to the extent necessary to guarantee the usefulness of the licensed patent.

11. To impose on the licensee a unilateral disadvantage in canceling a license agreement, such as to stipulate that the agreement is subject to immediate and unilateral cancellation, without

providing for an adequate grace period, for reasons other than the inability to perform (the agreement) on the part of the licensee due to insolvency or other justifiable causes.

12. To prohibit the licensee from contesting the validity of the patent.

Note: This item is held unlawful since if the patent is preserved on technology which is not patentable, the use of the technology by others is excluded thereby and competition is unduly restricted. It is also held unlawful if the licensee has to continue paying royalties on the technology which is in the public domain and which the licensee is entitled to use without paying royalties.

3. Items Which Are Likely To Be Held Unlawful

1. To set the resale price of the patented product in the domestic market.

Note: This restriction suppresses competition at the level of wholesalers and retailers of the patented product in the market and has no redeeming virtues. For this reason, this restriction is held to be unlawful in principle.

2. To set the sales price of the patented product in the domestic market.

Note: This item restricts the competitive ability of the licensee, and price competition of the patented product is suppressed. It is not absolutely necessary for the purpose of securing royalty payment. For the above reasons, this item is held unlawful in principle.

3. To prohibit the licensee from handling competing products or adopting competing technology after the term of the licensing agreement has expired.

Note: A restriction after the expiration of the licensing agreement cannot be justified for reasons of securing royalty payments and no other redeeming virtue is found. This item is likely to be held unlawful.

4. To prohibit the licensee from utilizing the technology incorporated in a patent, to restrict the use thereof after the patent has expired, or to impose the obligation on the licensee to pay royalties for use of the technology incorporated in a patent after the patent has expired.

5. To prohibit or restrict the licensee from engaging in research

and development either alone or jointly with others with regard to the licensed patent or competing technology.

6. To require the licensee to assign improvement inventions and applied inventions which have been achieved by the licensee to the licensor or to grant to the licensor an exclusive license thereof.

Note: This restriction tends to promote or maintain the market power of the licensor unduly and to limit the freedom of the licensee to use knowledge, experiences or improvements which have been developed by the licensee and to license them to third parties. This restriction also provides a disincentive to the licensee to engage in research and development and to promote the development of new technology. Also, if similar obligations are not imposed on the licensor, the licensor is deemed to be imposing unreasonable business conditions on the licensee. For this reason, this restriction is, in principle, held unlawful.

3. KNOW-HOW LICENSING AGREEMENTS

In this section, items involved in know-how licensing agreements are dealt with. The term "know-how" here means technological know-how which can be applied only in industrial technology and does not include knowledge or skill in management, marketing, and other non-technological matters.

1. Items That Are Lawful in Principle
1. To license know-how for a limited period.
2. To limit the application of know-how by the licensee within a certain technological field of use.
3. To set the minimum quantity for manufacture or sale by the licensee of the product in which the licensed know-how is incorporated or the minimum frequency of use of the know-how by the licensee.
4. To prohibit or restrict the licensee from handling a similar or substitute product which competes with the licensed product or adopting similar or substitute technology which competes with the licensed know-how for a short period (two years), when it is difficult to prevent the know-how from leaking out, by prohibiting its use after the expiration of the contract.
5. To require the licensee to report to the licensor knowledge

or experiences which the licensee has acquired with respect to the licensed know-how or to grant the licensor a non-exclusive license of improvement inventions or applied inventions which the licensee has developed, provided that the licensor bears similar obligations as the licensee and the substance of the obligations of the parties is generally balanced.

6. To set standards for the quality of raw materials and components or of the licensed product, provided that such standards are necessary to maintain the good will of the trademark or to secure the effective use of the licensed technology.

7. To require the licensee to purchase raw materials and components from the licensor or a party designated by the licensor, provided that the good will of the trademark or the effective use of the licensed technology cannot be maintained through other kinds of restriction or that such a restriction is necessary to maintain the confidentiality of the know-how, and provided that the obligations imposed remain within the scope necessary to guarantee the usefulness of the licensed know-how or to maintain the confidentiality of the know-how.

8. To prohibit the licensee from exporting to an area: (a) in which the licensor has registered the patent covering the licensed goods, (b) in which the licensor is constantly engaged in sales activities of the licensed product, or (c) in which the licensor has granted the exclusive right to sell the licensed product to a third party.

9. To set the export price or quantity of the licensed product exported by the licensee or to require the licensee to export through the licensor or a party designated by the licensor when the export areas restricted fall under any of the above-specified areas (a), (b), or (c).

10. To use, for the sake of convenience in computing royalties, the quantity of manufacture/sale of the finished product in which the licensed know-how or components are used or the quantity or frequency of use of raw materials or components thereof as the basis for computation when the licensed know-how relates to a part of the manufacturing process or to components.

11. To require the licensee to accept a license of plural items of know-how en bloc to the extent necessary to guarantee the usefulness of the licensed know-how.

12. To require the licensee to continue paying royalties for a short period during the term of the agreement after the licensed know-how becomes generally circulated, even though the licensee has not caused it, to the extent that such obligation is recognized as an installment payment or deferred payment of the royalty.

13. To provide that the license agreement will be canceled when the licensee contests the confidentiality of the know-how and claims that the know-how has come into general circulation.

14. To require the licensee not to disclose the licensed know-how to third parties while the know-how is kept confidential.

15. To require the licensee to exert its best efforts in utilizing the licensed know-how.

2. Items That May Be Held Unlawful

1. To prohibit the licensee from handling competing products or adopting competing technology during the term of the license agreement.

Note: This item is held unlawful when the business opportunity of competing enterprises is unduly restricted or the freedom of the licensee to select products and technology is unduly restricted.

2. To require the licensee to sell the licensed product through the licensor or a party designated by the licensor or to prohibit the licensee from selling the licensed product to parties designated by the licensor.

Note: This item is held unlawful when it unduly deprives the licensee of the freedom to choose sales outlets.

3. To require the licensee to inform the licensor of knowledge or experiences which the licensee has acquired with regard to the licensed know-how or to grant a non-exclusive license of improvement inventions and applied inventions which the licensee has developed, except for cases in which the licensor bears obligations similar to those borne by the licensee, and the contents of the obligations of both parties are generally balanced.

Note: This restriction is held unlawful when the licensor does not bear a similar burden to that of the licensee or the contents of the burden are unbalanced.

4. To require the licensee to use the trademark and other rep-

resentations designated by the licensor on the licensed product.

Note: This item is held unlawful when the freedom of the licensee to select the trademark is unduly restricted, and the business activities of the licensee are unduly hindered. Also, this item is held unlawful when continuous use of the trademark designated by the licensor is imposed on the licensee and, because of this continuous use, the licensee must use the trademark designated by the licensor after the licensed know-how has come into general circulation.

5. To set standards for the quality of raw materials, components, or the licensed product, except for cases in which such standards are necessary to maintain the good will of the trademark or the usefulness of the licensed technology.

6. To require the licensee to purchase raw materials and components from the licensor or a party designated by the licensor, except for cases in which guaranteeing the usefulness of the licensed know-how or the maintaining of the good will of a trademark through the restrictions on the quality of raw materials or components or other restrictions is difficult or such restriction is absolutely necessary to guarantee the usefulness of the licensed know-how, the maintenance of the good will of a trademark, or the confidentiality of the know-how.

7. To restrict the areas to which the licensee can export the licensed product, except for cases in which the areas to which export is prohibited: (a) where the licensor has registered the patent covering the licensed product, (b) where the licensor is continuously engaged in sales activities of the licensed product, and (c) where the licensor has granted a third party the exclusive right to sell the licensed product.

8. To set the export price or quantity of the licensed product by the licensee or to require the licensee to export through the licensor or a party designated by the licensor, except for cases in which the export in question is destined to areas (a), (b), or (c) specified above and the restriction is kept to the necessary minimum.

9. To require the licensee to pay royalties on products other than the licensed product, except for cases in which the computation of royalties is based, for the sake of convenience in computing royalties, on the quantity of manufacture/sale of the finished

product or the value of manufacture/sale thereof or on the quantity of use of raw materials or components or the frequency of use thereof when the licensed know-how is used in a part of the manufacturing process of the finished products or related to components.

10. To require the licensee to accept a license of a plural items of know-how en bloc, except for cases in which such obligation is kept within the scope necessary to guarantee the usefulness of the licensed know-how.

11. To impose unilaterally a disadvantageous condition for cancellation of a license agreement on the licensee, such as to provide that the license agreement is subject to immediate cancellation for reasons other than the inability of the licensee to perform the agreement or other justifiable reasons and without providing for an adequate grace period.

12. To require the licensee not to contest the confidentiality of the licensed know-how and claim that the licensed know-how has become publicly known.

3. Items That Are Likely To Be Held Unlawful

1. To set the resale price of the licensed product in the domestic market.

2. To set the sales price of the licensed product in the domestic market.

Note: By this item, the competitive position of the licensee will be considerably weakened, and competition in the market for the licensed product is likely to be adversely affected. This item cannot be justified by the argument that such a restriction is necessary to guarantee royalty payment.

3. To prohibit the licensee from handling competing products or adopting competing technology after the license agreement has expired, except for cases in which such a restriction is necessary to prevent the licensed know-how from leaking out and the term of the restriction is limited to a short period of time.

Note: This item cannot be justified for the argument that it is necessary to secure royalty payment.

4. To prohibit or restrict the licensee from using the technology incorporated in the licensed know-how when the licensed know-

how has become generally circulated without the responsibility of the licensee or to require the licensee to pay royalties for the use of the technology after the licensed know-how has become generally circulated, except for cases in which the obligation to pay royalties is imposed on the use of technology for a short period of time during the term of the agreement after the know-how has become generally circulated.

5. To prohibit or restrict the licensee from engaging alone or jointly with others in research and development of the licensed know-how or a competing technology.

6. To require the licensee to assign to the licensor the right to improvement inventions or applied inventions, which the licensee has developed or to grant an exclusive license thereof.

Note: This item tends to unduly enhance the market power of the licensor, deprives the licensee of the freedom to use the licensee's knowledge, experiences, or improvements or to license them to third parties and thereby acts as a disincentive to the licensee to engage in research and development. Such a restriction tends to hinder research and development in new technology and to reduce competition in the product market and the technology market. Also, if the licensor does not bear a similar burden as that borne by the licensee and the contents of the burden borne by both parties are unbalanced, this amounts to the imposition of unreasonable conditions on the licensee.

§ 8–5. DESIGNS

The Design Law protects the exclusive right to the commercial use of "the shape, pattern, color, or combination of these or an article which through the sense of sight arouses an aesthetic sensation."[25] A design may be registered with the Patent Office if it meets the legal criteria of novelty, utility, and creativeness.[26] An application for design registration must be filed with the Patent Office together with a drawing of the design. The application must also state the name and residence of the applicant, the date

---

[25] Ishō Hō, Law 125, 1959.
[26] Id., art. 3.

of the filing, the name and residence of the creator of the design, and the articles to which the design is to be applied.[27] A design right is effective for a period of 15 years after the date of its registration.[28] The owner of a design right has an exclusive right to work his or her registered design, and design rights are freely assignable and may be licensed on either an exclusive or non-exclusive basis.

§ 8–6. TRADEMARKS

A trademark may be "characters, letters, figures, or signs, or any combination of these and colors which are used on goods by a person who produces, processes, certifies, or assigns such goods in the course of trade."[29] Under this definition, virtually anything that has a distinctive quality or secondary meaning may be registered as a trademark; it is not necessary for a trademark to be actually used in order to be registered.[30] Certain types of trademarks, however, are not registerable because they lack a distinctive quality: generic names, marks indicating place of origin, place of sale, quality, raw materials, efficacy, use, quantity, shape, price, manner or time of production, or processing or use of goods; marks indicating a common surname or appellation; and marks by which consumers are unable to identify the business to which the goods are related.[31] Certain other marks such as flags or international symbols are not registerable on the grounds of public interest.[32]

To create trademark rights, Japanese law requires registration. Applications for trademark registration are filed with the Director General of the Patent Office. The application must designate one or more goods on which the trademark is to be used. Upon acceptance of registration, a trademark right comes into force for a period of ten years. It may be renewed unless prior to the renewal application neither the trademark owner nor a licensee

[27] Id., art. 6.
[28] Id., art. 20(1).
[29] Trademark Law (Shōhyō Hō), Law 127, 1959, art. 4(1). Franchising, in particular, involves licensing the use of the franchisor's trademark or other trade symbols.
[30] Id., art. 3(1).
[31] Id.
[32] Id., art. 4.

has been using the trademark for the designated goods in Japan.[33] Trademarks are assignable and can be licensed on either an exclusive or non-exclusive basis.

§ 8–7. SERVICE MARKS

A service mark is a mark representing services rather than a commodity. An example is JAL the well-known mark for Japan Airlines. The Trademark Law defines the term trademark as a symbol attached to a tangible commodity to represent the origin and quality of a commodity. Therefore, a service mark is not qualified to be considered a trademark and is not entitled to protection under the Trademark Law.

Nevertheless, the owner of a service mark can protect its mark under the Unfair Competition Prevention Law.[34] Article 1 (2) of this law provides that a party can file a suit for injunction if one's business is likely to be injured by an "act of a person to use a mark or representation identical or similar to the name, trade name, or other representation of another person's business widely known in the area in which this law applies and to cause confusion with that person's business facility or activity." This definition is broad enough to cover service marks, and, therefore, whenever there is an infringement of a service mark, the injured party can use this provision to stop the infringement and/or to recover the damage sustained thereby. Under this provision, the plaintiff must prove that by the infringement of his service mark, the business interest is "likely to be injured." However, this requirement should not be difficult to meet. Under article 5 of the law, a criminal penalty for infringement is provided.

---

[33] Id., arts. 18 and 19.

[34] Fusei Kyōsō Bōshi Hō, Law 14, 1934. This law forbids practices that lead to confusion regarding goods such as those with similar trade names, containers for packaging; practices leading to confusion with businesses such as those with similar trademarks, trade names, or indications; false representations regarding the place of origin; misleading representations or advertising regarding the place of manufacture or processing; misleading statements about the quality, content, or quantity of goods; false statements about another's business; and unpermitted use of a trademark by an agent. See, for example, National Football League Properties v. Marutake Shōji K.K., *Mutai Reishū*, Vol. 8, p. 441 (Osaka Dist. Ct., 5 Oct. 1976).

§ 8–8. Parallel Importation of Genuine Goods

The remedy for the violation of registered intellectual property rights is a lawsuit which can be filed in court. Relief may include an injunction, recovery of damages, and measures to restore the business reputation of the intellectual property rights owner. Criminal penalty can be attached to an infringement of intellectual property right. Another possible remedy is a suit filed under the Unfair Competition Prevention Law.

If imported goods infringe a registered intellectual property right, application may be made to the MOF under article 21 of the Customs and Tariff Law for an order excluding their importation and sale. The article prohibits the importation of goods which infringe upon patents, utility model rights, design rights, trademark rights, and copyrights. Counterfeit goods which infringe on duly registered trademarks and goods which infringe on duly registered patents, utility model rights, and design rights, therefore, may be excluded from importation upon the application of an interested party.

There are special problems with parallel importation. Parallel importation occurs when commodities produced by foreign manufacturers using their duly registered patent rights, or which bear the trademark duly owned by the foreign manufacturer in the foreign country are imported by a party other than the owner or the exclusive licensee in Japan of the corresponding patents or trademark rights. If this happens, can the Japanese owner of the exclusive licensee exclude importation of such a commodity? The situation depends on the type of intellectual property involved. In patent cases, parallel importation of goods covered by a patent registered in Japan can be blocked upon an application of the owner of the patent or the exclusive licensee thereof. In the Brunswick case, the owner of a patent in Japan successfully blocked a parallel importation of bowling pins covered by the patent and manufactured abroad.[35]

In trademark cases, parallel importation of genuine goods imported by any party other than the exclusive licensee of the mark must be allowed. In the Parker Fountain Pen case, the

---

[35] Brunswick Corporation v. Orion Kōgyō K.K., *Mutai Reishū*, Vol. 1, p. 160 (Osaka Dist. Ct., 9 June 1969).

Osaka District Court held that the exclusive licensee of a trademark registered in Japan could not stop parallel importation of the goods bearing the same mark imported by a third party as long as the goods were genuine.[36] The rationale of the decision was that whereas the basic functions of a trademark were the identification of the origin and the guarantee of the quality of the goods bearing the mark, parallel importation of genuine goods by a third party did not adversely affect any of those two basic functions of trademark and, therefore, no trademark infringement occurs through parallel importation. On August 25, 1972, the Finance Minister issued a directive to implement the Parker Fountain Pen decision and to allow parallel importation of genuine goods.

After this liberalization, prices of imported goods which bore famous trademarks did not go down significantly. It was suspected that the sole import distributors of such commodities were taking steps to prevent parallel importation. Responding to this situation, the FTC announced guidelines.

On November 22, 1972, the FTC announced the "Antimonopoly Law Guidelines for Sole Import Distributorship Agreements," in which the FTC enumerated major unfair business practices involved in sole import distributorship agreements. Before the Parker Fountain Pen decision and the directive of the MOF which allowed parallel importation of genuine goods, the AML could not be applied to practices of sole import distributors of quality goods from abroad designed to block parallel importation. Now that parallel importation was interpreted by the court not to violate the Trademark Law, practices which were designed to prevent parallel importation of genuine goods came to be regarded as violations of the AML.

The FTC Guidelines enumerate six general categories of conduct which constitute unfair business practices. They state that, among the restrictions which are likely to constitute unfair business practices in continuous import and sale agreements, including sole import distributorship agreement, the following are outstanding: (1) to set the resale prices of the goods

[36] N.M.C. v. Shriro Trading Co. Ltd., *Muta Reishū*, Vol. 2, p. 71 (Osaka Dist. Ct., 27 Feb. 1970).

covered by an agreement; (2) to specify the persons to whom the goods covered by an agreement are resold; (3) to impose an obligation to purchase parts, etc., for the goods covered by an agreement from a foreign party or person designated by such foreign party. . . ; (4) to unduly hinder parallel importation of the goods covered by the agreement; (5) to impose an unduly disadvantageous condition for the termination of the agreement; and (6) to prohibit the manufacture, use, or sale of goods competitive with those covered by the agreement. . . ."[37]

Not all the items relate to parallel importation of genuine goods. However, Item 5 specifically states that activities of the sole import distributor that unduly hinder parallel importation of the goods covered by the agreement amount to an unfair business practice. If, therefore, a Japanese sole import distributor has entered into an agreement with a foreign exporter in which the latter is obligated to turn down any party who wishes to purchase the commodity from the exporter, then such a provision is held to be an unfair business practice.

However, hindrance of parallel importation can be achieved by means other than a contractual provision in international agreements. In light of this, the FTC issued a memorandum on April 17, 1987, in which some of the practices which are regarded as unreasonable hindrances of parallel importation are listed. In the memo, the following practices are enumerated:

1. When the Japanese sole import distributor demands a foreign enterprise to refuse to deal with a Japanese parallel importer when the parallel importer requests supply of goods from the foreign enterprise.

Note: This item does not cover the situation in which the Japanese sole import distributor asks the foreign exporter not to sell the goods covered by the distribution agreement to any party in Japan, since the very essence of sole import distributorship is that the sole agency has the exclusive right to import the goods. However, if the domestic sole agency requires any foreign third party who purchased the goods to refuse to resell the goods to

---

[37] For details on these guidelines, see Matsushita, "Regulations of Sole Import Distribution Agreements under the Japanese Antimonopoly Law," *The Japanese Annual of International Law*, Vol. 18, No. 2, pp. 66–82 (1974).

a Japanese parallel importer, such a requirement is regarded as excessive and unlawful.

2. When the distributor sells the imported goods to wholesalers and retailers on the condition that they do not handle the same goods imported by parallel importers.

Note: This condition is regarded as an undue interference with the decisions of wholesalers and retailers to select their sources of supply and is unlawful.

3. When the distributor sells the imported goods to wholesalers on the condition that they do not engage in transactions with retailers who sell the same goods imported by parallel importers.

Note: Again, this is regarded as an undue interference into the decisions of wholesalers to select the sales outlets and is unlawful.

4. When the distributor demands sellers of the goods imported by parallel importers not to sell them, claiming that they are counterfeit goods and that they infringe on the trademark.

Note: If a commodity imported and sold by a parallel importer is counterfeit and constitutes a violation of the Trademark Law, of course the sole import distributor has the right to stop importation or to prohibit sales in the domestic market. This item, however, envisages the actions taken by the sole import distributor such as to claim, without sufficient evidence, that the goods imported are in violation of the trademark. Even though such a claim may not be legally successful, it may have a chilling effect on the enthusiasm of retailers selling the goods in question for fear of a possible infringement action by the sole import distributor. This item, therefore, states that action of this kind taken by the sole import distributor constitutes a violation if the claim for a trademark infringement is groundless.

5. When the distributor buys up the goods imported by parallel importers and removes them from the market.

Note: The removal of parallel imports which are usually priced much lower than goods sold by the sole import distributor tends to reduce price competition and is held unlawful.

6. When the distributor refuses to repair the goods imported by parallel importers.

Note: This kind of conduct is regarded as a de facto attempt by the sole import distributor to block parallel importation and is unlawful.

§ 8–9. COPYRIGHT

Copyright protection is granted to authors without official registration, but recording of copyrights may be carried out at the Culture Affairs Department of the Ministry of Education. The Copyright Law gives protection to works first published in Japan and works first published abroad and published in Japan within 30 days.[38] A copyright includes the following rights: the right to make the work public,[39] the right to preserve the integrity of the work against any mutilation, distortion, or other modification,[40] the exclusive right of reproduction,[41] the exclusive right of performance,[42] the exclusive rights of broadcasting and wire transmission,[43] the right of recitation,[44] the exclusive right of exhibition,[45] the exclusive rights of cinematographic presentation and distribution,[46] the exclusive right of translation and adaptation,[47] and rights regarding the exploitation of a derivative work.[48] The copyright endures for the life of the author and 50 years following the author's death. For films and photographic works, the duration is 50 years following the creation of the work.[49]

Japan is a member of the International Union established by the Berne Convention for the Protection of Literary and Artistic Works.[50] This treaty provides for a reciprocal protection of works originating in a foreign country if it is a member of the International Union. If the duration of the copyright granted by the country of origin is shorter than that provided under the

[38] Chosakuken Hō, Law 48, 1970, amended by Law 49, 1978; Law 46, 1984; Law 62, 1985; and Law 64, 1986.
[39] Id., art. 18.
[40] Id., art. 20.
[41] Id., art. 21.
[42] Id., art. 22.
[43] Id., art. 23.
[44] Id., art. 24.
[45] Id., art. 25.
[46] Id., art. 26.
[47] Id., art. 27.
[48] Id., art. 28.
[49] Id., art. 51.
[50] Signed 24 July 1971. Japan is also a party to the Universal Copyright Convention of 1952, revised in Paris, 1971. Under these conventions a work is protected in all of the member states upon its completion.

Copyright Law, the duration of the copyright is that granted by the country of origin.[51]

Article 10 of the Copyright Law sets out the categories of authors' works which are protected: (1) novels, dramas, articles, lectures, and other literary works; (2) musical works; (3) choreographic works and pantomimes; (4) paintings, engravings, sculptures, and other artistic works; (5) architectural works; (6) maps, charts, and models; (7) cinematographic works; (8) photographic works; and (9) program works including computer software.

Computer programs and software were granted explicit protection under the Copyright Law by an amendment added in 1985.[52] For purposes of this law, a computer program is defined as "an expression of combined instructions given to a computer so as to make it function and obtain a certain result.[53] Protection does not extend, however, to any programming language, rule, or algorithm used for making such works. Moreover, the owner of a copy of a program work may reproduce or adapt that work to the extent deemed necessary for using that work in a computer by himself.[54] In addition, Japan has passed a special law designed to protect circuit layouts (mask works) of semiconductor integrated circuits. A circuit layout right is protected upon registration for a period of ten years. This law, passed in May 1986,[55] is similar to the United States Semiconductor Chip Act of 1984.[56]

The Copyright Law gives special protection to performers through recognizing "neighboring rights" (*chosaku rinsetsuken*) that are independent of the copyright granted to authors.[57] The neighboring rights law was modeled on the provisions of the Rome Convention of 1961,[58] which gives performers rights in their unfixed live performances, including the unqualified right to authorize or forbid the recording of live performances.

[51] Copyright Law, art 58.
[52] Law 62, 1985.
[53] Id., art. 1.
[54] Id., art. 47(2).
[55] Law 64, 1986.
[56] 17 USC § 901 et seq.
[57] Copyright Law, arts. 89–104. Law 48, 1970.
[58] International Convention for the Protection of Performers, Producers of Phonograms, and Broadcasting Organizations, 26 Oct. 1961. Copyright Law, art. 91.

CHAPTER NINE

TAXATION

§ 9–1. The Tax System

The tax laws of Japan are administered by the Commissioner of the National Tax Administration Agency (Kokuzei Chō), which is a division of the MOF. Article 30 of the Constitution declares the "duty of the people to pay taxes as provided by law." Taxes are collected at the level of the national government, the prefecture, and the local government.

At the level of the national government, the principal taxes are the individual income tax[1] and the corporate tax.[2] There are also taxes on gifts and inheritance,[3] on the sales of certain commodities,[4] and on certain transactions, such as the use of official documents (deeds, articles of incorporation, etc.) and securities transfers. Individual taxpayers are classified into residents and non-residents of Japan. While resident taxpayers are taxed on their worldwide income, non-residents are taxed only on the portion of their income derived from Japan. Individual tax rates vary with the amount of taxable income.

At the prefectural level, there is an inhabitants' tax, taxes on entertainment, and taxes on the acquisition of real property and automobiles. Local government taxes include taxes on income,

---

[1] Shotokuzei Hō (Income Tax Law), Law 33, 1965.

[2] Hōjinzei Hō (Corporate Tax Law), Law 34, 1965.

[3] Sōzokuzei Hō (Inheritance Tax Law), Law 73, 1950.

[4] Buppinzei Hō (Commodities Tax Law), Law 48, 1962. This is an indirect sales tax payable at the wholesaler level. If a commodity subject to tax is exported, the tax paid is refundable.

property, and a variety of smaller taxes on certain consumption and transactions.[5]

§ 9–2. FOREIGN OPERATIONS

A foreign business has the option of doing business either as an entity incorporated under Japanese law (a subsidiary or a joint venture) or as a branch office. In either case, the permanent establishment in Japan will trigger tax consequences under Japanese law. Within two months of incorporation or the establishment of a branch office, a foreign company must submit a report and copies of its documents of establishment[6] to the district tax office.

Foreign subsidiaries and joint ventures with foreign participation are subject to tax on their worldwide earnings like other Japanese corporations. The standard tax rate for corporations is 40 percent and will be further reduced in fiscal 1990, but only a 32 percent tax rate is applied to income distributed as dividends.[7] Smaller companies with paid-in capital of ¥100 million or less are subject to reduced rates: 30 percent of the first ¥8 million if earnings are retained, and 24 percent on current dividends.[8] Income exceeding ¥8 million is taxed at the regular rates (40 and 32 percent).

There is a 20 percent withholding tax on cash or stock dividends paid.[9] Applicable tax treaties, however, commonly reduce this tax to 15 percent.[10]

---

[5] For more detailed treatment of taxation in Japan, see Otsuka, "Tax: Japan," *International Business Lawyer*, p. 440 (Nov. 1987).

[6] These include an authorized copy of the registration of the branch, the articles of incorporation, a balance sheet, and other corporate books and records. Corporate Income Tax Law, art. 141.

[7] Sozei Tokubetsu Sochi Hō (Tax Special Measures Law) art. 42(2), Law 26, 1957. The purpose of this reduced rate is to reduce the impact of the double taxation of dividends.

[8] Japanese law requires, however, that companies set aside a minimum of one-tenth of annual dividends paid as an earned surplus reserve until this reserve is equal to one-quarter of paid-in capital (Commercial Code, art. 288). Companies are restricted from declaring dividends that would impair this reserve (Id., art. 290).

[9] Income Tax Law, art. 212(1).

[10] See the U.S.-Japan Convention on the Avoidance of Double Taxation (8 March, 1971) 23 U.S.T., 7315 T.I.A.S., art. 12(2) (g).

A Japanese branch of a foreign company is taxed on all industrial and commercial profits from sources within Japan at a standard rate of 40 percent of taxable income.[11] If the foreign corporation has paid-in capital of not more than ¥100 million, the rate is 30 percent for the first ¥8 million of income.[12] There is no withholding tax on remittances of profits from the branch to the head office.

When goods are transferred between parent and subsidiary or between a branch and an offshore manufacturing facility, pricing must be in accordance with an "arms-length" standard of value. The arms-length price may be established according to a variety of methods: (1) comparable transactions between non-affiliates under similar circumstances; (2) cost plus reasonable profits; or (3) the resale price to third parties minus ordinary profits. Thus a reasonable profit margin may be included for purpose of establishing a deduction from the Japanese branch or subsidiary's gross income. Where goods are purchased offshore from a third party, however, no profit margin may be included upon an intercorporate transfer. The difference between the arm's-length transaction price and that actually declared by the taxpayer is deemed to constitute additional income or must be subtracted from a declared deductible expense. These rules affect not only sales and purchase transactions with a foreign affiliated company but also other transactions such as loans, licensing, and services.[13]

Foreign subsidiaries and branches must also pay two local government taxes imposed on business organizations: the inhabitants' tax (jūminzei) and the business activities tax (jigyōzei). These are deductible from the corporate income tax.

This pattern of taxation means that there is little difference from a tax standpoint in operating as a branch or subsidiary in Japan. It is usually more advantageous to operate as a subsidiary, however, because of the greater flexibility involved and to take advantage of the lower tax rate applied to earnings repatriated as current dividends.

---

[11] Corporate Income Tax Law, art. 143(1).
[12] Id., art. 143(2).
[13] See the Tax Special Measures Law, art. 66–5, 1986.

§ 9–3. TRANSFER PRICING TAXATION

Transfer pricing is the manipulation of prices by internationally related companies so as to minimize tax. It is often undertaken by multinational corporations to minimize income in countries where tax rates are high and maximize income in countries where tax rates are low, thereby attempting to maximize income after tax for the group as a whole. For example, when a foreign company which owns a subsidiary in Japan exports goods to the subsidiary at an artificially high price, a price higher than the arm's-length price, in order to "squeeze profits" of the subsidiary, then the corporate income tax to be paid by this subsidiary to the Japanese government is lower than it would be if price manipulation had not occurred.

Governments of various countries try to prevent this tax avoidance and have introduced transfer pricing taxation in which the actual price and transactions between related companies is disregarded for tax purposes, and tax is based on "constructed price" and "constructed transactions." The taxing authority sets a price which would be realistic if the companies in question were independent of one another and bases the tax on this price. This tax system exists in the United States, Great Britain, Germany, France, and Japan.

In 1986, the government introduced a transfer pricing taxation law, the Tax Special Measures Law. Under this law, when the income of a corporation is artificially squeezed due to price manipulation between the corporation and its related companies abroad, in order to keep the taxable income in Japan low, the tax authority disregards the actual transaction prices and bases taxation on a price that would have existed had the companies in question really been independent of each other. "A related company abroad" is defined as a company incorporated abroad which is related to a Japanese company through stockholdings of more than 50 percent.

If it is deemed that the price used between a Japanese company and its foreign affiliate in their transaction is kept artificially low or high, as the case may be, so as to avoid or minimize taxes, the Japanese tax authority disregards this transaction and the price and sets a price as if these companies were independent of each other. This "as if price" is computed by means of (1) the independent price comparison method, (2) the resale price method, or (3) the cost-plus method.

In the independent price comparison method, the tax authority considers similar transactions performed between third parties which are independent of each other and modifies the price formed in those transactions according to the differences in the quality of products involved, the conditions of the transactions, the time of the transactions, the stage of the transactions, and the geographic market. It then constructs a price to be used for taxation purposes.

In the resale price method, the taxing authority deducts an appropriate amount as a markup from the resale price charged by a purchaser who originally purchased the product from a taxpayer. Necessary adjustments are made and a constructed price is arrived at. In the cost-plus method, the tax authority adds profit to the manufacturing cost of the product and thus computes the constructed price which is used for taxation purposes.

The Corporate Income Tax Law provides that the tax authority can require taxpayers to answer questions posed by the authority and produce documents necessary for tax investigation. In the transfer pricing tax law, however, it is only provided that the Japanese taxpayer should do the utmost in obtaining documents related to its foreign transactions and affiliated companies abroad. In this way, extraterritorial investigation is avoided. However, if a taxpayer does not cooperate in producing documents from abroad, the tax authority can base the tax on the best information available.

§ 9–4. TAX TREATIES

Japan has concluded bilateral tax treaties with over 35 countries.[14] These treaties are based upon the OECD Model Convention for the Avoidance of Double Taxation and the Preven-

[14] For example, the following countries have signed tax treaties with Japan: Australia, Austria, Belgium, Brazil, Canada, China, Czechoslovakia, Denmark, Egypt, Finland, France, F.R. Germany, Hungary, India, Indonesia, Ireland, Italy, Malaysia, the Netherlands, New Zealand, Norway, Pakistan, the Philippines, Poland, R.O. Korea, Romania, Singapore, Spain, Sri Lanka, Sweden, Switzerland, Thailand, the United Kingdom, and the United States.

tion of Fiscal Evasion with Respect to Taxes on Income.[15] Under these treaties, Japan undertakes, on a reciprocal basis, to levy taxes only on foreign enterprises that have a permanent establishment in Japan. Furthermore, only earnings derived from permanent establishment in Japan are taxable. There are also agreed-on reduced tax rates with respect to dividends, interest, and royalties.[16] Japan also has implemented a system of allowing a credit against domestic taxes for foreign taxes paid.

§ 9–5. THE CONSUMPTION TAX

The consumption tax, introduced by the Consumption Tax Law,[17] was one of the major tax reforms since the establishment of the Japanese tax system after World War II. Before the introduction of this tax, the national revenue was heavily dependent on such direct taxes as individual and corporate income taxes. The tax reform of 1988 was designed to introduce the consumption tax, which is an indirect tax, on the one hand, and to reduce income tax, on the other. The consumption tax took effect on April 1, 1989.

A short definition of the consumption tax is a tax imposed on a transfer or lease of property for consideration (such as sale of goods). It is payable by the person who transfers the property and is shifted forward to the purchaser of the property; that is, the amount of the consumption tax is added on the price charged by the person transferring the property. If the property is transferred again, another consumption tax is imposed on the transfer and shifted forward again. Thus, the consumption tax is ultimately borne by the consumers. The rate of the consumption tax is 3 percent of the value of each transaction.

The following is an illustration of how the tax operates. Suppose there are transactions beginning from a manufacturer of a raw material of a product and ending in a purchase by a consumer. The parties are A (the manufacturer of the raw material), B (who purchases the raw material from A, manufactures the

---

[15] This convention was concluded in Paris in 1983.

[16] Typically, these rates are 15 percent for dividends, 10 percent for interest, and 10 percent for royalties.

[17] Shōhizei Hō, Law 108, 1988.

finished product, and sells it to the wholesaler), C (the wholesaler who purchases the finished product from B and sells it to the retailer), D (the retailer who purchases the finished product from C and sells it to a consumer), and E (the consumer of the finished product).

A sells the raw material to B for ¥20,000 and pays 3 percent consumption tax, which is ¥600. A shifts the burden to B by charging ¥20,000 plus ¥600. Therefore, the total charge to B is ¥20,600. B manufactures the finished product by using the raw material and sells it to C for ¥50,000. The consumption tax is ¥1,500. The total amount charged by B to C is ¥51,500. The consumption tax payable by B to the government is the amount equal to ¥1,500 minus ¥600 paid by A as the consumption tax, which is ¥900. C sells the product to D for ¥70,000. The consumption tax payable by C is ¥2,100 minus ¥1,500, that is, ¥600. D sells the product to E for ¥100,000. The consumption tax payable by D is ¥3,000 minus ¥2,100, that is, ¥900. D sells the product to E for ¥103,000. This means that the total amount of consumption tax payable by A, B, C, and D (600 + 900 + 600 + 900 = ¥3,000) is ultimately borne by E, the consumer.

1. Taxable Transactions

The consumption tax is imposed on a transaction that involves transfer and lease of an asset or offer of services: (1) performed in Japan, (2) performed by an enterprise as business, and (3) for consideration. The consumption tax is imposed only on a "domestic transaction," that is, a transaction performed in the Japanese territory. In transfers of assets, the test is the location of the asset. Therefore, the sale of a property in Japan by a foreigner is taxable, while the purchase of a property by a Japanese abroad is not taxable. In the case of an offer of services, the test is the location of the place where the offer is made. Therefore, while a performance by a Japanese actor abroad is not taxable, a performance of a foreign pianist in Japan is taxable.

The consumption tax is imposed on a transfer of assets or offer of services when it is executed by an enterprise "as business," which is defined as an economic activity in which the enterprise is repeatedly, continuously, and independently engaged. Therefore, an isolated and occasional sale by an individual of his property (such as selling his own car) is not business. A transaction in which no consideration is received is, in principle, exempted from the consumption tax.

2. Import Transactions

Import transactions are treated somewhat differently from domestic transactions. It is provided that a "foreign article withdrawn from the bonded area" is taxable, which would mean that an import transaction is taxable. There is no provision stating that a transaction is taxable only when engaged in an enterprise as business and for consideration. This means that an import transaction is taxable even if it is conducted by a person who is not an enterprise or who pays no consideration.

3. Non-taxable Transactions

There are some transactions which are regarded as non-taxable. They include: (1) transactions not suitable for the object of the consumption tax, (2) transactions for which a special consideration (such as social welfare policy consideration) is necessary, and (3) transactions on which a separate indirect tax is imposed.

Category 1 includes 11 items, such as a transfer or lease of land, a transfer of negotiable instruments and instruments of payment, or an interest which accrues from loan of money. The rationale for not taxing these items is not entirely clear. It is probably based on policy compromises rather than on consistent tax theory.

Category 2 includes three items: (1) medical treatment and related services, (2) social welfare activities and related services, and (3) tuition charged by educational institutions.

4. Export Transactions

Since the consumption tax is imposed on the transfer of articles and offer of services for domestic consumption, an export transaction is exempted. If a product is manufactured and distributed in Japan and then is exported abroad, the consumption tax is paid and shifted forward during the domestic transactions through which the exporter acquires the product, and it is ultimately borne by the exporter, while the export transaction itself is exempted from the consumption tax. To remedy this anomaly, the amount shifted forward and borne by the exporter is returned by the government to the exporter when the product is exported.

5. The Taxpayer

The consumption tax, as the name indicates, is ultimately borne by consumers as the prices they pay are inclusive of the consumption taxes paid by the sellers.

In domestic transactions, an enterprise which is engaged in a transfer and lease of property or an offer of services is a taxpayer. In import transactions, any person who imports an article from abroad is subject to the consumption tax.

However, a small enterprise whose total sales in the representative period (usually the preceding two years) is ¥30 million or less is exempted from consumption tax. It is said that as far as the number of enterprises is concerned, 70 percent of all enterprises are exempted from the consumption tax for this reason. However, those small enterprises occupy only 3 percent of the total sales value. Therefore, this exemption is not likely to impair the revenue objective of the tax.

6. Agreements Among Enterprises Concerning Consumption Tax

When the consumption tax was proposed and debated, there was great concern among enterprises, especially small enterprises, that although the consumption tax system was based on the premise that the taxpayer shifts the tax burden forward by adding the amount of tax on the price, such a forward shifting may not be possible due to intensive competition. To ease forward shifting of the consumption tax, article 30 of the Attached Rules of the Consumption Tax Law provides that small enterprises can enter into an agreement concerning forward shifting of the consumption tax and that such an agreement enjoys exemption from the AML.

A small enterprise is defined as an enterprise that employs less than 300 employees or whose capital is less than ¥100 million in manufacturing, less than ¥100 million or ¥30 million in wholesale, and less than ¥50 million or ¥10 million in the retail and service industry. Small enterprises can enter into an agreement to decide jointly ways to shift the tax burden onto the price they charge as long as in that agreement at least two-thirds of the participants are small enterprises. Similarly, a trade association in which at least two-thirds of the members are small enterprises can decide ways in which the members will shift the tax burden.

Examples of such an agreement would be to decide jointly that: (1) participants add the amount of the consumption tax on the existing sales price which has been independently decided by the participants; (2) they add the consumption tax on the sales price of a new commodity which they have decided independently; (3) they reduce or change the volume or quantity of goods or services while no amount is added to the sales price; and (4) they round off unit figures which accrue due to the imposition of the consumption tax on the sales prices.

Enterprises, whether small or large, can enter into an agreement to decide jointly ways to represent the consumption tax. Examples of such an agreement would be to decide jointly that: (1) participants use a uniform representation concerning the consumption tax, such as to represent the consumption tax separately from the price or include it within the price without representing the amount of tax separately; (2) they represent the amount of the consumption tax on receipts they issue; (3) they place a sign at the entrance of a shopping mall that the price represented in the shops all include the consumption tax; (4) they represent that the sales price does not include the consumption tax and the amount of tax is charged separately; or (5) they use a uniform format with respect to the representation of the consumption tax in invoices, bills, receipts, and similar documents.

It is specifically declared, however, that an exemption from the AML is not available if such an agreement causes a sharp rise of price by substantially restraining competition or if unfair business practices are used. The exemption from the AML is granted only between December 30, 1988, and March 31, 1991. To obtain exemption from the AML, an agreement must be filed with the FTC.

THE GOVERNMENT SYSTEM

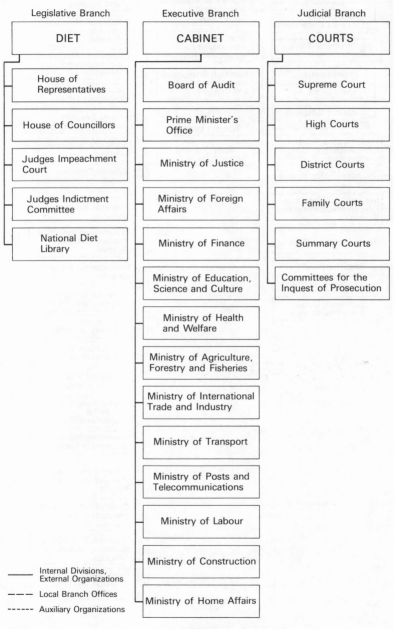

Legislative Branch	Executive Branch	Judicial Branch
DIET	**CABINET**	**COURTS**
House of Representatives	Board of Audit	Supreme Court
House of Councillors	Prime Minister's Office	High Courts
Judges Impeachment Court	Ministry of Justice	District Courts
Judges Indictment Committee	Ministry of Foreign Affairs	Family Courts
National Diet Library	Ministry of Finance	Summary Courts
	Ministry of Education, Science and Culture	Committees for the Inquest of Prosecution
	Ministry of Health and Welfare	
	Ministry of Agriculture, Forestry and Fisheries	
	Ministry of International Trade and Industry	
	Ministry of Transport	
	Ministry of Posts and Telecommunications	
	Ministry of Labour	
	Ministry of Construction	
	Ministry of Home Affairs	

————— Internal Divisions, External Organizations

— — — Local Branch Offices

- - - - - Auxiliary Organizations

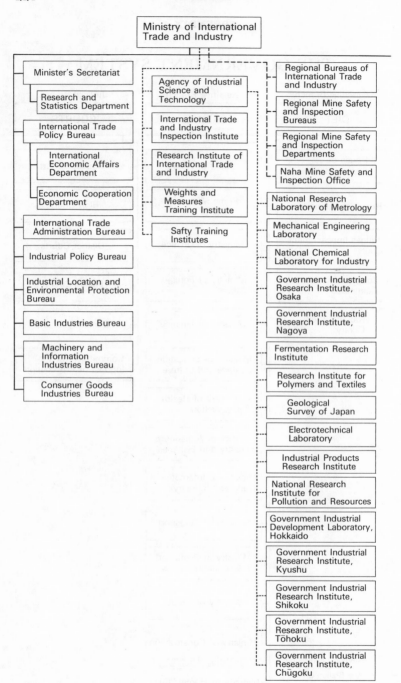

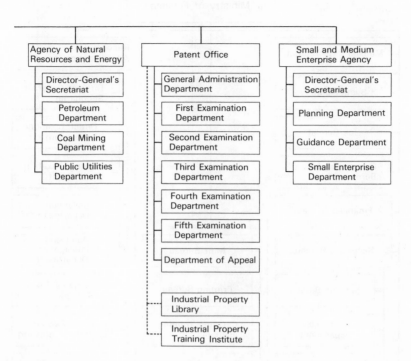

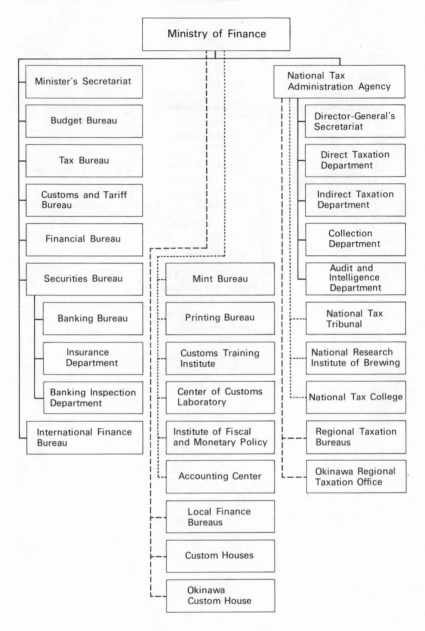

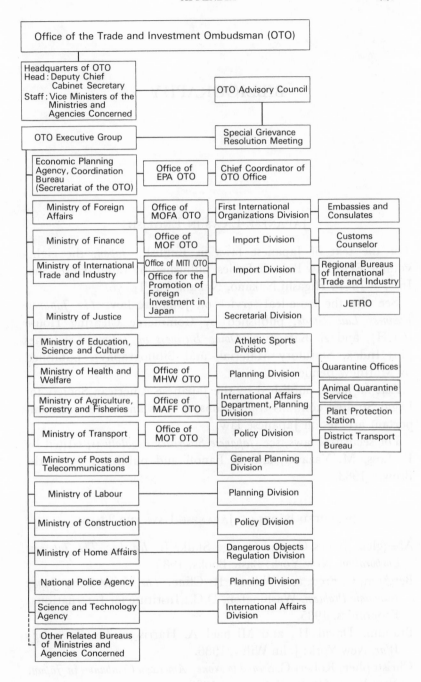

BIBLIOGRAPHY

Japanese Laws in English

For the text of Japanese laws in English, *Japan*, the eight-volume EHS Law Bulletin Series, published by Eibun-Hōrei-Sha, Inc., 4–18–14 Higashi Nakano, Nakano-ku, Tokyo.

See also the loose-leaf service on Japanese law, *The Japanese Business Law Guide*, published by Commerce Clearing House (CCH), and Z. Kitagawa, *Doing Business in Japan* (7 volumes plus Index, Statutory Material, and Bibliography), published by Matthew Bender.

Law in Japan, published by the Japanese American Society for Legal Studies, contains translations of cases and timely and important articles on Japanese law.

For securities laws, see *Japanese Securities Regulations*, edited by L. Loss, M. Yazawa, and B. Banoff and published by Little, Brown, 1983.

Selected Books on Japanese Law and Trade

Abegglen, James C., and George Stalk, Jr. *Kaisha: The Japanese Corporation*. New York: Basic Books, 1985.

Bergsten, C. Fred, and William R. Cline. *The United States–Japan Economic Problem*. Washington, D.C.: Institute for International Economics, 1985.

Brandin, David H., and Michael A. Harrison. *The Technology War*. New York: John Wiley, 1986.

Christopher, Robert C. *Second to None: American Companies in Japan*. New York: Crown Publishers, 1986.

Cohen, Stephen D. *Uneasy Partnership*. Cambridge, Massachusetts: Ballinger, 1985.

Drucker, Peter F. "Japan's Choices," *Foreign Affairs* (Summer 1987).

Fukushima, Glen S. "The U.S.–Japan Trade Conflict: A View from Washington," *Bulletin of the International House* 6(2): 7 (1986).

Gresser, Julian. *Partners in Prosperity*. New York: McGraw-Hill, 1984.

Hahn, Elliott J. *Japanese Business Law and the Legal System*. Westport, Connecticut: Quorum Books, 1984.

Inoguchi, Takashi, and Daniel I. Okimoto. *The Political Economy of Japan, Vol. 2: The Changing International Context*. Stanford University Press, 1988.

Ishizumi, Kanji. *Acquiring Japanese Companies*. Tokyo: The Japan Times, 1988.

Jackson, John H., Jean-Victor Louis, and Mitsuo Matsushita. *Implementing the Tokyo Round*. Ann Arbor, Michigan: University of Michigan Press, 1984.

Johnson, Chalmers, ed. *The Industrial Policy Debate*. San Francisco: Institute for Contemporary Studies Press, 1984.

———. *MITI and the Japanese Miracle*. Stanford: Stanford University Press, 1982.

Krugman, Paul R., ed. *Strategic Trade Policy and the New International Economics*. Cambridge, Massachusetts: The MIT Press, 1987.

Lincoln, Edward J. *Japan: Facing Economic Maturity*. Washington, D.C.: The Brookings Institution, 1988.

Monya, Nobuo. "International Protection of Intellectual Properties and Japanese Laws: In Particular Patent Law," *The Japanese Annual of International Law*, Vol. 30, p. 56 (1987).

Okimoto, Daniel I., and Thomas P. Rohlen, eds. *Inside the Japanese System: Readings on Contemporary Society and Political Economy*. Stanford: Stanford University Press, 1988.

Rosecrance, Richard. *The Rise of the Trading State*. New York: Basic Books, 1986.

Sawada, Toshio. "International Commercial Arbitration in Japan," *The Japanese Annual of International Law*, Vol. 30, p. 69 (1987).

Schlosstein, Steven. *Trade War.* New York: Congdon & Weed, 1984.

Shibata, Tokue. *Public Finance in Japan.* Tokyo: University of Tokyo Press, 1986.

Yamamura, Kozo, and Yasukichi Yasuba. *The Political Economy of Japan, Vol. 1: The Domestic Transformation.* Stanford: Stanford University Press, 1987.

Yoshihara, Kunio. *Sōgō Shōsha: The Vanguard of the Japanese Economy.* Oxford: Oxford University Press, 1982.

Zysman, John and Stephen S. Cohen. "Double or Nothing: Open Trade and Competitive Industry." *Foreign Affairs* (Summer 1983).

―――― and Laura Tyson, eds. *American Industry in International Competition.* Ithaca: Cornell University Press, 1983.

TABLE OF CASES

TABLE OF STATUTES

INDEX